✝ ✡ ✝ ✡ ✝ ✡ ✝ ✡ ✝ ✡ ✝ ✡ ✝ ✡ ✝ ✡ ✝ ✡ ✝

Copyright 2007 © John Aaron Lee

For Worldwide Distribution

Amazing Ministries

ISBN – 978-0-9815676-2-4

www.amazingministries.org
P. O. Box 3211
Brentwood, TN 37024

Sword and Spirit Publishing
SAN: 855-9007

First Edition 2008

Cover design by Kyle Lopez

i

Amazing
Review Quotations

"Excellent content, great applications, and very resourceful."

"I love the title; it's absolutely perfect. The title for Chapter One was also perfect, I thought, because, in a sense, what the entire book is about is the presence of God, not only in our own experiences and relationships with Him but also in the created order, right down to the details of the English language in Gmail."

"I thought that there were sentences throughout the book that popped up like spontaneous gems."

"Interesting and thoughtful. I loved this book."

"The lexicon was fascinating."

"I was especially glad that you included your own testimony in the book as it presents many spiritual truths in ways that people can relate."

"I have enjoyed reading the manuscript so much and feel so privileged to have been allowed a sneak-peak. Thanks so much!"

"I was also moved by your pivotal decision to seek true power with God rather than that of the world."

"*Amazing* gives the reader an opportunity to gain substantial Bible literacy from one easy to understand book."

"My prayer is that God will bless this book and speak to people through it."

Table of Contents

John the Baptist was prophesied by Isaiah over 700 years before his birth. The angel Gabriel announced to his father Zechariah that his prayer had been heard and Elizabeth, his wife, would bear a son. His name would be called John, and he would be filled with the Holy Spirit from his mother's womb. Because Zechariah and his wife were both quite old, he asked Gabriel for a sign. The sign came in a most unusual way. Zechariah was struck dumb (unable to speak) which lasted until eight days after John's birth.

Five months after Elizabeth conceived, the angel went to Mary and told her that she would miraculously conceive, and she gave birth to the Son of God. There are different opinions, but there is substantial scholarly evidence that John the Baptist was born on Passover and that Jesus was born on the first day of the Feast of Trumpets. John's purpose was to turn many Israelites to the Lord their God. John's purpose was for a preparation for the Messiah, Jesus, who has unquestionably had the greatest influence of any person that has ever lived.

Today, that need is there again for Israelites to turn to the Lord, but not just Israel. The peoples of the world primarily are neither living by nor being governed by Biblical precepts and statutes. God is a stranger to billions of the current inhabitants of this planet. At the time of Christ's birth the announcement by the angel was, "I bring you good tidings of great joy, which shall be to all people." (Luke 2:10) This good news is for the whole world!

The New Testament account of John the Baptist reveals a man with a unique ministry and strange characteristics. There are two kinds of prophets, some were speaking and some were writing. John was a speaking prophet. John had the ministry to make people ready by preparing the way for the Messiah, Jesus Christ. He wore camel hair clothing and a wide leather belt. His diet was locusts and wild honey. His place of ministry was the wilderness area around the Jordan River, north of the Dead Sea. This was not a very pleasant climate or environment, being over 1000 feet below sea level. John's message was quite strong, since he referred the

Israelites as a "generation of vipers." But, not withstanding his dress, diet, and location, the multitude came from Jerusalem and all of Judea.

Jesus, himself, praised this man that many considered to be common, and even a little strange at the least. He was even blessed to baptize Jesus, the one called Yeshua. Yeshua said that of those born of woman there was not a greater prophet than John the Baptist. John the Baptist was the first prophet in 400 years and he called the people of Israel to repentance to prepare the way of the Lord. John's calling and ministry was unique; I also believe that this is a book birthed from a unique calling. And, that it was made possible by divine revelations for an approaching end time period called, "the day of the Lord."

Twenty years ago, I spent some time in a rural area in a southern state. I met an older couple there that, at that time, had recently spent ten years traveling around the world on a beautiful yacht. The man was seventy years old, and was not a Christian. We had a discussion that disturbed him. I returned a couple of years later and this man saw me. He immediately proclaimed that he was at church all the time. And then he lowered his voice and advised me, "Around here you are known as John the Baptist." I knew I had some impact on a few people there, but I had no idea I had attained such unworthy recognition. Just as my name, John, means "The Lord is gracious," I believe that these divine revelations have been a gracious gift from the Lord.

I want to make the point that not everyone has the same spiritual experience, power, gifts or calling. Should not everyone be true to the light that they have received?!! I do not claim to be a prophet as my understanding is that all true prophets have been Jewish and they have spiritual infallibility. I have received many revelations and a little fore knowledge, but I lack the two primary qualifications of a prophet; that is, I am not Jewish, nor am I infallible. I do believe that God gifts some to proclaim or tell forth His truth and this book does contain revelations. In 1st Thessalonians Chapter 5, Paul instructs the brethren not to despise prophesyings. That is because this is a special type of Christian communication that needs to be given attention.

Well, besides a unique calling, "Does John the Baptist have anything else to do with this book written 2,000 years after his remarkable ministry?" I see a few other similarities. The preaching of John the Baptist was not just challenging to the religious elite of his day, but opened the eyes of thousands to repentance. John the Baptist was very blunt and that characteristic will be will be seen at the end of the last chapter of the book.

I would like for this book to make truth easier for many to see. Repentance is just a turning or a change in what you think or believe. No one is born believing in God. Since most of humanity has missed knowing the one God and the true God, I hope this book will be one more opportunity to assist individuals in finding the narrow way that leads to eternal life. My personal wake-up came from a spiritual book over a quarter century ago.

In Revelation, the last book of the Bible, the spiritual condition of the church at Laodicea was described. The picture is not complimentary. The church is supposed to convert the world, but this church has primarily been converted by the world. Most members of this church are not born again and saved for an eternity in heaven. God loves those few that are, but even they need to repent and be zealous. When you get some understanding of all the false religions and misleading doctrines today, you see why being zealous is so important. Christian zeal is needed, but for the most part it is missing. "Enter ye in at the strait gate: for wide *is* the gate, and broad *is* the way, that leadeth to destruction, and many there be which go in thereat:" (Matthew 7:13).

Most Bible scholars believe that the seven churches of Revelation represent churches of all ages, but each age is characterized primarily by one of these churches. Observation and statistics seem to verify that Laodicea is the church of our present time. Today, many Christians do not hold to many basic fundamental beliefs of the faith.

An example would be the Deity of Jesus Christ. Respect for Jesus or believing that he is a prophet does not go far enough and is not sufficient for salvation. Jesus was fully man and fully God. He claimed to be equal with God. Have you examined that claim? What you believe about Jesus Christ is crucial to your standing with God. For me and countless others, He is Lord, Savior, King of

Kings, the First born of the Resurrection and the unique Son of God. As He said, "He that has seen me has seen the Father." There is no neutral position – you either believe or you do not. Non believers are at enmity with the Almighty God.

Jesus sat His disciples down, "And beginning at Moses and all the prophets, he expounded unto them in all the scriptures the things concerning himself." (Luke 24:27) The Bible is profound and deep and God hides many secrets within the sacred scriptures for man to search out. As an early example, Jesus might have used Genesis Chapter 5 listing the genealogies of Adam through Noah. The study of a Hebrew lexicon of the root meanings of the names of these ten men produces a surprise. Using the root meaning of each of their names and taken in order, you get a sentence that states the New Testament gospel. Remarkably, *Amazing* does a similar thing through words throughout the Bible with this new holographic lexicon from Genesis to Revelation. This gives direct evidence from two witnesses – a Hebrew lexicon and this new discovery of the holographic lexicon. "In the mouth of two or three witnesses shall every word be established."

When I was age eleven I was required to regularly attend a neighborhood church. I remember you had to wear "Sunday clothes" and the wool pants I wore made me itch terribly. One day the pastor called me to his office. He suggested I consider the ministry. I laughed. He was offended because he was serious. He replied that whenever I spoke before the church everyone in the church sat up and listened, and they did not even do that for him. I said that I did not have anything important to say. He said that did not matter. Well, it is now decades later, and I am persuaded that I do have a lot that needs said. These are spiritual things to share, and I do want people to listen. I hope many people will listen and hear with their heart as well as their head.

Isn't it remarkable that approximately fifty percent of the current world's population claim either to be physically or spiritually related to Abraham? That is several billion people who include Catholics, Protestants, Muslims, Arabs, Jews and others. Thousands of years ago the God of Abraham asked him a question, and Abraham did not know the answer. You do not know the answer either. In this book you will get both the question, and because of divine revelation, you will get the answer. If you can not wait, the question is in Genesis 15:5.

I would hope that the billions of people that claim a kinship with Abraham might want to listen to the person who could answer a question that this great man of faith could not. This is a question that no one could correctly answer without the benefit of supernatural revelation. It is a question about the Cosmos that even NASA with super computers would be able to solve.

Christianity is not an esoteric religion; rather it is a personal relationship with the real God. By God's grace, I have had many answered prayers and personal experiences with the living God for a quarter of a century. I believe that because of God's amazing grace, this writer is a disciple that has been allowed to have some special privileges with the Creator. These privileges are to produce fruit that will be a blessing to others. The words of Jesus, "Feed my sheep" have been a motivation to write. Therefore, these privileges do not give pride, but rather a sense of responsibility. I have long realized that any spiritual work that I attempt should be started and finished through faith. I have seen works done with faith produce results far that exceed my natural abilities.

Faith is clarity, vision, belief, trust, dependence, and confidence. Not being a writer by profession (except grant writing, & articles), I undertook this writing on faith. I have experienced that God has given the grace to complete this work. "But God hath chosen the foolish things of the world to confound the wise; and God hath chosen the weak things of the world to confound the things which are mighty." (1 Corinthians 1:27)

In the Bible, God proclaims to Israel that He is a jealous God. He had that right because he was in a covenant relationship with Israel. This is just like jealousy that might occur in a marriage because the union is a covenant that pledges fidelity. I find that just as God is jealous, so am I jealous for the God of Abraham, Isaac and Jacob. I know that this is the true God and this God is really worth knowing.

I feel burdened for those that have not found God and entered into His experiences, peace and rest. I say with confidence that the advantages of being in God's family are superior to anything else that you could have in this world. God desires for you to seek Him. I pray you will seek truth and with God's grace find Jesus Christ, the second person of the Godhead (the Bible reveals one God, but three distinct persons of the Godhead that exist simultaneously).

Jesus is referred to this way - "In the beginning was the Word, and the Word was God and the Word was with God." (John1:1) Since Jesus Himself is called the Word, it would appear that words are very important to God. And what is important to God should be important to us.

As this book progresses into section two you will see an enormous amount of evidence to support that statement. Christians should have a reverence for a Holy God and also have the utmost appreciation for the Holy Bible. I believe that it is the inspired word of God, and that it is magnificent and miraculous. The Bible should be the final authority on all matters in the Christian faith.

This book is written to complement the sacred Scriptures and generate a refreshing interest in Scripture and a clearer understanding for many. The prayer is that your reading of this book will be a stimulating, strengthening, satisfying and significant spiritual blessing to you.

SECTION ONE

GMAIL was a term used to describe God mail which is faster than e-mail. The term was developed at least a couple of years before Google g-mail. Gmail developed from a discovery, by divine revelation, that English language words contain letters that when properly combined reveals deeper meanings. This is a type cryptic message or code within words that seems to have mostly been overlooked, missed or lost. There are more to our words than meets the eye.

Shortly after Gmail began, the person who first had the experience of meanings revealed within words stated, "I think that God and Noah Webster had fun together." To quote Noah Webster – "Language as well as the faculty of speech, was the immediate gift of God."

This author definitely agrees with Noah Webster. *Amazing* will provide extensive evidence that language reveals a pattern of design, so sophisticated, that it would surpass the ability of modern super computers to duplicate. This pattern in language shows further proof of God's design in yet another aspect of creation. Billions believe, including this author, that God created the universe. And the evidence of this divine design or fingerprints of God, are manifested in numerous ways.

God provides numerous clues to His reality. Many of these clues are not as clear as the physical laws of gravity and the sun always rising. There are aspects of human existence such as poverty, suffering, pain, and death that confuse many. Actually, suffering and death confirm that man is under a judgment curse because of sin. Lacking faith, they miss the clues and miss out on knowing God. These evidences of a power much higher than mankind have included, but are not limited to; the marvelous design of the cosmos, balance in nature, complex life on earth, and the Old and New Bible Testaments with hundreds and hundreds of accurately fulfilled prophecies.

There is astonishing evidence of God in both a macro (large) and a micro (small) examination of existence. As science advances, the macro view is expanded across trillions of miles of space and countless galaxies (estimate a trillion). In one of the most distant galaxies named Whirlpool Galaxy (or M51) a NASA photo shows a dark cross in a circle of white light. If, as Christians maintain the cross at Calvary does represent the single most important event in the history of planet earth, you might expect it to be showcased even in a distant galaxy.

Man's knowledge continues to increase in the micro universe as well. Science has discovered laminins, glycoproteins, which are the structural scaffolding in almost every human and animal tissue. Laminins are secreted and incorporated into cell-associated extra cellular matrices. These micro components are shaped like a cross. "And he (Jesus) is before all things and by him all things consist." (Colossians 1:17) Consist means that He holds everything together! Without laminins we would be a pile of jelly. Laminin - I am in man).

I have a cross story I would like to share. My wife likes diamonds and she had a white gold cross with diamonds. In a store she saw a more expensive diamond cross that caught her eye. She said to me that if I would buy her that cross I could give my daughter the cross she was wearing. I decided to go back and buy the new cross. I boxed and wrapped her first diamond and 14k gold cross and sent it to my daughter for Christmas. Later, after Christmas, I spoke with my daughter and I got the "Paul Harvey rest of the story." She said my young granddaughter asked her what she wanted for Christmas. She told her that the only thing she really wanted for Christmas was a cross. My daughter's daughter processed the request and told her mother that she did not have any money for a cross. My daughter told her that if she would just draw a picture of a cross that would be fine. When my granddaughter saw the shiny gold and diamond cross her mother opened, she enthusiastically said to her mother, "God does answer prayer."

Kabbalah, originated from ancient Jewish mysticism, and was the source for a line in the movie *Bee Season* starring Richard Gere. It states that the letters in words contain the secrets of the universe. This book agrees with, and provides verification, for that statement, but Kabbalah endorses a non-Biblical view of God. *Amazing* does support the Biblical view of God. A primary purpose of *Amazing* is to show the readers that words reveal a design structure that is beyond human ability. This would then add human language as one more component to the list of "God's clues or fingerprints."

In *Amazing,* you will see how words (162) contain the letters for other words which display the nature and wisdom of God. This book offers a new view of language that uncovers its divine construction and the spiritual DNA of language. This DNA of language supports the truth of Scripture. By the way – DNA that makes each and every person unique is in the word individual. This was not by accident!

The second person of the Godhead is called the Word, and "Heaven and earth shall pass away, but my words shall not pass away." There is clearly a divine essence within language; and Scripture provides the primary window with which God is revealed to mankind. Thus, it stands to reason that language that was with God before creation and is part of His being.

The Bible could be the only book you would ever have and it would be all you would need. It is so important that is why we have bibliography (Bible - Holy Graph)

> *"For now we see through a glass, darkly; but then face to face: now I know in part; but then shall I know even as also I am known."* - 1 Corinthians 13:12

Holy Scripture is a window to God. The result of *Amazing* is to bring a sharp focus view on one word at a time. *Amazing* provides a laser like light and magnifying glass for each word examined. Scripture reveals the truth and glory of God and this book shows the importance and significance of many words in that window view. Word has the letters phonetically for door. Each word in *Amazing* opens a door to a treasure room of understanding. *Amazing* gives the reader a thought provoking view of the divine DNA of language, and the uncanny ways in which God has left His fingerprints on words. If a regular English word dictionary is important, how valuable is a spiritual lexicon (special dictionary)?

The word hologram has meaning both from the definition of holocryptic and holograph. The first of these two words means to effectively conceal, and the second word means whole or entire.

The equipment for making a hologram includes a laser, mirror and diffusers. The hologram is a frequency record, and when viewed with a laser of the same frequency, it reveals a three-dimensional image of the original object. A profound quality of a hologram is that the image is distributed throughout the entire media. If the hologram is cut into pieces, each piece contains the complete image.

In his book, *Cosmic Codes*, Dr. Chuck Misler discussed the similarities between a hologram and the Bible. I do agree with Dr. Misler that the Bible is like a hologram, and that God's plan for redemption of mankind is distributed from Genesis in the Old Testament to Revelation in the New Testament. Even the idea of God in the form of a man started in Genesis. This man, God as a man, made three appearances to Abraham and Abraham worshiped him. If Abraham accepted and ran to meet this man in the form of God why shouldn't you do the same?

This hologram concept then makes words the smallest segment of the Bible that still conveys an accurate message or picture. Just like each piece of a hologram contains the complete image. When letters from words are reformed to make other words, it provides compelling evidence to the accuracy of the Bible and for the hologram theory.

Gmail got started in 2002 as instant revelations of words within words. People exposed to some of this Gmail recognized the significance of words from words, but many thought that they just came from tinkering around with the letters. Once you see examples of words from words you can "tinker with letters in words" and make interesting discoveries. But, this is not true Gmail. The most profound word examples in this book, including the title, did not come from tinkering with letters, but rather came from an instantaneous understanding, or revelation. Gmail is believed to be an instant communication from God.

For a Gmail example, I will use the word pirate. In the word there are the letters for words RAPE and TRAP. Rape means to seize by force, or plunder or have sex by force. Does that

14

describe pirates? Pirates are also known for setting traps for their victims; which is even still true today with increasing internet piracy. This example shows that the word has letters within the word that support the meaning and use of the word. Some of the Biblical words in the lexicon are far more profound than this example.

The following is a small sample list of Gmail words: **Universe** – (uni verse) One verse, and it is the first verse in the Bible. "In the beginning God created the heaven and the earth." There is a universe because God brought it into existence. **Earth** – (heart) This planet is called earth because it is of prime importance to God's heart. **World** – (word and Lord) It is appropriate to be here because of God's word and the Lord Jesus Christ. **Life** – (file) God has a file on every person that will ever live. The Bible refers to the Book of Life. **Person** – (per Son) You are who you are per the son. "No man cometh unto the Father, but by the Son." **Deity** - (Die) Can God die? The answer is yes because the second person of the Godhead, Jesus who was fully God and fully man did die on a cross in Jerusalem. If your God did not die you have the wrong god. **Character** – (heart chart) Character is evaluated by God, with a chart on everyone's heart (the essence of who you are and the seat of emotion and reason) **Bibliography** – (Bible holy graph) The Bible is the authentic sacred book and everyone's biography should be influenced by this divine inspired Holy book. **Scripture** – (your script). God's will is important for you to know, and there is a script for you from the Bible, and you are responsible for that script. If you stay ignorant that is no excuse. **Stone** – The word note is in stone. Every time you cast a stone at someone else God makes a note of it and it will come back to you. Jesus knew this and he said, "let he who is without sin cast the first stone." **Conservative** – Con (with verse) all conservatives use verse whether they are evangelical Christians, Orthodox Jews, Mormons, Jehovah Witness, Amish, or some Sunni or Shiite Muslims, etc. They also vote and are reactive to conserve their views. Some conservatives serve the true God, but many do not. **Liberal** – (libel, lie, rebel) these, as a group, believes a lie, and therefore they libel God (make and say false assumptions) and many are in a rebellion against God. Repentance might be a good option.

For several years, there was only one person that received regular Gmail. For this person, it started during a Henry Blackaby small group Bible study of *Experiencing God*. About the time that a group of three of us agreed to do some collaboration on this book lexicon, we all started getting regular and significant numbers of Gmail. This continued for about three months, and then we realized that all three of us had, at about the same time, stopped getting Gmail. Later, the Gmail started again, but they came at a slower rate. Later, the editor of this book, a fourth person received some Gmail. This further substantiates that this is not something that we are able to do or control merely just with our intellect. The four of us are convinced that there is a definite component of revelation with receiving Gmail.

I would like to share an experience I had several years ago in a medical doctor's office. The doctor is an endocrinologist, and I was there waiting for an appointment. His first name is George, and I started writing all the words that I could make with the letters in his name. I had written several, and then I saw the word ego. I placed it at the top of the list even though I had written several other words before I saw this one. When the doctor entered the room he immediately saw the list and asked if I had made it. I said yes. He quickly went to the telephone and made a call. When he returned, he said, "Last night my wife and I had a long conversation about my ego." This example, though not exactly Gmail, illustrates God using a word from a word to get a doctor's attention. I believe it was not a coincidence or accident that ego was placed at the top of the list.

It is hoped readers will find these words within words insightful, inspiring, and thought provoking. Christian and Messianic pastors and apologists should find these many word examples to be a valuable tool to compliment their ministries. Other Christian believers should enjoy the many insights from word revelations that support the God of the Bible, and the Christian worldview. Anyone who values the Bible should love the Gmail lexicon as a Biblical aide.

Jesus said, "Feed my sheep." (John 21:17) These words of instruction by Jesus were convicting enough to encourage the completion of this work. The book was written for God's sheep, both those that know they are sheep and those that will hear God and become sheep. Jesus said, "I am the good shepherd, and know my sheep and am known of mine." (John 10:14). It is hoped that those who are genuinely seeking to find meaning and purpose to life may discover some helpful answers from reading *Amazing*.

Also, it is suspected that God wants to leave enough important word codes unsolved so that some others might enjoy this same experience. Revelations from words are an exhilarating experience that you really want to share with others. When you receive a true Gmail you know it. It is both insightful and thrilling to hear from God in this special way. It is always great to experience the presence of God!

What do we know about the origin of language? Scientists cannot answer with 100% certainty questions of origin because they were not there. This is a question similar to the origin of the universe because we do not have any eye witnesses. In a book, *The Word*, written by Isaac Mozeson, evidence is presented that demonstrates that Hebrew is the patriarch of language. Mozeson's book demonstrates that all languages come from a single original source. Mozeson supports language having a divine origin. And, as quoted earlier, Noah Webster believes that language and speech were both instant gifts from God.

This writer takes as accurate and inspired revelation, the Biblical accounts of both the origin of the universe and the origin of language. As the reader progresses through this book, he will encounter a lot of evidence to support both of these Biblical claims through many Gmail examples, along with additional information. The following is what the Word of God says about the source of language.

"And the whole earth was of one language, and of one speech. And it came to pass, as they journeyed from the east, that they found a plain in the land of Shinar; and they dwelt there. And they said one to another, Go to, let us make brick, and burn them thoroughly. And they had brick for stone, and slime had they for mortar. And they said, Go to, let us build us a city and a tower, whose top may reach unto heaven; and let us make us a name, lest we be scattered abroad upon the face of the whole earth. And the

LORD came down to see the city and the tower, which the children of men built. And the LORD said, Behold, the people is one, and they have all one language; and this they begin to do: and now nothing will be restrained from them, which they have imagined to do. Go to, let us go down, and there confound their language, that they may not understand one another's speech. So the LORD scattered them abroad from thence upon the face of all the earth: and they left off to build the city. Therefore is the name of it called Babel; because the LORD did there confound the language of all the earth: and from thence did the LORD scatter them abroad upon the face of all the earth. (Genesis 11:1-9) *These are the families of the sons of Noah, after their generations, in their* <u>nations</u>*: and by these were the* <u>nations</u> *divided in the earth after the flood.*" (Genesis10:32)

Separate nations are God's plan for this planet, and this necessitated many different languages. According to this account written by Moses and recorded in the first chapter of the Old Testament, the languages (thousands) in the world came directly from God early in human history. Of course, over time there are additions and changes to language, but each original language had a divine origin. Gmail will provide evidence to help substantiate that claim.

It is understood there are many individuals that do not have personal experiences with God. That is unfortunate because the Bible gives assurance that true believers have direct access to God.

"*Let us therefore come boldly unto the throne of grace, that we may obtain mercy, and find grace to help in time of need.*" (Hebrews 4:16)

Some believers do not think that God provides any new revelations since the Bible is complete. The writer's position is that the Bible is the inspired word of God and the ultimate authority. Anything contradicting the inspired Word of God should be rejected. However, through a personal relationship with the God of Abraham, Isaac and Jacob, I am convinced, both by experiences and Biblical text, there is divine help with understanding and new spiritual revelations. The original word for "word" in the New Testament substantiates just this. The Greek word 'logos' refers to the written Word of God. And the word 'rhema' refers to 'words' or revelations from God that are always based on Scripture. Throughout history, God has revealed Himself not only through the written word, but through divine revelation.

In 1905, when Albert Einstein was only 26 years old, he published a paper on relativity. At the time of the publication on the theory of relativity, it was met with skepticism and ridicule. As other papers were published, they were viewed the same way. Since these papers were so advanced, only a few physicists even understood them. Only slowly over time did people start to realize that Einstein was actually a true genius. He developed the theory of relativity. The greatest result of relativistic physics was Einstein's famous relation, $E=mc^2$. The equation demonstrates that for a small amount of mass you get an enormous amount of energy. That is precisely what occurs with an atomic bomb. Did you know that Einstein claimed to have gotten his understanding for $E=mc^2$ from the Bible? He said that you will not see it, but it is there in the first book, the Book of Genesis. Using letters in the name of the Jewish Albert Einstein you are able to spell <u>liberate Israel</u>.

Besides being a great physicist, Albert Einstein is also famous for his many quotes. One quote is, "One cannot help but be in awe as he [one] contemplates the mysteries of eternity, of life, of the marvelous structures of reality." For many years, prior to $E=mc^2$ and the atomic bomb, skeptics made fun of the Bible because of a verse that said the *"elements shall melt with a fervent heat."* (2 Peter 3:10) This contradicted the science of the day. Today, if you ask a physicist to describe an atomic reaction, they will talk about tremendous heat that occurs in a split second, because of the energy released when atoms split. The heat parallels that of our sun. So once again, the Bible proved to be right – elements, indeed, shall melt. The more science discovers, the smarter the Bible becomes. Since this period of the explosion of knowledge began, the Bible has proven to be hundreds or even thousands of years ahead of its time on many issues.

Isaac Newton died 280 years ago and is the scientist known for laying much of the foundation for modern physics, astronomy, math (calculus) and optics. This man considered by many to be the world's greatest scientist, had an intense interest in the Bible. Newton studied the Book of Daniel and concluded that the world would not end earlier than 2060. In 2001, from my study of end times, I arrived at the date of 2050 before the world could end. That is not much difference, and his calculations were 300 years ago. Newton was convinced that the Bible contained cryptic messages and I think he would enjoy this book that reveals cryptic messages in language! As you read, I hope that this decoding of words will be an enjoyable and informative adventure for you. You may even find yourself decoding some words yourself.

CHAPTER TWO
HOW EVERYTHING BEGAN

Gmail from the following words (36) will be in this chapter: Adam, atom, began, breath, character, creation, dimension, dominion, earth, elements, evolution, galaxy, genes, genesis, history, image, individual, knowledge, life, live, moon, nature, origin, person, planet, philosophy, reality, serpent, sound, species, stars, sun, time, universe, wisdom, and world.

When I was a young boy lying in bed at night, I sometimes would meditate on the question, "What would be here if what is here did not exist?" I just could not understand how I and everything else came into being. This question and one other, have held the fascination of philosophers, scientists and most of mankind for centuries. These two questions are: From where did everything originate? And what is the meaning of life?

This chapter presents direct evidence from the thirty-six English words listed above to support answers to these two age old questions. This presentation should provide you with much to think about, and some interesting new insights into both theology and science.

Over twenty-five years ago, I realized that the written Bible was the inspired revelation from God for the benefit of man and the glory of God. A year later, I became fascinated in learning more about creation. I accepted Genesis as being both accurate and historical. This first book in the Bible explained how the universe got here, the origin of all life on the earth, and man's fall by disobeying God.

I thought I would take the time to study creation, and to learn a lot more about God's word over that summer. A few days after I decided to start my studying, I got a call from a dear

Christian lady that taught a high school Sunday school class in a Lutheran Church. She asked me if I would be able to teach her class because she had temporary blindness. Their next lesson started with the study of the beginning of Genesis, which covered the account of creation. Her blindness continued for the four weeks that I taught the verses from the Sunday school lesson plan. After I had finished, her sight returned. Just as I believe that God called me to teach twenty-five years ago, I am convinced that God wants me to teach this subject of creation again.

Origins present a particular difficulty of uncertainty because none of us were there at the time. The attempt by scientists to explain the universe and many life forms on earth, without direct evidence, seems to blur into philosophy and therefore, becomes a type of faith or belief that is based on their particular view of reality. Many start from the position that there is no God; therefore some other explanation must be sought.

In *Scientific American*, in 1959, two-thirds of those scientists surveyed, said when asked the age of the universe, "Beginning? The universe is eternal." Now the Big Bang is accepted, and science believes the universe had a beginning. The Bible stated that the universe had a beginning. It is profound to me just how much science is getting right when compared to Biblical statements. Science and the Bible go hand in hand, and do not contradict themselves, as much as many people have been mislead into believing.

For many years, scientists have used this Big Bang theory to try to prove that the universe was created by an explosion of matter from a single point. It states that there was nothing in the beginning. It goes further to say that a process known as Vacuum Fluctuation created a dime-sized singularity, or a dense mass of matter, which exploded to form the ever-expanding universe we see today. An expanding universe gets into complex and interesting physics. Does space and time dilate with expansion? Oh the mysteries and complexities of creation.

Was the universe formed from a big bang? On the surface, the Big Bang theory as stated by scientists looks like an absolute mockery of God's divine blueprint of the universe. And that generally is their whole aim: To try to remove God from His

22

creation. However, they may be closer to the scriptural truth of creation than they realize! Again, in accepting the Big Bang theory, these scientists also accept the event of a beginning, but they do not acknowledge God as the creator. We know that in the beginning there was "nothing," as the scientists say. That compressed mass of matter that exploded had to come from somewhere!

Matter is not eternal and it did have a beginning. God, not matter, is eternal. God is not matter. God is a spirit.

> *"God is a spirit: and they that worship him must worship him is spirit and in truth." (John 4:24)*
> *"For the invisible things of him from the creation of the world are clearly seen, being understood by the things that are made, even his eternal power and Godhead; so that they are without excuse."* - Romans 1:20

Now, if matter had a beginning where did it come from? Genesis, the first book in the Bible, was inspired by God, and written by Moses before 1,400 BC. The "beginning" Moses described was an absolute beginning before anything existed: except God and eternity, because God states that he is eternal. *"The eternal God is thy refuge..."* - Deuteronomy 33:27

The thing that confounded me for years was my understanding that God brought the creation ex nilo, out of nothing. My analytical brain could not understand that, because, how do you get something out of nothing? This issue also confounds science and philosophers because they do not have an answer. God did not use his essence to make the matter or material of Creation. I prayed for years for God to reveal to me how he brought something out of nothing.

There was a bumper sticker that said, "I Believe in the Big Theory: God said "Bang" and there it was!"

> *"By the Word of the Lord were the heavens made; and all the host of them by the breath of His mouth. He gathereth the waters of the sea together as an*

heap: He layeth up the depth in storehouses. Let all the earth fear the Lord: let all the inhabitants of the world stand in awe of Him. For He spake, and it was done; He commanded, and it stood fast." - Psalm 33:6-9

Finally, I got an answer this year, and I think that the bumper sticker was right. I heard a preacher on Christian radio; I did not catch his name, but he was explaining that God made the Creation out of sound. The Bible record does state that God spoke it into existence. The more he talked, the better I liked the explanation. Could God speak everything into existence? That night when I prayed, I asked God to show me what the building block of matter looked like. I instantly saw a vision of a perfect circle, a little larger than the size of a quarter, with uniform waves going all the way around the circle. The circle with the perfect symmetrical wave was connected, just like a ring that symbolizes eternity because it has no beginning or end.

Astronomers in the 1970's theorized that the universe was thick and gassy just after the Big Bang and that the heavens rang with sound, like cosmic bells. Dr. Daniel Eisenstein has continued studying this theory, part of the Sloan Digital Sky Survey and he has concluded that the distance of the many galaxies today, and the pattern of the sound waves of the early universe, match up precisely and the early cosmic sounds were like pebbles being thrown into a pond. Again, a scientist may have inadvertently found the result of God's speaking this universe into creation.

There is your "Big Bang." I believe that this sound from God might have extended for a trillion times a trillion miles. That would have made a really loud bang. Just in case you are still wondering – BEGAN has the letters for *bang*. One more little bit of evidence is the word SOUND. It contains *son* and *sun*. Therefore, the position is yes, there WAS a really big bang. Halleluiah, praise God!

"In the beginning was the Word (son), and the Word was with God, and the Word was God. The same was in the beginning with God. All things were made by Him; and without Him was not any thing made that was made." – John 1:1

A recent poll showed that in the United States only twelve percent of the population does not believe that life came from God. Recently, I read about a DNA study by researchers from the Broad Institute of MIT and Harvard. The study hypothesized that an ancestral ape species split into two isolated populations about ten million years ago, then got back together after a few thousand millennia. One thousand millennia would be a million years. They suggest that the human-chimp split was no earlier that 6.3 million years ago, and more likely in the neighborhood of 5.4 million. They also say that their data suggests this human-chimp split probably took millions of years to occur.

I have an idea for these researchers. Since they think that the species split and re-united once, shouldn't it be about time for them to do this again. Yes, it is about time for these ancient relatives to re-unite a second time. These guys should just either move in with the chimps or have the chimps move in with them. If given a few million millennia they just might be able to produce another new species for their family tree.

The writer of this book thinks that evolution research is a questionable use of valuable resources, and in fact we have a few questions for the researchers. First, where did the apes come from? How many splits did it take to get the apes and monkeys? How many thousands of millions of years did that take? What millennia did man get the gene for language? Animals do not laugh or cry; when did man acquire that gene? When did we get our gene for abstract thought? How many splits did it take to get the 5,000 species of birds on planet Earth, with a range in weight from a couple of ounces to 300 pounds? Sorry, this writer prefers the inspired Bible, a divine designed language, the enormous variety of complex life, and the astonishing human DNA code to your suggested conclusions.

The research conclusions on evolution frankly sound just plain impossible, and therefore ridiculous. It would be like throwing pieces of a watch into a field and waiting for them to evolve into a watch, instead of trusting in the careful hand of a watchmaker to craft the intricate masterpiece. How ridiculous a thought! And how impossible! We know that a watch would never just come from a pile of watch parts, unless crafted by the watchmaker. Even if we waited a million years, like the evolutionists say. So, why think the complexity of life would happen the same way?

If you want to believe in phenomenal species complexity, improvement, and advancement that occurred over thousands of millions of years; and that you are related to apes and chimps, you are free to do just that. But those of you doing evolution research are the blind leading the blind. Jesus healed a blind man and he said, when questioned by the Pharisees, *"One thing I know, I was blind and now I see."* Everyone that is born again, born spiritually, is able to make that statement. You are justified, not by works, but by faith. Faith is not blind. You must hear from God to have faith. The real blind are those without faith and therefore without hope. I would not trade real faith for a ton of gold.

Evolution is called a theory, but it lacks the observed phenomena to justify that scientific designation. It does not even have the foundation for a hypothesis. It is actually just a notion; which is a vague thought. I have one word for those that promote EVOLUTION, which is an *evil notion*, and that word is universe. The UNIVERSE exists because of one *verse* and it is the first verse in the Bible.

"In the beginning God (Elohim) created the heaven and the earth." - Genesis 1:1

This first Bible verse is a summary statement, and what follows are many details. This verse answers one of the two questions, "From where did everything originate?" by plainly stating that matter did have a beginning. And yes, evolution is not only false, but it is evil. Those that promote this feeble theory would be better served to seek eternal life. Fortunately, there have been evolution scientists that did see the light, and have become strong defenders of the Genesis creation account. One such well known scientist that supports Genesis is the published author Dr. Henry Morris. His doctorate in paleontology provided an academic evolution background. He became a creation apologetics (defender) author. If you do not believe this author please read a book or two written by Dr. Henry Morris.

There was a CREATION because of the Creator, the eternal God. This word was used because the creation demonstrates _art_. Also, CREATION includes the word _eat_ in the middle of the word. "And he said, Who told thee that thou wast naked? Hast thou eaten of the tree, whereof I commanded thee that thou shouldest not _eat_?" (Genesis 3:11) Because of that sin of disobedience to God the whole creation is under a curse.

> *"For we know that the whole creation groaneth and travaileth in pain together until now."* - Romans 8:22

There is a theory called "theistic evolution" which states that evolution and the Bible can both be believed at the same time without contradicting each other. About twenty years ago, I was riding in Virginia with a Navy Seal and he asked me this question, "John, can you believe in evolution and be a Christian?" My answer was simply, "Yes." He drove a little further and asked, "Would you be on the first team?" I said, "No." He drove a little further and said, "I have always been a first team guy." I said, "Good."

> *"And God called the light Day, and the darkness he called Night. And the evening and the morning were the first day."* - Genesis 1:5

In the Genesis account of creation, numerals are used for each day. This means that it is a literal twenty-four hour day and the entire creation, including man, was completed in six literal days. I believe that the Bible supports a young earth of thousands of years and not an earth of millions of years. I do not believe that real science has any way of contradicting that position. I like real science, but I do not like the philosophy of applied materialism represented through the theory of evolution, as being science. I am convinced that the millions or billions of years "scientific theories" hold require circular reasoning, conjecture and/or false assumptions. Circular reasoning goes something like this: The fossil is ten million years old. How do you know? The rock where it was found was ten million years old. How do you know the age of the rock? The fossil found there is ten million years old. Okay!!

I would like to offer a little Gmail insight into the Charles Darwin's book, *"Origin of the Species."* ORIGIN has _groin_ because that is the area of the body where reproduction is initiated. SPECIES rearranged gives you _pieces,_ because there is no "missing link." And there is not any chain, or any transitional species or pieces. Yes, after centuries of extensive archeology, thousands of these "transitional animals" should have been found if they had existed.

> *"And God said, Let the earth bring forth the living creature after his kind, cattle, and creeping thing, and beast of the earth after his kind: and it was so."*
> - Genesis 1:24

That is what man and animals do. They always reproduce their own kind from a genetics pool that provides for variety. That is what has always been observed, and that is also what the fossil record shows. Macro evolution, simple changing into complex, is not science. And if you like evolution I am so sorry, because you have accepted a lie and have fallen into darkness. There are no less than seven disciplines of science that disprove evolution.

> *"And the light shineth in darkness and the darkness comprehended it not."* - John 1:5

I am not being judgmental because I also needed to be convinced of sin and saved by God's marvelous grace. I just hope and pray that those of you, who have not before, will see the light of truth and believe before it is too late. Faith is not blind as some suppose. You receive faith by hearing from God. I do not know of anything that is clearer than real Biblical faith.

"Faith *cometh* by hearing and hearing by the word of God." - Romans 10:17

We got our *genes* on the sixth day of GENESIS. The genetic information coded in human DNA is so extensive, that if the instructions were regular language the material would fill the books in the average size library. The material would equal the equivalent of 2,000 books of 250 pages each. That is a message and anytime there is a message there is a messenger. That is compelling proof for design. I submit to you that in this case the messenger is none other than the eternal God. Wisdom is intelligence that is superior to knowledge.

"The fear of Lord is the beginning of wisdom." - Proverbs 9:10

What is more important to you, the world or your soul? You are not just a big pile of arranged molecules that developed by accident. You have purpose and value. HEART has the letters for the word *rate* for both physical and spiritual reasons. You need a heart beat (rate) to be physically alive, and you need the right heart rate or rating by God to be spiritually alive. God said let us make man in our image, after our likeness.

". . So God created man in his *own* image." - Genesis 1:27

IMAGE contains *I Am* and *me*. The image of you and me is in the likeness of I Am. God has revealed to man that He is one Godhead but with three distinct and equal persons – Father, Son, and Holy Spirit. So, if we are in his likeness, does man exhibit anything similar to this? We have a soul, a body and a spirit, or three in one. The Father represents the soul, Jesus, the body, and the Holy Spirit, the spirit. To quote Ravi Jacharias, "Our mind is to our souls, as our brain is to our body." The brain controls and directs the body, and our minds direct our hearts and souls. Has your mind directed you to Christ? If not, what is hindering you?

We also received BREATH, and from these letters you can spell *heart*.

> "And the Lord God formed man *of* the dust of the ground, and breathed into his nostrils the breath of life; and man became a living soul." Genesis 2:7
> "Jesus said unto him, THOU SHALT LOVE THE LORD THY GOD WITH ALL THY HEART, AND WITH ALL THY SOUL, AND WITH ALL THY MIND." - Matthew 22:37

I was a non-believer (not a Christian), but I still knew, as most people will also acknowledge, that there was too much complexity of design for random events to have been responsible for creation. I realized that a God, or some power and intelligence much greater than man existed. God makes no attempt to prove His reality rather He says it this way,

> "The fool has said in his heart *there* is no God." - Psalms 14.1

The Bible states that man does not fail to recognize God in nature because of reason or intellect, but because of his heart. The word CHARACTER contains *heart chart*. God knows you better than you know yourself, and has a chart of everyone's heart. Do you have a heart for the creator God? I was once this way: I did not know God and was not interested in God, because I enjoyed a secular life.

> "And this is the condemnation, that light is come into the world, and men loved darkness rather than light, because their deeds were evil." - John 3:19

30

By the way, for all the nature worshippers, it is called NATURE because it provides a glimpse into the *nature* of an all powerful and sovereign God. Be careful what you worship.

There is something about truth with which nothing else compares. Once you really experience truth, you would never want to live again without it. Jesus said,

> "I am the way, the truth, and the life: no man cometh unto the Father, but by me." - John 14:6

What a profound statement. My prayer is that if you do not have truth now, that the Spirit of God will draw you. I hope that you will find truth as I was blessed to do, over twenty-five years ago.

> "The wages of sin is death; but the gift of God is eternal life through Jesus Christ our Lord." - Romans 6:23

It is okay to be in the WORLD because it contains *Word* and *Lord*. EARTH rearranged spells *heart* because this is where God's heart is focused. It is a PLANET because it was from a *plan*. You were also planned and designed unique from anyone else that has or ever will live.

Moses had his first encounter with God on Mt. Sinai, "And said unto God, Behold when I come unto the children of Israel and shall say unto them, The God of your fathers, the God of Abraham, the God of Isaac, and the God of Jacob, hath sent me unto you; and they shall say unto me, What is his name? What shall I say unto them?"

> "And God said unto Moses, I AM THAT I AM: and he said, Thus shalt thou say unto the children of Israel, I AM hath sent me unto you. "- Exodus 3:14

These words express absolute and eternal being. About 1,400 years later you find that Jesus or Yeshua, his actual Hebrew name, arrives on the scene and is I am. Jesus said, I am the bread

31

of life, I am the good shepherd, I am the way, etc. Is it a coincidence that the name of the first human, ADAM contained *am*? I do not think that it was a coincidence, because God breathed life into Adam that made him a living soul. God <u>ad</u>ded AM when he created man.

Why do we have a LIFE? Because when you rearrange the letters you get *file*. Before you are saved or born again you are an enemy of God, but after spiritual birth you immediately receive eternal life. God has a file on every person that ever lives. The files of those that are saved have no sins recorded, but what is recorded is for the purpose of rewards. Every single thing that you have done that has any purpose for God's Kingdom will be in your file. Scripture states,

> *"For where your treasure is, there will your heart be also."* - Luke 12:34

If you are a believer you should be about building treasure in heaven. One of the standards for that is what you have done to help others.

> *"He that believeth on the Son hath everlasting life: and he that believeth not on the Son shall not see life; but hath the wrath of God abideth on him."* - John 3:36

You are who you are as a person *per* the *son*! You will either have an eternity with God; or an eternity of separation, loss or despair solely based on your standing with God per his only begotten Son.

You LIVE because the letters rearranged spell *evil*.

> "Behold, I was shapen in iniquity; and in sin did my mother conceive me. Psalm 51:5 "For all have sinned, and come short of the glory of God." - Romans 3:23

We are not capable of righteousness within ourselves, and that is why we need to have righteousness imputed to us through faith in the Savior.

> "For I am not ashamed of the gospel of Christ: for it is the power of God unto everyone that believeth; to the Jew first and also to the Greek (gentile)." - Romans 1:16

I would like to get back to the question of what, if anything would be here if the universe was not. I do have an answer to offer. God has revealed that He is omnipresent. God is everywhere at the same time, and God was here before time, space, and the universe. God is in eternity and is not limited by time, space, past or future. TIME is a *mite* to God. I find it interesting that time provides a type of space. We are in time and space with a spirit, a soul and a body. Time is present with matter and eternity is not just lots and lots of time. The spirit of God, the Holy Spirit, is like an invisible sea that extends throughout this entire expanse of universe. God is omnipresent. We *see* because of that *sea* of the Spirit of the eternal God.

Adam, the first man, was given DOMINIOM over the animal kingdom, but one of those animals, a serpent, was used by Satan to cause a *domino* effect of sin in man. SERPENT has *step*, *repent*, *tree* and *see*. Since the serpent did this, God cursed him, saying he would crawl on his belly and,

> *"I will put enmity between thee and the woman, and between thy seed and her seed; it shall bruise thy head and thou shall bruise his heel."* - Genesis 3:15

Satan used the serpent to trick Eve into eating the fruit of the *Tree* of Knowledge of Good and Evil, telling her:

> *"your eyes (see) shall be opened, and ye shall be as gods, knowing good and evil."* - Genesis 3:5

33

Man's fall came through Adam because he was not deceived, but rather made a willful decision. Adam and Eve ate the fruit and then, *"they knew that they were naked."* Genesis 3:7 Nakedness is now a problem, because sin is passed through the genitals by reproduction.

This Tree of Knowledge is a big deal to God. Why might God have forbidden something that does not appear that serious? Besides a test, being the only sin Adam could have committed, that he and mankind failed because Adam represented the human race. Why would a Tree of Knowledge be so bad? I think that the tree represents a false and perilous pursuit. It is human nature to be curious and to seek knowledge. The Bible even encourages man to search out the hidden. But this tree apparently represents seeking knowledge apart from God. Is it any surprise that countless millions of people still seek their understanding by this method and apart from God? Science (means knowledge) so this tree could be called the "tree of science." Unfortunately, this seems to be the Tree of Knowledge that so many think will advance man; and make humans the measure of all things instead of God, the Creator of this universe, and the Sovereign Supreme eternal being.

Knowledge, apart from humility through a relationship with God, can puff you up and make you prideful. Some theologians consider pride to be one of the worse sins. Many pursue knowledge and neglect God. Are you a doctor, lawyer, professor, scientist, jet pilot, CEO, etc. that has knowledge which gives you advantages? Your knowledge may have made you a multi-millionaire or even built a $25 billion foundation, but I would not trade places with you if you do not know God. And I promise God is really worth knowing!

> "For what is a man profitted, if he gain the whole world, and lose his own soul? Or what shall a man give in exchange for his soul?" - Matthew 16:26

Man's wisdom is foolishness to God, so WISDOM apart from God is *we is dumb*. The Bible warns against vain philosophies. PHILOSOPHY, separate from God, is *full of loss*. Wake up; wake up America and the rest of the world! Millions upon millions have continued to eat the forbidden fruit, and it is the same dead end now as it was for Adam. If you are one that has neglected God and followed only knowledge and philosophies of man, you need to repent (change your mind). You should fall on your face and apologize to the One that designed you and gave you the gift of life.

KNOWLEDGE is for _now_ and has a _ledge_ because it only goes so far. Wisdom helps you understand the proper application and limited aspects of knowledge. Textbooks constantly need updating and technology is still exploding. Each year ninety percent of Intel sales at the end of the year are for products that did not exist at the beginning of that year. Today, much of current technology and products produced fast become obsolete. It is so pronounced that the effect is that time and space are being compressed.

How many stars do you think are in the heavens? Until Galileo invented the telescope the number of observable stars was about 1,000 to 1,500. This seemed to contradict the Bible that stated that the stars were as the sand of the sea. Abraham received a word from the Lord in a vision.

> "And he brought him forth abroad, and said, Look
> now toward heaven, and tell the number of stars, if
> thou be able to number them: and he said unto him,
> So shall thy seed be." - Genesis 15:5

Scientists now know that GALAXIES (_axis_ –yes, galaxies must have an axis or it would not be in the word) contain millions or billions of stars, and with powerful modern telescopes they look out across many trillions of miles of space. They have determined that there are innumerable galaxies estimated at about a trillion. The Milky Way galaxy has approximately 200 billion stars. It is considered to more than the average number in all the galaxies. However, the galaxy 3C 236 is two hundred times the size of the Milky Way. Therefore, not only could Abraham not count the stars, but they still cannot be counted with a modern super computer. God not only knows the number, but:

"He calleth them all by *their* names." - Psalm 147:4

That is an omnipotent and powerful God. Man is not able to count the stars, but God knows them by name. Our star is called *sun* because of the *Son*. They both are the light the world.

Well this writer decided that since man could not count the stars that I would, in faith, just ask God in prayer for the answer. I instantly had a vision of 10^{10}. I thought that this might just be the format of the answer rather that the correct answer for this question. This number is only ten billion, so it is not the number of stars. About three months later on May 1, 2006, I believe that God revealed to me the answer. It is 10^{24}. That number represents a septillion. Starting at a million, then billion, then trillion, etc. to a septillion is seven numbers times a thousand. Seven is an extremely significant number appearing numerous times in Scripture. It represents covenant completeness. The four of the world (four limbs, four chamber heart, four seasons, etc.) plus the three of the trinity).

> *"And round about the throne were four and twenty seats: and upon the seats I saw four and twenty elders sitting, clothed in white raiment; and they had on their heads crowns of gold."* - Revelation 4:4

Could it be that each elder has the responsibility and privilege for oversight of 1/24 of the universe? Twelve is the number for fullness of completion, so then possibly twenty-four is the number for the complete universe.

STAR has the letters for the word <u>art</u>. The stars in the heavens have been an inspiration for poets and artists for thousands of years. About a 1,000 to 1,500 stars are visible to the naked eye on a very dark night. Are these stars randomly scattered in the sky as you would expect from an uncontrolled explosion, or might there be some order of design? Also, earth has the word <u>art</u> as well. Would you agree that all human art and all colors come from the observance of nature?

"The heavens declare the glory of God; and the firmament sheweth his handywork." - Psalms 19:1

Recently, physicists have theorized that there are actually 10 dimensions. The foundation for this is the mathematics of geometry. The word _dime_ means a tenth, and that is why a dime is ten cents. Therefore, I conclude, based on the word DIMENSION that the physicists are correct; and that there are ten dimensions. I suspect that if the creation was not in a fallen condition because of sin, that we would know and experience all of these dimensions.

If our very existence is by chance, then what real purpose, hope, or future could anyone have? Life would have no meaning. The agnostics and atheists can just eat drink and be merry, for after death there will be nothing. I have some news for them that may come as a surprise. Even though they do not realize it, they have an appointment scheduled with God. The worst possible event will be these words heard spoken by the King of the Universe.

"And then will I profess unto them, I never knew you: depart from me ye that work iniquity. (Matthew 7:23) "And these shall go away into everlasting punishment: but the righteous into life eternal." - Matthew 25:46

SECTION TWO

Section Two of this book will provide an alphabetical list of
GMAIL words with commentary and Bible verses.
This section is referred to as the

GMAIL Lexicon,

And Section Two is the reason for, and the heart of this book.

A

Abraham

Am - Bar (son) - Arab
Hebrew:
אברהם – Avraham – Father of Many
בר – Bar – Son
רב – Rav – Many
אמה – Umah – People, Nation
רם – Ram – High, Exalted
הר – Mountain

Abraham's name originally was Abram and God changed it to Abraham. This was very significant because it represented a change had occurred. His former name looked back to his father and pagan roots and his new name looked to a very different future. This future from his descendants would eventually include the Messiah and bring blessing to the entire world.

You might find it interesting that Abraham was from the area of modern day Iraq, and that he has Arab in his name. His parents would have been Arab. Bar means son and Abraham's name means father of many. When God gave Abraham his name he had not even fathered one child. Now, Abrahams' descendents would be in the millions. His two best known sons are Ishmael and Isaac. Many Arabs are descended from Ishmael, and Jews are descended from Isaac. He is a father of multitudes of Arabs, as well as, the father of the Jews. Jews are simply Arabs that God separated and made a distinct people group to serve His purposes. Israel is God's servant. The Jewish people and the Arabs are close relatives.

Abraham is a special man – God identified him as both "a friend of God" and "the father of faith." Today, over half of the world's population claims either a physical or spiritual connection to father Abraham. Abraham pleased God, and I wonder how many of the Arab, Jewish, Catholic, Christian/Protestant and other groups that identify with this man would receive similar compliments from God. I see evidence indicating God would like to see major spiritual changes in every one of these groups that claim Abraham as their Father. Being a physical descendent does not mean your father is Abraham. If you are not spiritually related to Abraham then your father is the devil.

God made a covenant with Abraham that is important to all of us. He promised to multiply Abrahams' descendents, and to bless all nations through his lineage. A faithful God has accomplished both of these promises in His covenant with Abraham. Twice Satan has tried unsuccessfully to eliminate the Jewish people in devilish ways. The first time Satan used Hiram, and the second time he used Hitler. Satan is not finished with attempts to accomplish this objective. Make sure you are not another pawn being used by Satan in his unholy spiritual war against these descendents of Abraham.

Satan is the main enemy of God, and he is also an enemy of mankind. Do you think Satan would spare the Ishmael side of Abraham's family tree? Could the Devil be pleased with any descendants from God's friend and this man of great faith? God desires to bless all of the descendants of Abraham. I have to believe that Abraham would be disappointed to see the fruit of his loins in so much division and opposition. I pray for the peace of Jerusalem and for the faith and blessing of Abraham for all his descendents.

God spoke to Moses from the burning bush over 3,500 years ago and told him that His name was "I am." Fourteen centuries after Moses heard the words "I am" the significance is revealed in God's only begotten Son. Jesus explained: "I am the Good Shepherd (lay down His life for the sheep), I am the Bread of Life, I am the Way, the Truth and the Life," etc. The blessing from God through Abraham's descendants was His own Son that became the perfect Lamb that died for the sins of the world. This lineage of God's Son, the Messiah, included Abraham, Isaac, Jacob, Joseph, Boaz, Jesse, David, Solomon, and Mary and Joseph of Nazareth.

"And I will make thy seed to multiply as the stars of heaven, and will give unto thy seed all these countries; and in thy seed shall all the nations of the earth be blessed;" - Genesis 26:4

"And as for Ishmael, I have heard thee: Behold, I have blessed him, and will make him fruitful, and will multiply him exceedingly; twelve princes shall he beget, and I will make him a great nation." - Genesis 17:20

"Ye are of *your* father the devil, and the lusts of your father ye will do. He was a murderer from the beginning, and abode not in the truth, because there is no truth in him. When he speaketh a lie, he speaketh of his own: for he is a liar, and the father of it." - John 8:44

"I am the good shepherd, and know my *sheep*, and am known of mine." - John 10:14

"I - am Alpha and Omega, the beginning and the ending, saith the Lord, which is, and which was, and which is to come, the Almighty." - Revelation 1:8

"That if thou shalt confess with thy mouth the Lord Jesus, and shalt believe in thine heart that God hath raised him from the dead, thou shalt be saved." - Romans 10:9

"they reached the place of which God had told him, Abraham built an altar there and arranged the wood on it. He bound his son Isaac and laid him on the altar, on top of the wood. Then he reached out his hand and took the knife to slay his son. But the angel of the Lord called out to him from heaven, "Abraham! Abraham!" Here I am," he replied. Do not lay a hand on the boy," he said. Do not do anything to him. Now I know that you fear God, because you have not withheld from me your son, your only son. Abraham looked up and there in a thicket he saw *a ram caught by its horns*. He went over and took the ram and sacrificed it as a burnt offering instead of his son. So *Abraham* called that place The Lord Will Provide.

And to this day it is said, "On the mountain of the Lord it will be provided." - Genesis 22:9-14

Accountability

Action – You – Ability - Account

You are accountable to God for your own actions, based on your God given ability. This principle has an effect both in time (now) and eternity (later). The credit in your account is determined on what you accomplished for the Master based on your ability.

Heaven is not earned by works, and is a privilege given by God's grace because it is a price that none of us could pay. I know that because Jesus asked his Father three times if there was any other way to let that cup pass from Him. The Father in Heaven did not know another way for mankind to be saved.

It does not matter how rich or poor you are one day, everyone's bank account on earth goes to zero. Then for those that have accepted God's free gift of salvation through Jesus, there will be a judgment that will only evaluate their good works. That is those works determined of value by God's standards value, not by man's standards. So heaven is not exactly general admission, the rewards there are based on what you have sent ahead by faith with good works.

"Oh let the wickedness of the wicked come to an end; but establish the just: for the righteous God trieth the hearts and reins."- Psalms 7:9

"And the Lord said, Who then is that faithful and wise steward, whom *his* lord shall make ruler over his household, to give *them their* portion of meat in due season?"- Luke 12:42

"For it is written, *As* I live, saith the Lord, every knee shall bow to me, and every tongue shall confess to God. So then every one of us shall give account of himself to God." - Romans 14:10-11

42

Adoration

Adorn - Radiant - Art

Adoration for God's beauty is a form of worship. His creation is a **radiant** work of **art** not only created for us to enjoy, but for us to recognize God's hand in it: so that we know that He is God. This brings Him glory. Every plant that sprouts vibrant, fragrant flowers, every colorful bird that sings long, captivating songs, and every clear blue tide that washes up on snow white sands should make us say "God, You are awesome! This beauty was not created by accident!" Even the complexity of living things should make us stop and praise God. We see this by realizing that only an all knowing God could create insects that look exactly like a thorn, or a leaf, or a stick; and creatures under the sea that create their own light; or are able to change the color of their skin to blend in flawlessly with rocks and coral. The Milky Way galaxy, and millions of other galaxies that **adorn** an otherwise cold and dark universe should be a reminder of how vastly far God's creation extends.

"For the invisible things of Him from the creation of the world are clearly seen, being understood by the things that are made, even His eternal power and Godhead; so that they are without excuse;" - Romans 1:20

"The heavens declare the glory of God; and the firmament sheweth his handywork." - Psalm 19:1

Almighty

I – Am – Light

When you flip on a light switch what happens? The dark disappears immediately. Darkness has no power against light and God is light. God is Almighty and by His power, He created everything we see and things that we can't see. When Moses asked

God what his name was, He replied, "I Am that I Am." We are to praise, worship, and exalt Him because without Him, we have nothing. In the New Testament, it says that Jesus is the light of the world. We should be drawn to him like moths to a flame; otherwise, we are just walking in the dark without anyone guiding us.

"And God said unto Moses, 'I Am that I Am' and He said, 'Thus shalt thou say unto the children of Israel, I Am hath sent me unto you" - Exodus 3:14

"This then is the message which we have heard of Him, and declare unto you, that God is light, and in Him is no darkness at all. If we say that we have fellowship with Him, and walk in darkness, we lie, and do not the truth: But if we walk in the light, as He is in the light, we have fellowship one with another, and the blood of Jesus Christ His Son cleanseth us from all sin."- 1 John 1:5-7

"Then spake Jesus again unto them, saying, I am the light of the world: he that followeth me shall not walk in darkness, but shall have the light of life." - John 8:12

Amazing

I am – A-Z – Gain – Again – In

Again, I am in A-Z. On a Sunday I had a discussion with one of the persons that helped add to the Gmail dictionary about the book title. I said that I would like it to be one word, but I had not gotten anything yet. The following Tuesday I received the word, again, and I knew that I now had the book title. This was his response to my email with the new title: "Amazing". That is great! I love it! Cheers to the Holy Spirit for that one. Very good! I received this Gmail complete at four a.m. on May 3, 2007. When you add up all the numbers in the date and time you get *twenty-one*. That is seven times three. One seven for each person in the

44

trinity, and each person of the Godhead is in the book. Seven is a special and important number in Bible numerology. That was not planned by the human author. God is truly amazing. Jesus is the light of the world, and without that light this world would indeed be very dark. If you would gain the whole world, but do not know the Lord Jesus and lose your soul, you would not have profited from the opportunity of life. Jesus has tried to make believing easy because He is in A-Z and is the "Alpha and Omega."

"For what shall it profit a man, if he shall gain the whole world, and lose his own soul?" - Mark 8:36

"I am Alpha and Omega, the beginning and the ending, saith the Lord, which is, and which was, and which is to come, the Almighty." - Revelation 1:8

John 11:25 Jesus said unto her, I am the resurrection, and the life: he that believeth in me, though he were dead, yet shall he live:12:26 If any man serve me, let him follow me; and where I am, there shall also my servant be: if any man serve me, him will *my* Father honour.12:46 I am come a light into the world, that whosoever believeth on me should not abide in darkness.13:13 Ye call me Master and Lord: and ye say well; for *so* I am.13:19 Now I tell you before it come, that, when it is come to pass, ye may believe that I am *he*.14:6 Jesus saith unto him, I am the way, the truth, and the life: no man cometh unto the Father, but by me.14:10 Believest thou not that I am in the Father, and the Father in me? the words that I speak unto you I speak not of myself: but the Father that dwelleth in me, he doeth the works.14:11 Believe me that I *am* in the Father, and the Father in me: or else believe me for the very works' sake.14:20 At that day ye shall know that I *am* in my Father, and ye in me, and I in you.15:1 I am the true vine, and my Father is the husbandman.15:5 I am the vine, ye *are* the branches: Pilate therefore said unto him, Art thou a king then? Jesus answered, Thou sayest that I am a king. To this end was I born, and for this cause came I into the world, that I should bear witness unto the truth. Every one that is of the truth heareth my voice.

45

Anxiety

Next – Yet – Exit

Anxiety is the fear of not knowing what will happen next, or what is yet to come. It is a form of worry, which is a sin because it shows a lack of trust in God. Therefore, the best way to get anxiety to exit your mind is to stop and realize that God has everything worked out for His divine purposes. He will take care of those things that are yet to come, because He knows all and sees all. Worry and anxiety may come about from many different circumstances, such as finances, job status, relationships, etc. All of these things, which we worry about, are things that can and will be provided by God. He will provide if we place our trust in Him, that He will take care of what we need. This allows us to have peace and joy in times that are normally stressful.

"Therefore I say unto you, Take no thought for your life, what ye shall eat, or what ye shall drink; nor Yet for your body, what ye shall put on. Is not the life more than meat, and the body than raiment? Behold the fowls of the air: for they sow not, neither do they reap, nor gather into barns; yet your heavenly Father feedeth them. Are ye not much better than they? Which of you by taking thought can add one cubit unto his stature? And why take ye thought for raiment? Consider the lilies of the field, how they grow; they toil not, neither do they spin: And Yet I say unto you, That even Solomon in all his glory was not arrayed like one of these. Wherefore, if God so clothe the grass of the field, which to day is, and to morrow is cast into the oven, shall he not much more clothe you, O ye of little faith? Therefore take no thought, saying, What shall we eat? or, What shall we drink? or, Wherewithal shall we be clothed? (For after all these things do the Gentiles seek:) for your heavenly Father knoweth that ye have need of all these things. But seek ye first the kingdom of God, and his righteousness; and all these things shall be added unto you. Take therefore no thought for the morrow: for the morrow shall take thought for the things of itself. Sufficient unto the day is the evil thereof."- Matthew 6:25-34

America - United States of America (USA)

I Am – Care – Merci (mercy) - USA

The nation of <u>America</u> was established on principles of faith and freedom, by men of strong conviction. God has given <u>America</u> an abundance of blessings, and this nation has served God and has shone to the world like a city on a hill. This nation has historically shown mercy and care to all areas of the world. <u>America</u> is an ally, friend and supporter of Israel, which is very important because God blesses and curses nations on this one issue. The city of Jerusalem, the Capitol of Israel, has <u>USA</u> in the middle of the word, and I believe that this is not a coincidence, but rather the plan of God. I Am is involved in the affairs and destiny of mankind. <u>America</u> owes her freedom and achievement to the providence of God. Unfortunately, as a nation, <u>America</u> has been sliding away from God for a long time. This is having, and will continue to have an adverse effect on continued blessings from God. God has and would love to continue to bless <u>America</u>. Nations that turn away from God eventually, rather than blessings, receive judgment. <u>America</u> may be there now!

"Ye are the light of the world. A city that is set on an hill cannot be hid." - Matthew 5:14

Argument

True men are great – Grate – Rage - Anger

Grate means to offend or irritate; as, harsh words grate the heart. An <u>argument</u> can escalate to the point of creating rage in one or both parties. Rage is anger on steroids, because it is furious and usually uncontrolled. This is why an <u>argument</u> might cause a response leading to injury or even death. The condition of rage is a sin or transgression against God. Any <u>argument</u> that reaches this level is another example of the sin nature that is in all mankind.

If a thing is true, it is not false, and it agrees with reality. In the Bible, men are telling Joseph, their brother who they did not recognize, that they are true men. Years earlier these brothers had sold him into slavery for twenty pieces of silver, and lied to their father that his son Joseph had been killed. They were not such true men back then.

Joseph tested his brothers to see if they had changed. They told Joseph that they were not spies, and that they were all sons of one man. Reality is the best <u>argument</u> for the truth. They were honest in what they told their brother Joseph, who had become a ruler in Egypt. They passed his testing and the family was reunited. This Old Testament account of Jacob, Joseph, and his brothers showed that true men are great. One reason they are great is that they are all in heaven.

"Then Job answered and said, Even to day *is* my complaint bitter: my stroke is heavier than my groaning. Oh that I knew where I might find him! *that* I might come *even* to his seat! I would order *my* cause before him, and fill my mouth with <u>argument</u>s. I would know the words *which* he would answer me, and understand what he would say unto me. Will he plead against me with *his* great power? No; but he would put *strength* in me. There the righteous might dispute with him; so should I be delivered for ever from my judge. Behold, I go forward, but he *is* not *there*; and backward, but I cannot perceive him: On the left hand, where he doth work, but I cannot behold *him*: he hideth himself on the right hand, that I cannot see *him*: But he knoweth the way that I take: *when* he hath tried me, I shall come forth as gold." - Job 23:1-10

We *are* all one man's sons; we *are* true *men*, thy servants are no spies. If ye *be* true *men*, let one of your brethren be bound in the house of your prison: go ye, carry corn for the famine of your houses: And we said unto him, We *are* true *men*; we are no spies: And the man, the lord of the country, said unto us, Hereby shall I know that ye *are* true *men*; leave one of your brethren *here* with me, and take *food for* the famine of your households, and be gone: And bring your youngest brother unto me: then shall I know that ye *are* no spies, but *that* ye *are* true *men: so* will I deliver you your brother, and ye shall traffick in the land." - Genesis 42:11-34

"It is an honour for a man to cease from strife: but every fool will be meddling." - Proverbs 20:3

"Where no wood is, *there* the fire goeth out: so where *there is* no talebearer, the strife ceaseth." - Proverbs 26:20

"An angry man stirreth up strife, and a furious man aboundeth in transgression." - Proverbs 29:22

"Be ye angry, and sin not: let not the sun go down upon your wrath:" - Ephesians 4:26

Atonement

One – Man - Amen – Meant

The Old Testament requirement of animal sacrifice for atonement was only a type, but was needed because "without the shedding of blood there is no remission of sin." Jesus was without sin and the only acceptable sacrifice acceptable to God the Father. The type was meant to point to Jesus, the Lamb of God.

"Wherefore, as by one man sin entered into the world, and death by sin; and so death passed upon all men, for that all have sinned:" - Romans 5:12

"Nevertheless death reigned from Adam to Moses, even over them that had not sinned after the similitude of Adam's transgression, who is the figure of him that was to come. But not as the offense, so also is the free gift. For if through the offense of one many be dead, much more the grace of God, and the gift by grace, which is

49

by one man, Jesus Christ, hath abounded unto many." - Romans 5:14, 15

"For as in Adam all die, even so in Christ shall all be made alive." - 1 Corinthians 15:22

"And all that dwell upon the earth shall worship him, whose names are not written in the book of life of the Lamb slain from the foundation of the world" - Revelation 13:8

"And walk in love, as Christ also hath loved us, and hath given himself for us an offering and a sacrifice to God for a sweet smelling savour." - Ephesians 5:2

"The next day John seeth Jesus coming unto him, and saith, Behold the Lamb of God, which taketh away the sin of the world." - John 1:29

"I am Alpha and Omega, the beginning and the ending, saith the Lord, which is, and which was, and which is to come, the Almighty." - Revelation 1:8 Amen!

Authority

Author – Truth

God's Word, the Holy Bible, is the ultimate <u>authority</u> because He is the author of truth. God is not only the author of the Bible (Through the divine inspiration of 40 men covering a period over 1,500 years), but is the author of all life. Unbelievers cannot accept the Bible as <u>authority</u> because they see it through the world's eyes. They think it is foolish, but through the Spirit, we can see and understand clearly. Some people think that faith is blind, but nothing is clearer because you have to hear from God to have faith.

"So then faith *cometh* by hearing, and hearing by the word of God." - Romans 10:17

"Looking unto Jesus the author and finisher of *our* faith; who for the joy that was set before him endured the cross, despising the shame, and is set down at the right hand of the throne of God." - Hebrews 12:2

"Now we have received, not the spirit of the world, but the spirit which is of God; that we might know the things that are freely given to us of God. Which things also we speak, not in the words which man's wisdom teacheth, but which the Holy Ghost teacheth; comparing spiritual truth with spiritual words. But the natural man receiveth not the things of the Spirit of God: for they are foolishness unto him: neither can he know them, because they are spiritually discerned. But he that is spiritual judgeth all things, yet he himself is judged of no man. 'For who hath known the mind of the Lord, that he may instruct him?' but we have the mind of Christ."- 1 Corinthians 2: 12-16

"Sanctify them through thy truth: thy word is truth"- John 17:17

Awesome

Awe – Some

Only some have awe for God, but all should.

"For it is written, *As* I live, saith the Lord, every knee shall bow to me, and every tongue shall confess to God." - Romans 14:11

"Let all the earth fear the Lord: let all the inhabitants of the world stand in awe of him." - Psalm 33:8

B

Baptism

Past

Baptism is an important part of becoming a follower of Jesus. It's important to know that baptism alone does not save one's soul, but it does serve an important purpose. Many people struggle with the guilt of past sins, and though those sins are forgiven as soon as one has saving faith in the Lord Jesus Christ, most times it takes something physical for a new believer's mind to grasp the spiritual. Baptism provides a physical means in which one can feel the washing away of that guilt. It represents a spiritual death of our past nature, and resurrection in the Holy Spirit, buried with Christ to be raised with Him as a new creation. It is a symbolic action that Jesus has "wiped the slate clean" so to speak, and the guilt of past sins washes away. This is not to say that a born again, baptized Christian will not sin. Because of our human nature, we will all inevitably sin until we are perfected in Heaven. However, we are no longer slaves to sin because its power has been broken. Even death's power is a thing of the past.

"What shall we say then? Shall we continue in sin, that grace may abound? God forbid. How shall we, that are dead to sin, live any longer therein? Know ye not, that so many of us as were baptized into Jesus Christ were baptized into his death? Therefore we are buried with him by baptism into death: that like as Christ was raised up from the dead by the glory of the Father, even so we also should walk in newness of life. For if we have been planted together in the likeness of his death, we shall be also in the likeness of his resurrection: Knowing this, that our old man is crucified with him, that the body of sin might be destroyed, that henceforth we should not serve sin. For he that is dead is freed from sin." - Romans 6:1-7

"The like figure whereunto even baptism doth also now save us (not the putting away of the filth of the flesh, but the answer of a good conscience toward God,) by the resurrection of Jesus Christ."- 1 Peter 3:21

Believed

Bled – Die – Live

The Lord Jesus suffered and bled on a Roman cross to die, so that we may live. He was resurrected to show that He could overcome death; and to show those who <u>believed</u> in Him that they could do the same. As Christians, we have Jesus' resurrection power through his precious blood. When we believe through faith that He gave His life for our forgiveness and salvation, and we die a physical death, we will be resurrected to live with Him eternally.

"Jesus said unto her (Martha, regarding Lazarus), 'I am the resurrection, and the life: he that believeth in me, though he were dead, yet shall he Live: And whosoever Lives and believes in me shall never Die. Do you believe this?" - John 11:25-26

Began

Bang

For many years, scientists have used the Big Bang theory to try to prove that the universe was created by an explosion of matter from a single point. It states that there was nothing in the beginning. It goes further to say that a process known as Vacuum Fluctuation created a dime-sized singularity, or a dense mass of matter, which exploded to form the ever-expanding universe we see today. On the surface, the Big Bang theory as stated by scientists looks like an absolute mockery of God's divine blueprint of the universe. And that generally is their whole aim: To try to disprove God's hand in creation. However, they may be closer to the scriptural truth of creation than they realize! In accepting the Big Bang theory, scientists also accept the event of a beginning, which is what is stated in Genesis 1:1. We know that in the beginning there was "nothing", as the scientists say (That compressed mass of matter had to come from somewhere!), but rather there was God who spoke the universe into existence. The key word here is "Spoke". This would obviously indicate a sound of some sort, be it actual words, or a simple bang. There was a bumper sticker that said, "I believe the Big Bang Theory: *God* said, 'Bang!' and there it was!"

"By the Word of the Lord were the heavens made; and all the host of them by the breath of His mouth. He gathereth the waters of the sea together as an heap: He layeth up the depth in storehouses. Let all the earth fear the Lord: let all the inhabitants of the world stand in awe of Him. For He spake, and it was done; He commanded, and it stood fast."- Psalm 33:6-9

"In the beginning was the Word, and the Word was with God, and the Word was God. The same was in the beginning with God. All things were made by Him; and without Him was not any thing made that was made. In Him was life; and the life was the light of men. And the light shineth in darkness; and the darkness comprehended it not. There was a man sent from God, whose name was John. The same came for a witness, to bear witness of the Light, that all men through Him might believe. He was not that Light, but was sent to bear witness of that Light. That was the true Light, which lighteth every man that cometh into the world. He was in the world, and the world was made by Him, and the world knew Him not. He came unto His own, and His own received Him not. But as many as received Him, to them gave He power to become the sons of God, even to them that believe on His name: Which were born, not of blood, nor of the will of the flesh, nor of the will of man, but of God. And the Word was made flesh, and dwelt among us, (and we beheld his glory, the glory as of the only begotten of the Father,) full of grace and truth." - John 1:1-14

Benevolence

Be - Noble - Love

It is easy to see that <u>benevolence</u>, or kindness, is tied tightly with all other fruit of the Spirit. One can't have kindness without love, and kindness and love birth goodness. All three of these together help each of us to be noble to our neighbors and to God. The definition of the word noble is *"possessing, characterized by, or arising from superiority of mind or character or of ideals or morals."* Our noble character as Christians should reflect the love that God showed to us.

"For God so loved the world, that he gave his only begotten Son, that whosoever believeth in him should not perish, but have everlasting life." - John 3:16

"For we ourselves also were sometimes foolish, disobedient, deceived, serving divers lusts and pleasures, living in malice and envy, hateful, and hating one another. But after that the kindness and love of God our Saviour toward man appeared, Not by works of righteousness which we have done, but according to his mercy he saved us, by the washing of regeneration, and renewing of the Holy Ghost;" - Titus 3:3-5

Bibliography

Bible – Biography - Holy

A <u>bibliography</u> is a compilation of works by a specific author. The Holy Bible is compiled of the writings of forty men who were inspired by the Holy Spirit to give us history, knowledge, wisdom, and guidance directly from God.

A biography is a written account of someone's life composed by someone other than the subject of the biography. A biography written about another person may have flaws and misinformation, but the Bible is an infallible biography because it was inspired by the Holy Spirit. It's a paradox, in that it is fully the Word of God, but fully penned by the hands of men. God is the author, yet man is the author. The mystery in this paradox is revealed in the person of Jesus Christ, the living word: fully God, and fully man.

"And the Word was made flesh, and dwelt among us, and we beheld his glory, the glory as of the only begotten of the Father, full of grace and truth" - John 1:14

"All scripture is given by inspiration of God, and is profitable for doctrine, for reproof, for correction, for instruction in righteousness."- 2 Timothy 3:16

Blameless

Lamb

In the Old Testament at the Passover Feast, the high priest brought an unblemished lamb to the altar to be sacrificed as an offering to God, in order for sins to be forgiven. The blood of the unblemished Lamb (or other animals) was a symbol of a pure, clean life. And the spilling of the blood symbolized death, because the wages of sin is death. The act of offering this sacrifice was done once a year. When Jesus came to this world, He lived a sinless life. He was blameless, yet He was condemned to die for sins He did not commit, but rather for the sins which we committed. He became as a sacrificial Lamb. The blood which was spilled covered all of our sin, not just for the year, but for all time. This is why we can rejoice as Christians because we know that what Jesus did for us justifies us as righteous before God. All sins, past, present and future are forgiven and not remembered (called to account for action) by God.

"And almost all things are by the law purged with blood; and without shedding of blood is no remission." - Hebrews 9:22

56

"And he shewed me a pure river of water of life, clear as crystal, proceeding out of the throne of God and of the Lamb. In the midst of the street of it, and on either side of the river, *was there* the tree of life, which bare twelve *manner of* fruits, *and* yielded her fruit every month: and the leaves of the tree *were* for the healing of the nations. And there shall be no more curse: but the throne of God and of the Lamb shall be in it; and his servants shall serve him:" - Revelation 22:1-3

Blessed

Bleed – Seed

Jesus Christ had to be crucified on the cross, pierced and bleed to death to take away the sins of the world. Jesus was of the seed of David and fulfilled the covenant that God made with Abraham that through him all nations would be <u>blessed</u>.

"And I will make thy seed to multiply as the stars of heaven, and will give unto thy seed all these countries; and in thy seed shall all the nations of the earth be blessed;" - Genesis 26:4

"I am the door: by me if any man enter in, he shall be saved, and shall go in and out, and find pasture" - John 10:9

"Of this man's seed hath God according to *his* promise raised unto Israel a Saviour, Jesus:" - Acts 13:23

But with the precious blood of Christ, as of a lamb without blemish and without spot:"- 1 Peter 1:19

Blood

Bold

Under the old covenant, no one was allowed to enter the

Holy of Holies. This was the innermost area of the temple, where God's presence dwelt behind a thick curtain. Only the high priest could enter, and only then if he brought <u>blood</u> to sprinkle on the Holy Seat. Otherwise, he would be struck dead because of his sinful nature. When Jesus died on the cross, his blood replaced that of the animals that were sacrificed under the Old Covenant laws. It covered our sins and made us clean, allowing anyone who has accepted Jesus' sacrifice to enter into God's presence whenever and wherever, without fear of being struck down. We can boldly come before God because of the <u>blood</u> of Jesus.

"Having therefore, brethren, boldness to enter into the holiest by the blood of Jesus" - Hebrews 10:19

Boundaries

Sound – Around – Abide – Sad – Sin - End

Skeptics and unbelievers have a misunderstanding about the commandments, precepts and laws of God. They see God as a kill-joy that takes away their fun. God acknowledges that there is "pleasure in sin for a season." However, God knows the ultimate consequence of disobedience and sin. Respect for <u>boundaries</u> and honoring boundaries actually increases freedom. Traffic lights establish legal <u>boundaries</u>, but they improve traffic flow and safety. It is the same with God's <u>boundaries</u> because they bring about a better society and richer, fuller, longer lives.

<u>Boundaries</u> should be sound, not established by man but by God. A nation built around sound <u>boundaries</u> will prosper, but if the people of that nation depart it will bring a sad end. Today, it appears that most of the nations of the world have not continued to abide in God's boundaries. This falling away is exactly what the Bible describes as the end approaches.

"But we are bound to give thanks to God always for you, brethren beloved of the Lord, for that God chose you from the beginning unto salvation in sanctification of the Spirit and belief of the truth:" - 2 Thessalonians 2:13

"See that none render unto any one evil for evil; but always follow after that which is good, one toward another, and toward all." - 1 Thessalonians 5:15

"Let no man beguile you in any wise: for *it will not be,* except the falling away come first, and the man of sin be revealed, the son of perdition," - 2 Thessalonians 2:3

Breath

Heart

God is love with a heart for human life that is sacred and distinguished from animals. Because we are made in the image and likeness of God and we have a living soul. Man became a living soul when he received the breath of life from God.

"But God, who is rich in mercy, for his great love wherewith he loved us," Ephesians 2:4

"The Spirit of God hath made me, and the breath of the Almighty hath given me life." - Job 33:4

C

Character

Heart – Chart – React – Rate - Tear

Because of original sin by Adam in the Garden of Eden, mankind inherited a fallen sin nature. The Bible states, "Jesus wept." Our character has been corrupted by sin and that causes weeping and tears. In a conversation with Cain, God said,

"If thou doest well, shalt thou not be accepted? And if thou doest not well, sin lieth at the door. And unto thee *shall be* his desire, and thou shalt rule over him." - Genesis 4:7

God will never lower His standard and excuse sin, so Cain was told that he must conquer sin. No one that has ever lived has done that except for Jesus Christ, the anointed Messiah. That is why our own righteousness or works is never adequate to meet God's standard. That is why we all need a Savior that does meet the righteous standard of God. In salvation that righteousness is applied to us and never removed.

The sin nature has an effect on our character and on how we react to circumstances, events and choices in life. God knows your heart better than you do and has a "heart chart" on you and everyone else. You have heard the expression he/she has a good heart. Yes, even people will rate the heart of others, but it is God's view that really counts. What does God think of your heart? Is it hardened toward God? Does it have hatred, envy, or covetousness? Does your heart demonstrate the fruit of the Holy Spirit?

The Finisher – Devie Anderson (American)

o o o For "The Finisher" is the author of faith
The completer of all
The essence
The "Way"
For better for worse
For winning the stand
"The Finisher" looks
At the heart of the man.

"But the fruit of the Spirit is love, joy, peace, long-suffering, gentleness, goodness, faith," - Galatians 5:22

"The heart *is* deceitful above all *things*, and desperately wicked: who can know it?" - Jeremiah 17:9

"For out of the heart proceed evil thoughts, murders, adulteries, fornications, thefts, false witness, blasphemies:" - Matthew 15:19

Children
Heir – hide

Just as <u>children</u> naturally enjoy playing hide-an-seek, there is need to seek a God that is hidden from the five senses. The loving creator God wants to draw us into a relationship with Him. He hides, but wants to be found. When you do find God through faith you become an heir of righteousness. All true believers are included in God's family, and in the New Testament are referred to as <u>children</u> because we are God's children. In heaven, there will be people from every kindred, tongue, people, and nation on this planet. This means that they will be heirs and receive eternal reward.

"My little children, these things write I unto you, that ye sin not. And if any man sin, we have an advocate with the Father, Jesus Christ the righteous:" - 1 John 2:1

"And if children, then heirs; heirs of God, and joint-heirs with Christ; if so be that we suffer with *him*, that we may be also glorified together." - Romans 8:17

"By faith Noah, being warned of God of things not seen as yet, moved with fear, prepared an ark to the saving of his house; by the which he condemned the world, and became heir of the righteousness which is by faith." - Hebrews 11:7

Christian

Christ – In – His

When we have faith to believe the divinity Jesus and the truth of His death and resurrection, we become <u>Christians</u>. We are in Christ, and we as the church function as His body. The Bible says that we are "the light of the world."

"So we, *being* many, are one body in Christ, and every one members one of another." - Romans 12:5

"For we must all appear before the judgment seat of Christ; that every one may receive the things *done* in *his* body, according to that he hath done, whether *it be* good or bad." - 2 Corinthians 5:10 (Rewards only and applies to all who are saved)

Committed

Come – Tied – To – Time

I come tied to time (we are only able to commit for a time). In this world, time is very short, just a breath, compared to eternity. Unfortunately, many trade time for eternity. Like the television show, "Deal or No Deal." Would you trade your short time or life span here for an eternity that you do not understand very well? Eternity is like the case that is holding ten billion dollars, and your case here has only ten cents. That is a reasonable analogy, and yet many trade their eternal birthright (salvation is eternal life) for the short time they might have in this fallen and corrupt world. Men reject light because their deeds are evil. They make a bad deal.

"I would seek unto God, and unto God would I commit my cause:" - Job 5:8

"But, beloved, be not ignorant of this one thing, that one day *is* with the Lord as a thousand years, and a thousand years as one day." - 2 Peter 3:8

"And saying, The time is fulfilled, and the kingdom of God is at hand: repent ye, and believe the gospel." - Mark 1:15

Compassion

Compass – Son

Christians should have <u>compassion</u> for those who are in need, be it physical or spiritual; and show them care in the way that Jesus showed us He cares while He was here on Earth. Through our <u>compassion,</u> we allow them to see Christ in us, pointing their eyes in the direction of Jesus. God will use a compassionate Christian as a compass to point the lost to His Son.

"And Jesus, moved with compassion, put forth *his* hand, and touched him, and saith unto him, I will; be thou clean." - Mark 1:41

"Then we which are alive *and* remain shall be caught up together with them in the clouds, to meet the Lord in the air: and so shall we ever be with the Lord." - 1 Thessalonians 4:17

Complete

Temple – Come

Most evangelical Christians have an expectation for the return of Jesus, and this is referred to as the "second coming." According to Bible prophecy, the Jewish Temple in Israel will be desecrated by the Anti-Christ exactly three and one half years before the Battle of Armageddon. The last Temple was destroyed by the Roman army in 70 A.D. So if there is no temple how could it be desecrated? The answer is that the Temple must be rebuilt for prophesy of its desecration to be fulfilled. There is probably a connection between the rebuilt Temple and Christ's return for believers, which is commonly called the Rapture.

"But when ye shall see the abomination of desolation, spoken of by Daniel the prophet, standing where it ought not, (let him that readeth understand,) then let them that be in Judea flee to the mountains:" - Mark 13:14

"Then we which are alive *and* remain shall be caught up together with them in the clouds, to meet the Lord in the air: and so shall we ever be with the Lord." - 1 Thessalonians 4:17

Consecrated

Sacred - Center - Secret

The word sacred is not in the Bible, but <u>consecrated</u> is a synonym for sacred. To have fear (awe, respect, and reverence) of the Lord opens a gate of understanding to the secret of His covenant. New Age practitioners like to refer to being "centered." What you really need is for the center of your being (heart) to understand a secret that makes you sacred (belong to God) by a covenant relationship with the Lord.

"For Moses had said, Consecrate yourselves to day to the LORD, even every man upon his son, and upon his brother; that he may bestow upon you a blessing this day." - Exodus 32:29

"The secret of the LORD *is* with them that fear him; and he will shew them his covenant." - Psalms 25:14

Conscience

Con – Science

Knowledge (science) alone only yields an unbeliever, but faith in God and science (knowledge) yields a believer. The human conscience exists universally, and is another witness to the existence of God. Values of morality are understood instinctively through the conscience producing general agreements of right and wrong. If man was the product of random organization through processes of nature, why would any moral values exist? Those relying only on science have been conned and are blind to spiritual truth.

"But have renounced the hidden things of dishonesty, not walking in craftiness, nor handling the word of God deceitfully; but by manifestation of the truth commending ourselves to *every man's* conscience in the sight of God." - 2 Corinthians 4:2

Conservative

Con (with) Verse – Vote – Reactive

All conservatives use verse whether they are Evangelical Christians, Orthodox Jews, Mormons, Jehovah Witness, Amish, or Sunni or Shiite Muslims, etc. They also vote and are reactive to conserve their views. Some conservatives serve the true God, but many do not. Many that use verse are deceptive and wicked.

Most of America's founding Fathers were greatly influenced by the Christian Bible (1611 King James Version). This influence resulted in the recognition of the Creator God and the establishment of freedom and liberty in the Declaration of Independence and the Constitution of the United States. A foundation in moral principals and religious freedom was an important part of their concept of self-government.

Consume

Come - Use - Me

When we let the Holy Spirit <u>consume</u> us, we are saying to God, "Come use me." The Holy Spirit is the part of the Godhead that lets Him be within us so that He can work on us to build character, faith, obedience, and wisdom. This is so that He can use us as part of the body of Christ to build His Kingdom.

"And the servant of the Lord must not strive; but be gentle unto all *men*, apt to teach, patient," - 2 Timothy 2:24

"So we, *being* many, are one body in Christ, and every one members one of another." - Romans 12:5

Converse (con-with)

Con – Verse

Your conversation should be influenced by verse from the Bible.

"But as he which hath called you is holy, so be ye holy in all manner of conversation;" - 1 Peter 1:15

"All scripture *is* given by inspiration of God, and *is* profitable for doctrine, for reproof, for correction, for instruction in righteousness:" - 2 Timothy 3:16

"For the word of God *is* quick, and powerful, and sharper than any two edged sword, piercing even to the dividing asunder of soul and spirit, and of the joints and marrow, and *is* a discerner of the thoughts and intents of the heart." - Hebrews 4:12

Covenant

One – Tent – Conven *(Convene)* – Ten

A <u>covenant</u> is a formal sealed agreement between two parties. Our God is a <u>Covenant</u> God, as we can see throughout the entire Bible. He made <u>covenant</u>s with mankind including Noah, Abraham, Moses, David, and believers in Jesus, the anointed Messiah. All of the promises God made in these <u>covenant</u>s have been kept by Him, because God is not a <u>covenant</u> breaker. The Old Testament contains the <u>covenant</u> revealed to Moses in the form of the Ten Commandments. The new <u>covenant</u> by Jesus' blood is different, however. It is not only for one group of people (the Jews), but for all who accept it and enter into the <u>covenant</u> and promises through Jesus Christ. The new covenant allows us to come together as one people, not Jew and Gentile, but as one new man, and convene as one body.

Moses was commanded by God to create a place for his people to worship, called the Tabernacle. The very first Tabernacle was a tent, called "The tent of Meeting", where all of his people came together. The Christian church is much like this tent of Meeting in the Old Testament. Since we are one body through Christ, we are all under His tent. He is the High Priest of the Tabernacle which resides in every Christian's heart. This tent covers every church that is rooted in His truth and acknowledges God's only son as High Priest, Prophet and King.

"And the bow shall be in the cloud; and I will look upon it, that I may remember the everlasting <u>covenant</u> between God and every living creature of all flesh that *is* upon the earth." - Genesis 9:16

"And the LORD said unto Moses, Write thou these words: for after the tenor of these words I have made a <u>covenant</u> with thee and with Israel. And he was there with the LORD forty days and forty nights; he did neither eat bread, nor drink water. And he wrote upon the tables the words of the <u>covenant</u>, the ten commandments." - Exodus 34: 27, 28

"For he is our peace, who hath made both one, and hath broken down the middle wall of partition *between us*;" - Ephesians 2:14

Creation

Art – Ate – Reaction – Action

The word creation has eight letters and eight is the spiritual number for a new beginning. A week is seven days and the eighth day starts a new week. In music, seven notes complete an octave and the eighth note starts a new octave. Noah and his family that survived the Genesis flood were a total of eight souls. Creation was something entirely new because it required a cause; and was not there until that cause or beginning took place. The creation is certainly a masterpiece of art, containing both phenomenal design and beauty. Now, this masterpiece of God is in a fallen condition because Adam ate fruit of the Tree of Knowledge of Good and Evil, which was forbidden. God did not create sin, but did create the potential for sin because man was equipped with a free will. Because of this freedom we also have the potential to generate real love for others and for the Creator. What is your reaction to this creation that you have the privilege of experiencing? I believe God is worth knowing, loving and worshiping beyond words. If you have not already, you should take action and pursue the Creator.

"In the selfsame day entered Noah, and Shem, and Ham, and Japheth, the sons of Noah, and Noah's wife, and the three wives of his sons with them, into the ark;" - Genesis 7:13

"And thou shalt love the LORD thy God with all thine heart, and with all thy soul, and with all thy might." - Deuteronomy 6:5

D

Daniel

I – And - El (God) **- Land**

Daniel had a life that fulfilled God's purposes for him, because Daniel was in a relationship with the true and living God of Israel. He had confidence in God's power, even when facing hungry lions. Daniel was a Prophet that God revealed precise information to about all the future kingdoms of the world. Of course, kingdoms involve land. Also, he spoke with King Cyrus who had conquered the Babylonian Empire and showed him that he had been prophesied by name in the Bible. King Cyrus allowed the Jews to return to Jerusalem and their land.

"Now God had brought Daniel into favour and tender love with the prince of the eunuchs." - Daniel 1:9

"In the third year of Cyrus king of Persia a thing was revealed unto Daniel, whose name was called Belteshazzar; and the thing *was* true, but the time appointed *was* long: and he understood the thing, and had understanding of the vision." - Daniel 10:1

"Thus saith Cyrus king of Persia, All the kingdoms of the earth hath the LORD God of heaven given me; and he hath charged me to build him an house in Jerusalem, which *is* in Judah. Who *is there* among you of all his people? The LORD his God *be* with him, and let him go up." - 2 Chronicles 36:23

Deceitful

Lie –Feud (strife) – Life – Die

The first deceit took place in the Garden of Eden when Satan deceived Eve. Today, the worst deceits are still the deceptions that lead away from the true God, and into serious errors like secularism, materialism, humanism or any false gods.

"Take heed to yourselves, that your heart be not <u>deceived</u>, and ye turn aside, and serve other gods, and worship them;" - Deuteronomy 11:16

"Who is a liar but he that denieth that Jesus is the Christ? He is antichrist, that denieth the Father and the Son." - 1 John 2:22

"It *is* an honour for a man to cease from <u>strife</u>: but every fool will be meddling." - Proverbs 20:3

"But of the tree of the knowledge of good and evil, thou shalt not eat of it: for in the day that thou eatest thereof thou shalt surely die." - Genesis 2:17 "And the serpent said unto the woman, Ye shall not surely die:" - Genesis 3:4

"By mercy and truth iniquity is purged: and by the fear of the LORD *men* depart from evil." - Proverbs 16:6

"With him *is* strength and wisdom: the <u>deceived</u> and the deceiver *are* his." - Job 12:16

"Be not <u>deceived</u>; God is not mocked: for whatsoever a man soweth, that shall he also reap." - Galatians 6:7

"And he said, Take heed that ye be not <u>deceived</u>: for many shall come in my name, saying, I am *Christ*; and the time draweth near: go ye not therefore after them." - Luke 21:8

Default

Fault – Ate

In the beginning, man was created as a blameless soul, with a sinless nature. He was without fault. But when Satan tempted Adam and he ate the fruit that was forbidden to eat, all mankind had inequity or sin from that point on. Through the fault of man, we forfeited our perfect nature and our natural default is now that of sin. We are born of the flesh when we enter the world. Our natural inclination is that of sin, and we are separated from God. When we are born again through belief in the deity and sacrifice of Jesus Christ, the righteousness of Christ is applied to us, and we are free from bondage to sin.

"But of the tree of the knowledge of good and evil, thou shalt not eat of it: for in the day that thou eatest thereof thou shalt surely die." - Genesis 2:17

"For if by one man's offence death reigned by one; much more they which receive abundance of grace and of the gift of righteousness shall reign in life by one, Jesus Christ.)" - Romans 5:17

Denial

A - Lie - End – Die

In the Garden of Eden Satan made a denial of the truth of the word of God. Faith comes by hearing the word of God – everyone either accepts God's word, or like Satan, denies God's word. All die because the wages of sin is death, and in the end you will either have eternal life or experience the second death.

"Ye are of *your* father the devil, and the lusts of your father ye will do. He was a murderer from the beginning, and abode not in the truth, because there is no truth in him. When he speaketh a lie, he speaketh of his own: for he is a liar, and the father of it." - John 8:44

"If we suffer, we shall also reign with *him*: if we deny *him*, he also will deny us:" - 2 Timothy 2:12

Dependence

Deepen – Need – Depend

We need God and should depend on Him for everything. Greater <u>dependence</u> will deepen our relationship with Him.

"Were not the Ethiopians and the Lubims a huge host, with very many chariots and horsemen? yet, because thou didst rely on the LORD, he delivered them into thine hand." - 2 Chronicles 16:8

"Cast thy burden upon the LORD, and he shall sustain thee: he shall never suffer the righteous to be moved." - Psalms 55:22

"For all these things do the nations of the world seek after: and your Father knoweth that ye have need of these things." - Luke 12:30

Desire

Reside

<u>Desire</u> can be a longing, an appetite, including sexual <u>desire</u> which is lust; or a wish to obtain something. <u>Desire</u> can be selfish or unselfish. You might wish for something good for someone else. <u>Desires</u> seem to reside in the heart, and they can produce cravings and emotions to attain that which is desired. The <u>desire</u> of something sinful and morally wrong can be difficult to overcome, because of this tendency for <u>desire</u> to reside with us. Even born again believer's that have been set free from sin could

slip into fleshly desires that war against the spirit. Therefore, "Put on the whole amour of God."

"If thou doest well, shalt thou not be accepted? and if thou doest not well, sin lieth at the door. And unto thee *shall be* his desire, and thou shalt rule over him." - Genesis 4:7

"He will fulfil the desire of them that fear him: he also will hear their cry, and will save them." - Psalms 145:19

"Better *is* the sight of the eyes than the wandering of the desire: this *is* also vanity and vexation of spirit." - Ecclesiastes 6:9

"For thus saith the LORD of hosts; Yet once, it *is* a little while, and I will shake the heavens, and the earth, and the sea, and the dry *land*; And I will shake all nations, and the desire of all nations shall come: and I will fill this house with glory, saith the LORD of hosts." - Haggai 2:6-7

"Brethren, my heart's desire and prayer to God for Israel is, that they might be saved." - Romans 10:1

"But now, after that ye have known God, or rather are known of God, how turn ye again to the weak and beggarly elements, whereunto ye desire again to be in bondage?" - Galatians 4:9

"For if after they have escaped the pollutions of the world through the knowledge of the Lord and Saviour Jesus Christ, they are again entangled therein, and overcome, the latter end is worse with them than the beginning." - 2 Peter 2:20

Devil

Lived

When Jesus was in the wilderness for forty days he was tempted by the devil (Satan), and if you have lived then you too have been tempted by the devil.

"And he was there in the wilderness forty days, tempted of Satan; and was with the wild beasts; and the angels ministered unto him."
- Mark 1:13

Deity

Yet – I – Die

Why would die be in <u>deity</u>? Can you kill God? No, you cannot kill God, but when God became fully man while still fully God (hypostatic union) he was killed on a cross. Jesus, the second person of the trinity, was fully God and this was attested to by Old Testament scripture, John the Baptist, the Apostles, by Jesus, by the Angles and by God the Father. Jesus himself declared that he was equal to God. Since about 2000 years ago when he died, was buried and rose again after three days, millions of believers have accepted that as fact and believe it with all their heart. It is part of the Good News that Jesus, the Lamb of God, died in our place and took the sins of mankind upon him.

"Jesus saith unto him, Have I been so long time with you, and yet hast thou not known me, Philip? he that hath seen me hath seen the Father; and how sayest thou *then*, Shew us the Father?" - John 14:9

"In whom we have redemption through his blood, *even* the forgiveness of sins: Who is the image of the invisible God, the firstborn of every creature:" - Colossians 1:14-15

Dimension

Dime – Mind – Men – Son

The concept of the Trinity, one God, but three distinct persons in the Godhead is hard for many people to comprehend. This pattern of one thing with three components is demonstrated over and over in nature. Matter exists in one of three states, either solid, liquid, or gas. Men have a body, mind, and spirit, but are one person. All matter has the three <u>dimensions</u> of length, width and height. A line drawn on a sheet of paper that might look two dimensional actually has three <u>dimensions</u>.

Scientists have a theory that was developed from advanced geometry that there are ten <u>dimensions</u>. Because dime means a tenth, I agree that reality probably has 10 <u>dimensions</u>. The Trinity; Father, Son, and Holy Spirit, is a complex concept, but for me it is easier to grasp than 10 <u>dimensions</u>.

"For God hath not given us the spirit of fear; but of power, and of love, and of a sound mind." - 2 Timothy 1:7

"Whosoever therefore shall be ashamed of me and of my words in this adulterous and sinful generation; of him also shall the Son of man be ashamed, when he cometh in the glory of his Father with the holy angels." - Mark 8:38

Disciple

Is – Led

Faith is not developed or nurtured by force or compulsion. Following is a calling for those that had the faith to become a believer. Believing and being a <u>disciple</u> are two separate things with different Bible verses for each. The salvation from believing is by grace alone, but discipleship involves following a call to be fishers of men. You could actually be a <u>disciple</u> and not be a believer – be saved. An example would be Judas Iscariot. He was a disciple, but will spend eternity in Hell because he never believed in Jesus.

The true God does not use force to win followers. Cattle can be driven, as seen in many old Hollywood westerns, but sheep cannot. Sheep need a shepherd, and they are required to be led. The Spirit of God draws, convicts, reveals, and leads, but does not force. Whenever the method is force, you can be sure that this is the beast, or Satan, and not God. God does not force His will upon you and violate the self-will that you were given.

You have been misled if you are told that if you do not give a tenth to the church that God will not bless you. That statement is a type of control that is not appropriate under grace. The New Testament is silent on tithing for Christian believers. I will say though that generosity was a characteristic of believers in the early church. Giving should be a cheerful and pleasant experience. God knows that a person's following and love needs to be because they want to, and not because of fear, force or no choice.

Being led by God is by far the best choice, but everyone has the freedom to reject God and sadly many do just that. First, a Christian disciple is a person who believes in the Jesus of the Bible. This Jesus is the Messiah, the Savior, the Lord and the King of Kings. He became a man, but was always God, the second person of the Godhead. Disciples follow Jesus' examples and teachings. They are commanded to share the gospel (good news) throughout the world.

Essentially, a disciple is indwelt by the Holy Spirit and is led by Jesus Christ. Disciples should have a love for God and demonstrate love to others, especially other believers. Christians are supposed to become more Christ like through fellowship (with man and God) and discipleship by the Good Shepherd. Discipleship is a lifelong process, because our character will never be perfected until we reach Heaven. Regardless of the condition or maturity of true believers Jesus said that we are the light of the world. That is important – all other religion is darkness because Christians are the light on this planet called Earth.

"I am the good shepherd: the good shepherd giveth his life for the sheep." - John 10:11

76

"The disciple is not above *his* master, nor the servant above his lord." - Matthew 10:24

"Ye are the light of the world." - Matthew 5:14

"Go ye therefore, and teach all nations, baptizing them in the name of the Father, and of the Son, and of the Holy Ghost:" - Matthew 28:19

"Every man according as he purposeth in his heart, *so let him give*; not grudgingly, or of necessity: for God loveth a cheerful giver." - 2 Corinthians 9:7

"And that no man might buy or sell, save he that had the mark, or the name of the beast, or the number of his name." - Revelation 13:17

Dominion

Domino

Man has a God given authority to rule over the earth. That right was compromised, or usurped, by Satan when Adam sinned in the Garden of Eden. Now all of creation is under a curse and in a fallen state, so really there is no paradise anywhere. Today, you can just look at the nightly news to see the domino effect of sin.

"And God blessed them, and God said unto them, Be fruitful, and multiply, and replenish the earth, and subdue it: and have <u>dominion</u> over the fish of the sea, and over the fowl of the air, and over every living thing that moveth upon the earth." - Genesis 1:28

"Thou madest him (Jesus) to have <u>dominion</u> over the works of thy hands; thou hast put all *things* under his feet:" - Psalms 8:6

"For sin shall not have <u>dominion</u> over you: for ye are not under the law, but under grace." - Romans 6:14

E

Earth

Heart – Art

This universe is so enormous that our minds really cannot grasp the distances involved throughout space and galaxies. The light from our closest star travels at 186,000 miles per hour for four years before it reaches the earth – traveling 24 trillion miles. Scientists estimate that there are 200 billion stars in the Milky Way galaxy, and now with modern telescopes approximate the number of galaxies at one trillion. With all of this enormity, the amazing thing is that the <u>earth</u> is where God's heart is. Of course, the art the <u>earth</u> displays is astonishing. Just the variety of colors and patterns in the atmosphere are remarkable. Not to mention that the <u>earth</u> primarily is watered by the atmosphere, and by the various happenings of our weather. Who does not think that a beautiful sunset is anything but art?

"Of old hast thou laid the foundation of the earth: and the heavens *are* the work of thy hands." - Psalms 102:25

"For God so loved the world, that he gave his only begotten Son, that whosoever believeth in him should not perish, but have everlasting life." - John 3:16

Entirety

Enter – Ten - Eternity

We will not know God in His <u>entirety</u> unless we have an eternity with God once we enter Heaven. The <u>entirety</u> of the law of God is contained in the Ten Commandments.

"And he was there with the LORD forty days and forty nights; he did neither eat bread, nor drink water. And he wrote upon the tables the words of the covenant, the ten commandments." - Exodus 34:28

"And after these things I heard a great voice of much people in heaven, saying, Alleluia; Salvation, and glory, and honour, and power, unto the Lord our God:" - Revelation 19:1

Established

Stable – Slab –Base – Able - Blessed

In Ephesians, Paul talks about being rooted and <u>established</u> in love. To describe God is to describe Love. He is fully love. If we are <u>established</u> in love, we are <u>established</u> in God. Most homes today are built on what is called a slab foundation. This is the base on which the home is built and supported. If the slab is not poured on stable ground, the foundation will sink. The home will have problems ranging from cracked walls and ceilings, unleveled flooring, separated brick joints, and a host of other issues. It is the same in our spiritual walk. If we become <u>established</u> in the Love that God is, the slab foundation is poured on stable ground, and we will be able to support the wood and bricks that make our hearts a home to Jesus and the Holy Spirit. Being firmly <u>established</u> with Love as our base, we will also become able to be used by God. And we will be blessed, as will others in our lives.

"For this cause I bow my knees unto the Father of our Lord Jesus Christ, Of whom the whole family in heaven and earth is named, That he would grant you, according to the riches of his glory, to be strengthened with might by his Spirit in the inner man so that Christ may dwell in your hearts by faith; that you, being rooted and established in love, may be able to comprehend with all saints what is the breadth, and length, and depth, and height, and to know the love of Christ, which surpasses knowledge, that you might be filled with all the fullness of God." - Ephesians 3:14-19

Eternal

God (El) – Tern (sounds like turn) – Al (sounds like All)

God is eternal and did not have a cause or beginning as we did. Eternity has no end, and those born again receive eternal life at the time of their salvation. The Bible reveals that all will have their turn with God. Another way to say that is, whether you know it or not, you have an appointment with God. Unfortunately, the lost will have an appointment for judgment at the Great White Throne. After that they will have an eternal separation from God that is called the second death. Believers will have eternal access and relationship to the Everlasting God of Glory.

"I am Alpha and Omega, the beginning and the end, the first and the last." - Revelation 22:13

Evangelist

Save - Give - Live – Gentiles – Angel

The primary responsibility of an evangelist is to preach the gospel as presented in the New Testament. Usually an evangelist travels and brings the gospel to the Gentiles to save their souls. The Bible says that the Jews are enemies for the gospel's sake. And their spiritual blindness was imposed by God for the "times of the Gentiles." As a nation they were restored to their Promised Land in unbelief, but in God's timing their blindness will be lifted. The remnant of Jewish believers is increasing. So it appears that we might be in a transitional time as it was 2,000 years ago, when the transition was going from the Jews to the Gentiles. The nations will benefit from a spiritual Israel.

The word for angel signifying, both in the Hebrew and Greek, a "messenger," and hence employed to denote any agent God sends forth to execute His purposes. I have heard many evangelists and find that the great majority are excellent messengers for God. Their primary message, the gospel (good news), will give the believer eternal life.

"But watch thou in all things, endure afflictions, do the work of an evangelist, make full proof of thy ministry." - 2 Timothy 4:5

"As concerning the gospel, *they are* enemies for your sakes: but as touching the election, *they are* beloved for the fathers' sakes." - Romans 11:28

Examine

I am man – I test (exam) me

Christians have a responsibility to do a self-exam where they confess and agree with God regarding sin in their lives. This process is not just important for spiritual health, but for physical health as well. In some cases it is a matter of life and death. Probably, the process could include some chastening by God to change the behavior. If that did not solve the problem then more serious consequences might follow.

Unfortunately, I do not care how good modern medicine is it will not be effective in this situation. So, the physical or medical problem would actually have a spiritual cause. Therefore, It would need a spiritual solution before it became too late!

"Wherefore whosoever shall eat this bread, and drink *this* cup of the Lord, unworthily, shall be guilty of the body and blood of the Lord. But let a man <u>examine</u> himself, and so let him eat of *that* bread, and drink of *that* cup. For he that eateth and drinketh unworthily, eateth and drinketh damnation to himself, not discerning the Lord's body. For this cause many *are* weak and sickly among you, and many sleep. For if we would judge ourselves, we should not be judged." - 1 Corinthians 11:27-31

F

Faithfulness

Fasten - Lean – Safe

Fasten your eyes on the Lord and lean on Him to be safe.

"Thy <u>faithfulness</u> *is* unto all generations: thou hast established the earth, and it abideth." - Psalms 119:90

Father

Fear - Hear - Heart

The similarities between our earthly <u>father</u>s and God, our Heavenly <u>Father</u>, are amazing. Naturally, parents hold a special place in a child's heart, and love for their father is different than love for their mother. Yet, at the same time, they are equal. Just as a child loves their earthly father, we are commanded to love God with all of our heart, with a love even greater than that for our parents. A <u>father</u>'s role in the family is vital. He offers protection, discipline and direction, just like God the Father. Just as an earthly father tells his child what is best for him, so God speaks to His children in the same fashion. It is our responsibility as children of God to hear and apply what He is telling us. Our natural response is to not listen, thinking we know what is best for ourselves, which often results in mistakes and/or discipline.

A child should fear his <u>father</u>. This doesn't mean they should be scared of them or afraid for their safety, but rather a fear out of respect knowing that their father has authority over them. <u>Fathers</u> should be, as God is, slow to anger. An angry <u>father</u> raises an angry, frightened, discouraged child. We fear God out of reverence knowing that He is the ruler of all creation and we are under His authority. A fear of the reality we would face if we weren't in Christ.

"Hear, ye children, the instruction of a father, and attend to know understanding."- Proverbs 4:1

"For ye have not received the spirit of bondage again to fear; but ye have received the Spirit of adoption, whereby we cry, Abba, Father. The Spirit itself beareth witness with our spirit, that we are the children of God: And if children, then heirs; heirs of God, and joint-heirs with Christ; if so be that we suffer with him, that we may be also glorified together." - Romans 8:15-17

"Fathers, provoke not your children to anger, lest they be discouraged" (Some translations; Lose Heart) - Colossians 3:21

Fear

Far – Ear

Do you <u>fear</u> God and do you hear God? God does not want your heart to be far from Him. And when it is perfect (wholly) toward God, He will make astonishing demonstrations for the sake of His name.

"The <u>fear</u> of the LORD *is* the beginning of wisdom: and the knowledge of the holy *is* understanding." - Proverbs 9:10

"Wherefore the Lord said, Forasmuch as this people draw near *me* with their mouth, and with their lips do honour me, but have removed their heart far from me, and their <u>fear</u> toward me is taught by the precept of men:" - Isaiah 29:13

Feelings

Life – Lies –Flee - Sing

You could have strong <u>feelings</u> about a person, politics, religion, an issue, or about God.   What are your <u>feelings</u> or convictions about life? What are your <u>feelings</u> about God? What is your perception of God, and do you have any emotion about God?

Sometimes <u>feelings</u> are emotional, or based on false perceptions or biases. Therefore, <u>feelings</u> are not are always rational or reliable. The Christian faith is not based on changing emotions, or an exciting experience. Faith is based on revealed knowledge of God and a relationship with God through Jesus Christ.

It would be impossible for me not to believe in God and the Jesus Christ of the Bible. Flee anything and everything that would keep you from knowing God for yourself. Believe in the Son of God and receive eternal life. You will be glad you did, because one day you will be heaven and will sing a new song.

"Who being past <u>feeling</u> have given themselves over unto lasciviousness, to work all uncleanness with greediness." - Ephesians 4:19

"For we have not an high priest which cannot be touched with the <u>feeling</u> of our infirmities; but was in all points tempted like as *we are, yet* without sin." - Hebrews 4:15

Fellowship

Fish – Flow - Whole - Self – Help - Ship - Fellows

Fellowship is a very important part of the Christian life. Fellowship applies both to a Christian's relationship with God and with other believers. That real and personal relationship with God provides extraordinary fellowship. Yet, while every Christian should set aside a quiet time to study Scripture and talk with God on their own, it's not a wise idea to think that because you have Jesus you need no other fellowship. There should be no such thing as a 'lone ranger Christian'. The Bible encourages us to put others above self and to love your brothers and sisters in the faith. We are commanded in the Bible to fellowship with other believers. We, as Christians, are like a school of fish. If we stay close to the other believers God has put around us, we have a better sense of where we are going. But if we try to swim alone and not go with the flow of the "school", we lose the guidance, encouragement and help that they offer. The church cannot be whole without fellowship. Likewise, a solitary Christian cannot be whole without it, either. Through fellowship, we get encouragement from other believers. We also get help in tough times, we have an outlet to which we can share our praises and our needs, and we learn to grow in grace and knowledge of His truth. These are all made possible by our unique spiritual gifts. Jesus made a promise that if two or more people should come together in His name, He would be there with them. So when we fellowship with others, we are fellowshipping with Jesus, as well. We are all fellows in a ship, and that ship is headed for golden shores. We may be able to make it to the shores in our own little dingy, but it's going to be one rough ride!

"That which we have seen and heard we declare unto you, that you also may have fellowship with us: and truly our fellowship is with the Father, and with his Son Jesus Christ." - 1 John 1:3

"For where two or three are gathered together in my name, there am I in the midst of them."- Matthew 18:20

"Two are better than one; because they have a good reward for their labor. For if they fall, the one will lift up his Fellow: but woe to him that is alone when he falls; for he has not another to help him up. - Ecclesiastes 4:9-10

Flesh

Self - Shelf

Natural man is primarily interested in self and his attention is focused on the flesh. If you were to look at the essence of sin it would be the desire to be your own captain – to put yourself in the position of independently setting your own course. The natural man is on the shelf – put aside, out of use to God. There is no neutral ground, and until a person is born again they are an enemy of God. Also, I do not believe that a person earns any eternal rewards until after they have been born again. They may do lots of good works; give away large sums of money, etc. But they will receive no eternal credit until after their salvation. Believer's privileges begin after the spiritual birth.

"But the natural man receiveth not the things of the Spirit of God: for they are foolishness unto him: neither can he know *them*, because they are spiritually discerned." - 1 Corinthians 2:14

"My flesh and my heart faileth: *but* God *is* the strength of my heart, and my portion for ever." - Psalm 73:26

"No man can serve two masters: for either he will hate the one, and love the other; or else he will hold to the one, and despise the other. Ye cannot serve God and mammon." - Matthew 6:24

Fruits

First - Ruts *(Ph: Roots)*

The Bible uses the word fruit to represent the visible action of the Holy Spirit in our lives, and also prosperity from God's blessings. They come from God and only God, which means they should be given back to Him by us. The first Fruit of the Spirit is love, and from it comes the rest of the fruits: Joy, Peace, Patience, Benevolence (Kindness), Faithfulness, Meekness, and Temperance (Self Control). The Holy Spirit allows this fruit to grow in us so that the seeds may be planted in others around us. But those seeds will not grow into fruit-producing vines without the Spirit; and for the Spirit, you need Jesus. This is the essence of loving your neighbor. By bearing fruit, we let people see that there is something different about the way we live. In order that they may seek what we have in Jesus Christ, and truly live. Christians want to share their joy with all. Yet, sadly, many Christians are hated because of their joy. God is love, but the Adversary is a murderer. How will there be peace when the "Prince of Peace" is rejected and hated?

Jesus says that we are like a branch on a vine, and that He is the vine and we are the branches. Each branch has the ability to produce fruit. But those that are dead will not produce fruit, so God cuts them off. A dead branch on a vine will draw nutrients away from the branches that are producing fruit. So if they are removed, the fruit producing ones will be able to bear more fruit and grow new branches. The implications of Jesus as the vine are very important because, He was sent by God as our source. The vine is nourished by roots and fed by God. This allows us, through Jesus Christ, to be rooted in love.

"But the fruit of the Spirit is love, joy, peace, longsuffering, gentleness, goodness, faith," - Galatians 5:22

"And other fell on good ground, and did yield fruit that sprang up and increased; and brought forth, some thirty, and some sixty, and some an hundred." - Mark - 4:8

G

Gifts

Fits – Fit

According to Scripture, every believer receives at least one spiritual gift at the time of his salvation. Believers have nothing to do with which gift(s) they receive. These gifts are supernatural and remain with each believer throughout his earthly life, regardless of behavior. Their purpose is to benefit the church. Scripture explains that the church functions as the body of Christ on earth, and Christ is the head of the church. The church is a supernatural organization that is fit together by the Holy Spirit. The spiritual gifts that the members bring to the church provide the church with multiple supernatural strengths. The gifts vary, but each is important just as it is with our physical bodies. One person's spiritual gift(s) may make them a hand, or an eye, or a mouth while another's may make them a foot, or an arm, or an ear. Understanding of your particular spiritual gift(s) help a Christian in knowing where he or she fits in the church body for service. The gifts are numerous; a few are prophecy, pastoring, evangelism, teaching, knowledge, wisdom, service, giving, exhortation, mercy, administration, etc.

"Now concerning spiritual gifts, brethren, I would not have you ignorant. Ye know that ye were Gentiles, carried away unto these dumb idols, even as ye were led. Wherefore I give you to understand, that no man speaking by the Spirit of God calleth Jesus accursed: and that no man can say that Jesus is the Lord, but by the Holy Ghost. Now there are diversities of gifts, but the same Spirit. And there are differences of administrations, but the same Lord. And there are diversities of operations, but it is the same God which worketh all in all. But the manifestation of the Spirit is given to every man to profit withal. For to one is given by the Spirit the word of wisdom; to another the word of knowledge by the same Spirit; To another faith by the same Spirit; to another the gifts of healing by the same Spirit; To another the working of miracles; to another prophecy; to another discerning of spirits; to another divers kinds of tongues; to another the interpretation of tongues: But all these worketh that one and the selfsame Spirit, dividing to every man severally as he will. For as the body is one, and hath many members, and all the members of that one body, being many, are one body: so also is Christ." - 1 Corinthians 12:1-12

Glorified
God - Lord - Life

It is appropriate for God to be in the word <u>glorified</u> because the greatest honor and praise belongs to God, and God only is worthy of worship. There is none other like God. A magnificent 15th century castle in England has glory. A mansion is glorious, and there are large and beautiful churches that show glory. Thomas Roads Baptist Church in Lynchburg, Virginia has a beautiful lobby that is over 23,000 square feet. And, think of the glory throughout nature. Have you ever stood in awe at the glory in the sunset, or in a starry night sky? There is glory on earth, but it is inferior to heavenly glory and God's glory.

Lord is in the word glory, because Jesus honored and glorified the name of the Father; and the Father has exalted Him above all others. The greatest glory comes from God, and without God there would be no glory. In heaven, authentic (real), Christians will be <u>glorified</u> by God. The sum of eternal truths of life and God are revealed in the Lord. Every religion must answer four questions: Origin, meaning, morality, and destiny. The coherent answers that Christianity provides cannot be matched by any other religion, philosophy, or science. Other religions make claims, but Jesus claimed to be equal with God and He backed it up by glorious works. Not only was His claim the greatest, but the amount of evidence for the truth of His claim is unequaled in all of history. Maybe this is why some of the countless millions in the past and present have encountered the Lord and believed in Him.

"Then Moses said unto Aaron, This *is it* that the LORD spake, saying, I will be sanctified in them that come nigh me, and before all the people I will be glorified. And Aaron held his peace." - Leviticus 10:3

"And said unto me, Thou *art* my servant, O Israel, in whom I will be glorified." - Isaiah 49:3

"Insomuch that the multitude wondered, when they saw the dumb to speak, the maimed to be whole, the lame to walk, and the blind to see: and they glorified the God of Israel." - Matthew 15:31

"And if children, then heirs; heirs of God, and joint-heirs with Christ; if so be that we suffer with *him*, that we may be also glorified together." - Romans 8:17

"Wherefore God also hath highly exalted him, and given him a name which is above every name:" - Philippians 2:9

"Now unto him that is able to keep you from falling, and to present *you* faultless before the presence of his glory with exceeding joy" - Jude 1:24

Grace

Care – Race

God's unfailing grace shows that He cares for us, enough to redeem us by sending Jesus to die on the cross for our sins. In Greek, the word for grace is *charis.* Sounds a lot like care, doesn't it? His grace is poured out over every nationality and race because He cares for all whom He created. Some grace is common, like rain that falls on all. Other grace is reserved for those that are in the family of God.

I also like grace as the following acronym (not original by this author): **G**od's **R**iches **A**t **C**hrist's **E**xpense.

90

"Concerning His Son Jesus Christ our Lord, who was made of the seed of David according to the flesh; And declared to be the Son of God with power, according to the spirit of holiness, by the resurrection from the dead: By whom we have received <u>grace</u> and apostleship, for obedience to the faith among all nations, for His name." - Romans 1:3-5

Gratitude

Great – Atitude (Attitude)

<u>Gratitude</u> is the joyful feeling one has when a favor is done for him undeservingly. <u>Gratitude</u>, as a Christian, is grace reflected back to the Father in the joy that we have in Jesus, and His grace towards us. It should give us a great attitude, even in difficult circumstances. Paul had such gratitude even when he was in prison.

In Greek, Grace is *Charis* and <u>gratitude</u> is *eucharistian.* Notice that the Greek word for care is in the word for <u>gratitude</u>. This is because gratitude is a response to grace. So be grateful, *You Christian! (euchiaristian)* Unfortunately, much of the human race blasphemes God instead of expressing <u>gratitude</u>. That will ultimately bring God's wrath upon the earth and the unbelievers.

"For all things are for your sakes, that the abundant grace might through the thanksgiving of many redound to the glory of God."- 2 Corinthians 4:15

"And said to the mountains and rocks, Fall on us, and hide us from the face of him that sitteth on the throne, and from the wrath of the Lamb:" - Revelation 6:16

Good

God

God is in <u>good</u> because only God is truly <u>good</u>. The word <u>good</u> as we use it today is from the Old English word for God.

When we say "Goodbye" to someone, we are actually using the Old English contraction for "God Be With You". But the word good is often used today as a way to describe things that are simply acceptable by man's standards. For example: A good movie, a good game of golf, good luck, good food, or a good argument. These things may not have anything at all to do with God, but we still use the word good for everything and anything that isn't necessarily bad. So knowing the true origin of the word good, we can clearly see that Scripture uses the word to describe things that are of God. When the word good is found in the Bible, you can put "of", "by" or "from" in front of it and see the implications of the word as it is meant to be read. A good person in the Bible is essentially being described as Godly.

"And Jesus said unto him, Why callest thou me good? *There is* none good but one, *that is*, God." – Mark 10:18

Guidance

Aid – Nudge

A nudge is a gentle touch, which is the method of the true God. There is a tremendous contrast because the self-serving Satan, and the God that loves us. Satan says to hell with you, but Jesus left heaven and went to hell for us. What a contrast! Jesus came to our aid by paying a price, with a blood sacrifice, that no one could pay by themselves. God nudges us to seek and to find Him because that is to our greatest benefit. Do not take your council from the ungodly. But seek to follow God. He will guide you.

"Blessed *is* the man that walketh not in the counsel of the ungodly, nor standeth in the way of sinners, nor sitteth in the seat of the scornful." - Psalms 1:1

H

Harvest

Earth – Star – Save – Have – Heart - Tares

The earth is going to continue to have a <u>harvest</u> of food as long as it exists. Besides a <u>harvest</u> time for food, there will be a time of spiritual harvest and the wheat (saved) will be separated from the tares (lost). God has a heart for a large harvest because He takes no delight in the death of the wicked. And in fact, there will be people of faith from the four corners of the world and from every spoken language on earth. Do you know the "Star out of Jacob" and the "seed of David?" Jesus is called the "Bright and Morning Star" and He is the "Lord of the <u>Harvest</u>."

"While the earth remaineth, seedtime and <u>harvest</u>, and cold and heat, and summer and winter, and day and night shall not cease." - Genesis 8:22

"He that gathereth in summer *is* a wise son: *but* he that sleepeth in <u>harvest</u> *is* a son that causeth shame." - Proverbs 10:5

"When thou cuttest down thine <u>harvest</u> in thy field, and hast forgot a sheaf in the field, thou shalt not go again to fetch it: it shall be for the stranger, for the fatherless, and for the widow: that the LORD thy God may bless thee in all the work of thine hands." - Deuteronomy 24:19

"Pray ye therefore the Lord of the <u>harvest</u>, that he will send forth labourers into his <u>harvest</u>." - Matthew 9:38

"And another angel came out of the temple, crying with a loud voice to him that sat on the cloud, Thrust in thy sickle, and reap: for the time is come for thee to reap; for the <u>harvest</u> of the earth is ripe." - Revelation 14:15

"I shall see him, but not now: I shall behold him, but not nigh: there shall come a Star out of Jacob, and a Sceptre shall rise out of Israel, and shall smite the corners of Moab, and destroy all the children of Sheth." - Numbers 24:17

"Neither is there salvation in any other: for there is none other name under heaven given among men, whereby we must be saved." - Acts 4:12

"Remember that Jesus Christ of the seed of David was raised from the dead according to my gospel:" - 2 Timothy 2:8

"As therefore the tares are gathered and burned in the fire; so shall it be in the end of this world." - Matthew 13:40

Hatred

Heart – Death

Hatred is an intense ill will toward a person, persons, or even God. Hatred causes harm. Any hatred always shows a heart problem, and hating harms you. Everyone is made in the image of God, receives their life from God, has a soul, and has a sacred value. Humans will not even be annihilated by God and will exist forever in either heaven or hell. The choice is ours, not God's. He has already made a way: Jesus. Even though He has made us, loves us, and has made a way for salvation, many still hate Him. Do you know that many people actually hate God? Jesus said that you are either for Him or against Him. There is no neutrality toward God, so you are on one side or the other.

"Thou shalt not bow down thyself to them, nor serve them: for I the LORD thy God *am* a jealous God, visiting the iniquity of the fathers upon the children unto the third and fourth *generation* of them that hate me;" - Exodus 20:5

94

"Blessed are ye, when men shall <u>hate</u> you, and when they shall separate you *from their company*, and shall reproach *you*, and cast out your name as evil, for the Son of man's sake." - Luke 6:22

"But I say unto you which hear, Love your enemies, do good to them which <u>hate</u> you," - Luke 6:27

"He that saith he is in the light, and <u>hate</u>th his brother, is in darkness even until now." - 1 John 2:9

"He that is not with me is against me: and he that gathereth not with me scattereth." - Luke 11:23

"But he that sinneth against me wrongeth his own soul: all they that <u>hate</u> me love death." - Proverbs 8:36

Heart

Hear - Hate – Rate - Heat

The human <u>heart</u> is regarded as the seat of emotions, personality, will, disposition, conscience, feelings, and thoughts. This is the center or core of your soul, of who you are as a person. The Lord God knows your heart better than you do. God wants you to hear Him in your <u>heart</u>. God wants you to have His Word in your <u>heart</u>. God wants you to fear Him in your <u>heart</u> because "the fear of God is the beginning of wisdom." God commands that we love him with all our <u>heart</u>. That is passion and heat or fire for God. You have a heart rate which determines your pulse. God also takes your rate or pulse, which reveals your opinions and feelings. If you have any hate in your heart for anyone, including God, you have a heart problem.

"The <u>heart</u> *is* deceitful above all *things*, and desperately wicked: who can know it?" - Jeremiah 17:9

"Idolatry, witchcraft, hatred, variance, emulations, wrath, strife, seditions, heresies," - Galatians 5:20

History

This - Is - His - Story

When we are reading the Bible, we can clearly see that "This Is His Story". The Bible is a book that reveals Jesus Christ, and it is a book about Jehovah. Everything from before creation, the six day creation itself, all the way through the last days of earth, and the end of time is recorded in the Bible. Even in the Old Testament there is carefully woven evidences of Jesus throughout. The Bible is truly the story of His glory. It tells His Story. There is no such thing as "Prehistory" since we have the Holy Bible. Job was on earth at the same time as the dinosaurs. A dinosaur called behemoth is described in the thirty-ninth chapter of the Book of Job.

About one-third of the Bible is actually future <u>history</u>, which is called prophecy. God is omniscient, all knowing, and that includes complete knowledge of the future. The atomic bomb, satellites, Israel's return to the land, the explosion of knowledge, and transportation are all foretold in the Bible. All these just mentioned occurred after I was born. The Bible contains at least one hundred fifty accurately fulfilled prophecies about the first coming of Jesus. There are an even greater number of prophecies regarding His return, or second coming. The Bible explains both our <u>history</u>, and our future from God's perspective. The Bible is a great treasure, and the greatest <u>history</u> and only accurate prophecy book ever written. It is a huge benefit to have an understanding of all of the most important events that lie in the future.

"For the prophecy came not in old time by the will of man: but holy men of God spake *as they were* moved by the Holy Ghost." - 2 Peter 1:21

"Behold, I come quickly: blessed *is* he that keepeth the sayings of the prophecy of this book." - Revelation 22:7

Holograms

Logos – Goal – Solo

Words must be important to God because the second person of the Godhead is called the Word. The Greek word that Word was translated from is the word logos. "In the beginning was the Logos, and the Logos was with God and the Logos was God." (John 1:1) This Logos accomplished the goal of submitting to the Father's will to be the solo acceptable and perfect Lamb of God to take away the sins of the world.

The word hologram has meaning both from the definition of holocryptic and holograph. The first of these two words means to effectively conceal, and the second means whole or entire. The equipment for making a hologram includes a laser, mirror and diffusers. The hologram is a frequency record, and when viewed with a laser of the same frequency it reveals a three-dimensional image of the original object.

A profound quality of a hologram is that the image is distributed throughout the entire media. If the hologram is cut into pieces, each piece contains the complete image. A hologram also can reflect the full color spectrum of the rainbow. The rainbow is a symbol of a covenant God made with Noah. Sometimes holograms are used to prove that something of value is authentic. You might see a hologram on a driver's license or on credit cards.

I agree with the concept that the Bible is like a hologram, and God's plan for the redemption of mankind is distributed from Genesis in the Old Testament to Revelation in the New Testament. This then makes words the smallest segment of the Bible that still conveys an accurate message or picture. When letters from words are reformed to make other words, it provides compelling evidence to the accuracy of the Bible and the hologram theory. Like a hologram for words to be converted to Gmail they need to be seen with the correct frequency, and these writers believe that frequency to be the Spirit of God.

"And the Word (Logos) was made flesh, and dwelt among us, (and we beheld his glory, the glory as of the only begotten of the Father,) full of grace and truth." - John 1:14

"And this is the Father's will which hath sent me, that of all which he hath given me I should lose nothing, but should raise it up again at the last day." - John 6:39

"Enter ye in at the strait gate: for wide *is* the gate, and broad *is* the way, that leadeth to destruction, and many there be which go in thereat:" - Matthew 7:13

"And I saw another mighty angel come down from heaven, clothed with a cloud: and a rainbow *was* upon his head, and his face *was* as it were the sun, and his feet as pillars of fire:" - Revelation 10:1

I

Idolatry

Lord - Dolar (Dollar) - Dirty - Try – A - Idol

Idolatry is certainly a serious matter to God because two of the Ten Commandments dealt with this issue. In its strictest form, idolatry denotes worship of deity in a visible form. This is a satanic counterfeit, because the essence of God is spiritual and unseen. Satan tried to get the Lord to commit idolatry because he asked Jesus to bow down and worship him. You can bet that Satan is involved in idolatry. Satan's message is try an idol, and everyone has. In the broadest sense, idolatry would be anything that persons or nations elevate above God. Much of modern idolatry is less obvious than ancient forms. But whatever is sought and valued above God is idolatry. It could be pleasure, wealth, materialism, science, sports, education, politics, national defense, religion, etc. These are not bad in themselves, but if they replace God they are idolatry. Wealth is not bad, but if the pursuit of wealth or if the wealth is put above God it would be sinful. I consider atheism to be idolatry because the person is stubbornly putting their unbelief above God. Denial of God is a category of ignorance. Agnostics are stubbornly skeptic, which is another one of the three forms of ignorance described in the Bible. Stubbornness is identified in the Bible as idolatry. If a nation relies more on its own defenses for protection than on God, it is idolatrous.

God takes idols very seriously because idolatry is misleading, and is always in competition with truth and the real Creator of the universe. The first example of idols among the Israelites is Genesis 31:19, where Rachael stole her father's gods. Idolatry has, and does appear, all over the world in nations and in all religions, even including some that profess to be Christian. The Israelites, despite severe warnings, had a past with multiple influences of idol worship. The nations that become more reliant on resources and dollars (U$A) than on the Sovereign God are idolatrous nations.

The worship of heavenly bodies, such as the sun and moon, were the most prevalent in systems of idolatry. Idols are carved from stone and made with hands. Idols started in the plains of Chaldea (Babylon) and spread through Egypt, Greece, Roman Empire, Asia and the whole world. Idols seduce others to false worship. Idols are attractive, because they are an outward sign, that attracts the senses of man. The Christmas season that is widely practiced in our culture is a mix of pagan custom and Christianity. This holiday is extremely popular and many individuals get quite caught up in either the pagan and spiritual aspects, or both. Easter is likewise a mix of pagan custom (eggs - fertility) and Christianity. Wealth, luxury, pageantry, parades, artistry, and the licentious revelries that accompanied much of false worship, appealed to a natural attraction to sensual passion and gave idolatry broad appeal. The amount of internet pornography and the explosion of and sale of pornography and pornographic materials in America, is an example of how addictive these desires can be. They are not called dirty books and movies for nothing. This is a gross industry and if you are in it you should repent and get out fast. This includes large hotel chains that sell pornography to guests in their rooms. Do not think there is not a judgment for idolatry. After the Israelites made and worshipped a golden calf, God required men with swords to go throughout the camp and about 3,000 were killed that day.

"Thou shalt have no other gods before me. Thou shalt not make unto thee any graven image, or any likeness *of any thing* that *is* in heaven above, or that *is* in the earth beneath, or that *is* in the water under the earth:" - Exodus 20:3-4

"Now while Paul waited for them at Athens, his spirit was stirred in him, when he saw the city wholly given to idolatry." - Acts 17:16

"For all the gods of the nations *are* idols: but the LORD made the heavens." - Psalms 96:5

"Cursed *be* the man that maketh *any* graven or molten image, an abomination unto the LORD, the work of the hands of the craftsman, and putteth *it* in *a* secret *place*. And all the people shall answer and say, Amen." - Deuteronomy 27:15

"And the devil said unto him, All this power will I give thee, and the glory of them: for that is delivered unto me; and to whomsoever I will I give it. If thou therefore wilt worship me, all shall be thine. And Jesus answered and said unto him, Get thee behind me, Satan: for it is written, Thou shalt worship the Lord thy God, and him only shalt thou serve." - Luke 4:6-8

Immanuel

El (Eloheim - God) - I Am – Man — Name

Jesus Christ is God (El) incarnate. He is the visible image of the invisible God, who is I Am. He was the Lamb slain before the foundation of the world. The Messiah, a sinless sacrifice, was God's divine plan for salvation by grace. He took on flesh and became the "Son of Man." The religion of Islam teaches the virgin birth of Christ, but belief in His birth does not save you. It is faith in His deity, death, resurrection and shed blood for your sin that saves you. Jesus was rejected, condemned, and nailed to the cross and crucified. He rose from the grave and He is the Resurrection and the Life. He has been given all power in heaven and on earth, and His name is above every name. The Christian hope is that we live because He lives. He is with us, and He and God are one (one God, but three persons of the Godhead). The word Immanuel literally means "God with us."

"Therefore the Lord himself shall give you a sign; Behold, a virgin shall conceive, and bear a Son, and shall call his Name Immanuel." - Isaiah 7:14

"Who being the brightness of *his* glory, and the express image of his person, and upholding all things by the word of his power, when he had by himself purged our sins, sat down on the right hand of the Majesty on high;" - Hebrews 1:3

"And every creature which is in heaven, and on the earth, and under the earth, and such as are in the sea, and all that are in them, heard I saying, Blessing, and honour, and glory, and power, *be* unto him that sitteth upon the throne, and unto the Lamb for ever and ever." - Revelation 5:13

Individual

DNA – Dual – In Al (ALL)

A discovery in 1953 found that each person has contained in their microscopic cells a language called Deoxyribon Nucleic Acid (DNA). If this language were written it would fill a thousand books. This language is the genetics design in all physical life. DNA is an extremely complex message and any message requires a messenger. This message was from the Giver of Life, the one true Living Almighty Creator God.

Each person is unique, one of a kind, and no two <u>individuals</u> are alike. DNA is an <u>individual</u> code that produces a unique person for a relationship with God and for a special job. The Creator holds the patent/copyright, and each human life is sacred because we are made in the image of God. We owe eternal allegiance and gratitude for this gift of life.

Every person is born in sin and has a sin nature. Man in this state is called the natural man. Only those <u>individuals</u> that have a second birth, a spiritual birth, have a dual nature. They still have the natural side. But they have the precious advantage of having a spiritual nature, and they are reconciled to God. Scripture says that we are partakers in the Divine Nature, so maybe DNA = "Divine Nature Applied." This is so important and that is why it is on the front cover.

"God created man in his *own* image, in the image of God created he him; male and female created he them." - Genesis 1:27

"And they went in unto Noah into the ark, two and two of all flesh, wherein *is* the breath of life." - Genesis 7:15

"But the natural man receiveth not the things of the Spirit of God: for they are foolishness unto him: neither can he know *them*, because they are spiritually discerned." - 1 Corinthians 2:14

"For the invisible things of him from the creation of the world are clearly seen, being understood by the things that are made, *even* his eternal power and Godhead; so that they are without excuse:" - Romans 1:20

"For this cause shall a man leave his father and mother, and shall be joined unto his wife, and they two shall be one flesh." - Ephesians 5:31

"Whereby are given unto us exceeding great and precious promises: that by these ye might be partakers of the divine nature, having escaped the corruption that is in the world through lust." - 2 Peter 1:4

Insight

His - In - Sight - Sign

Without God there would be no sight, period. The Holy Bible was written by forty men over a period of approximately 1,500 years. The first five books were written by Moses, and the last book by the Apostle John around 95 AD. God's ways are not simple, and God's true Word was not produced in a simple way. These writers had an unparalleled insight into the mysteries of God's ways, because they were being led and inspired by the Holy Spirit. The profoundness and prophecy contained in the Bible are astonishing. The Holy Spirit allowed the writers to see reality in His sight, through His eyes. As opposed to seeing it through their own flawed, human eyes that could not grasp the full truth and wonder of God's mind and heart. This special insight allowed some of the Biblical writers, notably prophets, to receive a vision or sign through a dream that uncovered a mystery, or foretold a future event. Hundreds of prophecies have been fulfilled that provided many exact details. Israel's dispersion and return to the land is one of those prophecies that was fulfilled in detail. Nations need to pay attention because you may think that you are measuring Israel, but the Sovereign God is measuring you by Israel. Nations, religions, churches, and individuals are being weighed in the balances.

"For the LORD *is* good; his mercy *is* everlasting; and his truth *endureth* to all generations." - Psalms 100:5

"All scripture *is* given by inspiration of God, and *is* profitable for doctrine, for reproof, for correction, for instruction in righteousness:" - 2 Timothy 3:16

"For the word of God *is* quick, and powerful, and sharper than any two-edged sword, piercing even to the dividing asunder of soul and spirit, and of the joints and marrow, and *is* a discerner of the thoughts and intents of the heart." - Hebrews 4:12

"Receiving the end of your faith, even the salvation of your souls. Of which salvation the prophets have enquired and searched diligently, who prophesied of the grace that should come unto you: Searching what, or what manner of time the Spirit of Christ which was in them did signify, when it testified beforehand the sufferings of Christ, and the glory that should follow. Unto whom it was revealed, that not unto themselves, but unto us they did minister the things, which are now reported unto you by them that have preached the gospel unto you with the Holy Ghost sent down from heaven; which things the angels desire to look into." - 1 Peter 1:9-12

"And I will bless them that bless thee, and curse him that curseth thee: and in thee shall all families of the earth be blessed." - Genesis 12:3

Inspiration

Anoint – In - Spirit – Pastor

The writers of the Bible were inspired by the Holy Spirit to write out the thoughts of God Almighty. The writing, though inerrant, was flavored by their personality and era in which they were living. Also, that divine inspiration didn't stop with the Apostles Peter, Paul or John. God still to this day, uses the Spirit to inspire His people. Believers are sealed by the Holy Spirit at their time of salvation, through faith in Jesus Christ. The Spirit is able to anoint our hearts and minds to be instruments of encouragement, teaching, and further inspiration to others. The Holy Spirit will work through all believers that allow Him to do so, and divine inspiration can come to anyone who is in the Spirit. When led by the Spirit you are not under the law. For where the Spirit of the Lord is there is freedom. God can take the weak and confound the wise. Spiritual gifts are supernatural. So a regular musician, writer, speaker, artist, teacher, doctor, athlete, or any other individual, may become a spiritual giant that will be used for God's purposes. One can be even greater than he could ever imagine, all for the glory of God. A spiritual gift(s) remains with an individual during his entire life. Yet they are not needed on the other side of eternity, since we will be with the Lord in our glorified state.

But to whom much is given, much is required. There is a certain responsibility that comes with this transformation from ordinary to extraordinary. When it comes to writers, teachers, evangelists, and pastors, this inspiration should be used very wisely. Teachings and writings regarding anything spiritual must be backed up by Scripture, the original Divine inspiration of God. This is so that the truth that was revealed to those original writers will be fortified and supported as opposed, to being changed for an agenda or any other purpose that would take away from the truth of God's Word. It is important to keep in mind that God's Spirit is what inspires, so we know that it is from God and not our own minds. This is so that He gets the glory only He is worthy to receive.

"For it is not ye that speak, but the Spirit of your Father which speaketh in you."-Matthew 10:20

"Are they not all ministering Spirits, sent forth to minister for them who shall be heirs of salvation?"-Hebrews 1:14

"And grieve not the holy Spirit of God, whereby ye are sealed unto the day of redemption." - Ephesians 4:30

Intimate

In - Time - Mate - Team

To be <u>intimate</u> is to be in close association, be very familiar, or to be in a close relationship. Usually, in an intimate relationship things are exclusively shared. You and your mate are a team and should be in an intimate relationship. In time you and your mate should learn more and more about each other, and grow stronger as a team. This team should make each of you stronger than you would be alone.

These same principles work in a relationship with God. A close personal, intimate relationship with God is something that is attainable. In time, God wants you to find Him, learn about Him, and grow into a personal relationship with Him. To be on God's team has amazing advantages. You have a soul and God has a soul. Your soul mate is supposed to be the Living Almighty God.

"For I determined not to know any thing among you, save Jesus Christ, and him crucified." - 1 Corinthians 2:2

"And the scripture was fulfilled which saith, Abraham believed God, and it was imputed unto him for righteousness: and he was called the Friend of God." - James 2:23

"For ye have not received the spirit of bondage again to fear; but ye have received the Spirit of adoption, whereby we cry, Abba, Father." - Romans 8:15

"Let us therefore come boldly unto the throne of grace, that we may obtain mercy, and find grace to help in time of need." - Hebrews 4:16

"And thou shalt love the LORD thy God with all thine heart, and with all thy soul, and with all thy might." - Deuteronomy 6:5
"I will greatly rejoice in the LORD, my soul shall be joyful in my God; for he hath clothed me with the garments of salvation, he hath covered me with the robe of righteousness, as a bridegroom

decketh *himself* with ornaments, and as a bride adorneth *herself* with her jewels." - Isaiah 61:10

Image

I Am – Me – Game - Age

    The <u>image</u> you have of yourself may be different from the <u>image</u> that God has of you. Many people get the spiritual <u>image</u> of themselves by comparing themselves with others. Many think that this is the standard that God uses for entrance into heaven. Where did they get that standard? Is it God's standard? It is not God's standard according to the Bible. Standing before God is different from standing before men. Based on your merit the standard is 100% sinless perfection. Do you measure up to that standard? No, you do not measure up to God's standard. If you could, Jesus would not have had to been crucified for sin. He is God's only acceptable standard, therefore, His righteousness must be applied to you. The formula for righteousness is not works, but faith in Christ and in His perfect sacrifice. Quit playing a game because without I AM you are all me (self), and none of God. The best image is Me + I AM. That way you will not have to worry about age because you will have eternal life.

"And God said unto Moses, I AM THAT I AM: and he said, Thus shalt thou say unto the children of Israel, I AM hath sent me unto you." - Exodus 3:14

"For all have sinned, and come short of the glory of God;" - Romans 3:23

"And have put on the new *man*, which is renewed in knowledge after the <u>image</u> of him that created him:" - Colossians 3:10

Israel

El (God) – Is - Real - Seal

Make no mistake about it; Israel has a special place in God's heart and in His plans. Israel is the "apple of God's eye." God has established an everlasting covenant with Israel, so His seal is on this nation. Israel is the center of the earth to God, and all nations on earth are located in reference to the small nation of Israel. Borders and destinies of nations are determined by God, based upon their stance concerning Israel. Regrettably, Israel as a nation, is still secular. The Jewish people were called back to the land in unbelief, but that will change. Already, there are many signs that this is a spiritual transition period for Israel. Be a part of this process through prayer and support. Every true church should have passion for Israel, as well as connections to Israel. The nation was given its name because the God of Abraham, Isaac and Jacob is the one true and Living God. Make no mistake, El is real.

"And I will establish my covenant between me and thee and thy seed after thee in their generations for an everlasting covenant, to be a God unto thee, and to thy seed after thee." - Genesis 17:7

"For thus saith the LORD of hosts; After the glory hath he sent me unto the nations which spoiled you: for he that toucheth you toucheth the apple of his eye." - Zechariah 2:8

J

Jesus

Use(s) – Us

The Lord is in the process of building the Kingdom of God on earth by salvation and sanctification of those who believe. His method to accomplish this important work is to use us, who ourselves, became born again believers. The Lord, while seated at the right hand of the Father, uses believers as His body on earth. The Lord's organization is the local church where believers assemble together. Without, faith in Jesus no one is able to please God or serve God.

When you receive Jesus you are sealed with the Holy Spirit, you are saved, and you are also called to serve God. The beneficial results from Christian service biblically are identified as fruit. As Christians, there are many ways, big and small, that God uses us, to the benefit of family, brethren, church, community, nation, world, and ultimately the Kingdom of God.

"So we, *being* many, are one body in Christ, and every one members one of another." - Romans 12:5

"Wherefore, my brethren, ye also are become dead to the law by the body of Christ; that ye should be married to another, *even* to him who is raised from the dead, that we should bring forth fruit unto God." - Romans 7:4

"But without faith *it is* impossible to please *him*: for he that cometh to God must believe that he is, and *that* he is a rewarder of them that diligently seek him." - Hebrews 11:6

"And other fell on good ground, and did yield fruit that sprang up and increased; and brought forth, some thirty, and some sixty, and some an hundred." - Mark 4:8

"Verily, verily, I say unto you, He that believeth on me, the works that I do shall he do also; and greater *works* than these shall he do; because I go unto my Father." - John 14:12

Jerusalem

USA - Rule - Real

Jerusalem is located in a small nation and it does not have a port, river or a major industry. So what is the big deal? Does it astonish you how important this city is to so many groups of people that represent billions of the world's population? It has important historical and spiritual significance to the three largest religious groups in the world; Catholics, Protestant Christians, and Muslims. There is a lot of emotion for this great city from the three groups sited above. It also is important to the Jews.

Abraham demonstrated his faith by bringing his son of promise, Isaac, to Jerusalem to offer the boy to God as a sacrifice. The Messiah or Christ had a real crucifixion and resurrection in Jerusalem. The Wailing Wall is all that is left exposed of the magnificent and Holy Temple, which was destroyed by a Roman army in 70 AD. The Muslim Dome of the Rock is located in Jerusalem, close to the Temple site. Jerusalem is called the City of David and is the capital city of Israel. The Jewish people regained control of Jerusalem in 1967, and this is the first time the city has been under Jewish control since the 70 AD conquest. There is a spiritual battle being waged between light and darkness, and Jerusalem has been, and will continue to be, very important in that battle. Pray for the peace of Jerusalem.

The United States of America (USA) has been very important for Israel and the Jewish people. President Truman played an essential role in the UN resolution passing that chartered Israel as a nation in May, 1948. The USA has provided the Jewish people with their longest stability, and greatest prosperity of any nation. In other lands, persecution eventually begins and pogroms and the Jewish residents have to flee. The reasons for Jewish acceptance are the Christian foundations in the USA, and the recognition of the heritage shared by Christians and Jews. If a religion is not able to flourish through a free choice environment, it is a worthless religion. If the USA foundations erode, then the peace and prosperity that the Jews have enjoyed in the USA will erode as well. There is a tremendous amount of Biblical history and prophecy regarding Israel and Jerusalem. Israel and Jerusalem are important in Eschatology, the study of end times. The Book of Revelation states that during the tribulation two witnesses are killed in Jerusalem. And that their dead bodies will be seen by many kindreds and tongues (languages) and nations. It would require television, internet, and satellite communications for that prophecy written over 1,900 years ago to take place. Israel, its capital of Jerusalem, and the Jewish people group are prominent in end time prophecy. When the "I am the Alpha and Omega" returns at the Battle of Armageddon, He will defeat the armies of the world assembled against Israel (really against Jesus) and led by the Antichrist. The Lord will then establish His rule, a thousand year kingdom, over the entire earth, and the capitol will be Jerusalem.

"And the children of Benjamin did not drive out the Jebusites that inhabited Jerusalem; but the Jebusites dwell with the children of Benjamin in Jerusalem unto this day." - Judges 1:21

"And these were born unto him in Jerusalem; Shimea, and Shobab, and Nathan, and Solomon, four, of Bathshua the daughter of Ammiel:" - 1 Chronicles 3:5

"O Jerusalem, Jerusalem, *thou* that killest the prophets, and stonest them which are sent unto thee, how often would I have gathered thy children together, even as a hen gathereth her chickens under *her* wings, and ye would not!" - Matthew 23:37

"For we wrestle not against flesh and blood, but against principalities, against powers, against the rulers of the darkness of this world, against spiritual wickedness in high *places*." - Ephesians 6:12

"And it shall come to pass in the last days, *that* the mountain of the LORD'S house shall be established in the top of the mountains, and shall be exalted above the hills; and all nations shall flow unto it. And many people shall go and say, Come ye, and let us go up to the mountain of the LORD, to the house of the God of Jacob; and he will teach us of his ways, and we will walk in his paths: for out of Zion shall go forth the law, and the word of the LORD from Jerusalem." - Isaiah 2:2-3

"And I John saw the holy city, new Jerusalem, coming down from God out of heaven, prepared as a bride adorned for her husband." - Revelation 21:2

Joyfulness

Enjoy/Joy- Soul - ful (full) – Luv (Ph. - Love)

True spirituality, sound doctrine, and a love for the Lord are accompanied by unspeakable joy. Joy is a delight (God is light) that seems to be beyond happiness. It makes your soul full and satisfies the deepest human need for unconditional love.

"And David spake to the chief of the Levites to appoint their brethren *to be* the singers with instruments of music, psalteries and harps and cymbals, sounding, by lifting up the voice with joy." - 1 Chronicles 15:16

"Then the people rejoiced, for that they offered willingly, because with perfect heart they offered willingly to the LORD: and David the king also rejoiced with great joy." - 1 Chronicles 29:9

"Yet I will rejoice in the LORD, I will joy in the God of my salvation." - Habakkuk 3:18

"But the fruit of the Spirit is love, joy, peace, longsuffering, gentleness, goodness, faith," - Galatians 5:22

"Whom having not seen, ye love; in whom, though now ye see *him* not, yet believing, ye rejoice with joy unspeakable and full of glory:" - 1 Peter 1:8

Judgmental

El (God) – Meant – Mean

Everyone will have to give their own account before God, so Scripture warns against us judging others. We should not be judgmental of others, because that is not meant for our role or responsibility. God is able to love the sinner and hate the sin; however, humans have difficulty making that clear distinction.

John Newton was a slave ship captain, and in that position he would have been part of tremendous cruelty and injustice to many dark skinned victims of the salve trade. This man, who had been among the greatest of sinners and enemy of God, experienced Jesus and converted to Christianity. Afterwards, he worked against the slave trade and he wrote one of the greatest hymns ever written, *Amazing Grace*.

During his lengthy career in the slave trade, how easy it would have been for people to have been judgmental regarding this man or have been mean to him. A judgment that slavery was sinful and immoral would have a correct ethical position, but being judgmental of the sinner is not appropriate. We are all sinners and have all "come short of the glory of God." Every single person has the seeds for every sin, and these seeds can bring forth evil fruit.

"And he shall judge among the nations, and shall rebuke many people: and they shall beat their swords into plowshares, and their spears into pruninghooks: nation shall not lift up sword against nation, neither shall they learn war any more." - Isaiah 2:4

"Judge not, that ye be not judged. For with what judgment ye judge, ye shall be judged: and with what measure ye mete, it shall be measured to you again."- Matthew 7:1-2

"Judge not, and ye shall not be judged: condemn not, and ye shall not be condemned: forgive, and ye shall be forgiven:" - Luke 6:37

"But after thy hardness and impenitent heart treasurest up unto thyself wrath against the day of wrath and revelation of the righteous judgment of God;" - Romans 2:5

"But the heavens and the earth, which are now, by the same word are kept in store, reserved unto fire against the day of judgment and perdition of ungodly men." - 2 Peter 3:7

"And I saw a great white throne, and him that sat on it, from whose face the earth and the heaven fled away; and there was found no place for them. And I saw the dead, small and great, stand before God; and the books were opened: and another book was opened, which is *the book* of life: and the dead were judged out of those things which were written in the books, according to their works. And the sea gave up the dead which were in it; and death and hell delivered up the dead which were in them: and they were judged every man according to their works. And death and hell were cast into the lake of fire. This is the second death. And whosoever was not found written in the book of life was cast into the lake of fire." - Revelation 20:11-15

Justifies

Just - Jesus – Us

To be justified by God is to be accepted by God as righteous, and to be free from any blame and penalty for sin. All have sinned and come short of God's required standard. So, who is justified, and how do you become justified? Simply put, Jesus justifies us. It is just by grace through faith in Jesus Christ. There is no work you can do to pay the penalty for sin. Jesus already paid the penalty for the sins of the whole world, but you need that payment personally applied to your sin. Believe. Just believe.

114

"Keep thee far from a false matter; and the innocent and righteous slay thou not: for I will not <u>justify</u> the wicked." - Exodus 23:7

"He (Jesus) shall see of the travail of his soul, *and* shall be satisfied: by his knowledge shall my righteous servant <u>justify</u> many; for he shall bear their iniquities." - Isaiah 53:11

"And the scripture, foreseeing that God would <u>justify</u> the heathen through faith, preached before the gospel unto Abraham, *saying*, In thee shall all nations be blessed." - Galatians 3:8

"For by grace are ye saved through faith; and that not of yourselves: *it is* the gift of God:" - Ephesians 2:8

K

Kingdom

Kin – God

The Bible states that when we accept Jesus, we inherit the <u>Kingdom</u> of God. We are also told that being born again we become brothers and sisters in Christ. That makes us spiritual kin to everyone who is in Christ. Those in the <u>Kingdom</u> of God are now our immediate family. Abraham is called the "father of faith"; so those of faith in the God of Abraham, Isaac, and Jacob are spiritually kin to Abraham. Being in the family of God brings many special privileges, including access to God and eternal life.

In many cultures, there is a special value on family. People will go out of their way to make sure their kinfolk are safe and well cared for. It should be no different with our Christian brothers and sisters. We should help, care for, encourage, and love our kin in Christ. This is what God commands. By being light that shines in darkness, Christians assist God in building His <u>Kingdom</u>.

Though it is not presently a visible <u>kingdom</u>, God is in the process of increasing His <u>kingdom</u> by adding believers from all over the world. Following the Battle of Armageddon, described in Revelation, the "Lamb of God", Jesus the Christ, will inherit the Davidic Throne and be King for a thousand years. This <u>Kingdom</u> will have rule and authority over all nations and will be located in Jerusalem.

"But seek first the <u>kingdom</u> of God, and his righteousness; and all these things shall be added unto you." - Matthew 6:33

"And he said unto them, When ye pray, say, Our Father which art in heaven, Hallowed be thy name. Thy <u>kingdom</u> come. Thy will be done, as in heaven, so in earth." - Luke 11:2

"And if children, then heirs; heirs of God, and joint-heirs with Christ; if so be that we suffer with *him*, that we may be also glorified together." - Romans 8:17

Knowledge

Now – Ledge

<u>Knowledge</u>, apart from humility through a relationship with God, can puff you up and make you prideful. Some theologians consider pride to be one of the worse sins. Many pursue knowledge alone, and neglect God. Are you a doctor, lawyer, professor, scientist, jet pilot, CEO, etc. that has knowledge which gives you advantages? Your knowledge may have made you a multi-millionaire or even built a $25 billion foundation, but I would not trade places with you if you do not <u>know</u> God. And I promise God is really worth knowing!

<u>Knowledge</u> changes, so it is just for now, and it only takes you so far until you end up at a ledge where you are not able to go any farther. I was sitting on an airplane beside a pharmacy student that was graduating in two months. I asked him about his field and how current the text books needed to be. He said last years book

would be out of date. Then I asked him a hypothetical question: If a person graduated from pharmacy school twenty years ago and had not done any learning since . . . He interrupted and said their education would be worthless.

Eating fruit from the Tree of <u>Knowledge</u> is the only sin that Adam could have committed. This Tree of <u>Knowledge</u> was a big deal to God. But why might God have forbidden something that does not appear that serious? Why would a Tree of Knowledge be so bad? I think that the tree represents a false and perilous pursuit. This tree apparently represents seeking knowledge apart from God. Is it any surprise that countless millions of people still seek their understanding by this method apart from God? Science means knowledge, so this tree could be called the "tree of science." Unfortunately this seems to be the Tree of <u>Knowledge</u> that so many think will advance mankind, and make humans the measure of all things instead of God, the Creator of this universe, and the Sovereign Supreme eternal being.

"And out of the ground made the LORD God to grow every tree that is pleasant to the sight, and good for food; the tree of life also in the midst of the garden, and the tree of <u>knowledge</u> of good and evil." - Genesis 2:9

"For what is a man profited, if he gain the whole world, and lose his own soul? Or what shall a man give in exchange for his soul? - Matthew 16:26

L

Learn(ing)
Earn

<u>Learning</u> is a gain of knowledge, and spiritual <u>learning</u> is identified as growth. New converts are called babes in Christ. All believers

are referred to as children of God. Spiritual maturity develops from a complex combination that includes an increase in Bible knowledge and understanding, fellowship, answered prayer, service, giving and worship. This whole process is called sanctification. After you are saved, God begins to work in your life to build your faith and ability to bear spiritual fruit. What a privilege to be able to learn more and more about the Person that created the entire universe.

Education or learning usually improves your ability to earn more money and enjoy a higher standard of living. Spiritual learning also improves your ability to earn more in terms of an eternal rewards. Those saved will not be judged for sin, but will be judged only to reveal their contributions to God's kingdom. The reward that they will receive will be based on the eternal good that they accomplish after being saved. You will not earn any heavenly reward until you have learned just enough to have saving faith in God. The most important things to learn are not mathematical skills, music, proper grammar, etc., but wisdom, principals for living, guidance, truth, and most importantly, more and more about the eternal Eloheim.

"But continue thou in the things which thou hast learned and hast been assured of, knowing of whom thou hast learned them; And that from a child thou hast known the Holy Scriptures, which are able to make thee wise unto salvation through faith which is in Christ Jesus. All scripture is given by inspiration of God, and is profitable for doctrine, for reproof, for correction, for instruction in righteousness: That the man of God may be perfect, thoroughly furnished unto all good works."- 2 Timothy 3:14-17

"But seek ye first the kingdom of God, and his righteousness; and all these things shall be added unto you." – Matthew 6:33

"And I, brethren, could not speak unto you as unto spiritual, but as unto carnal, *even* as unto babes in Christ." – 1 Corinthians 3:1

Liberal

Libel – Lie - Rebel

These, as a group, believe a lie, and therefore they libel God (make and say false assumptions) and they rebel against God. Those that do not believe in God or oppose the light that came into the world actually hate God. Repentance might be a good option.

"Ye are of *your* father the devil, and the lusts of your father ye will do. He was a murderer from the beginning, and abode not in the truth, because there is no truth in him. When he speaketh a lie, he speaketh of his own: for he is a liar, and the father of it." - John 8:44

"God forbid that we should rebel against the LORD, and turn this day from following the LORD" - Joshua 22:29

Liberty

El (God) – Try

Freedom is found in truth and America became a nation of freedom and liberty because it was founded on Biblical principals. The correct fight is not to establish a state religion, but to establish freedom for all religion. If you have not already done so, I suggest that try God and be set free. "It is impossible to enslave, mentally or socially, a Bible reading people. The principles of the Bible are the groundwork of human freedom." Horace Greeley

"The Spirit of the Lord GOD *is* upon me; because the LORD hath anointed me to preach good tidings unto the meek; he hath sent me to bind up the broken hearted, to proclaim liberty to the captives, and the opening of the prison to *them that are* bound;" - Isaiah 61:1

"And ye shall know the truth, and the truth shall make you free." - John 8:32

119

Life

File

You have a <u>life</u> because God has a file on you and on everyone else. In your file even the hairs on your head are numbered. Human life is sacred because mankind is made in the image of God. God gave you the breath of <u>life</u> and you will always exist as a human somewhere. There are only two options, heaven or hell. In heaven, you will experience the presence of God, and in hell, there is separation from God. You want to be sure that you have eternal <u>life</u>, which a person receives at their time of salvation. This guarantees ones eternal security. Once you have eternal life there is no sin remembered against you. In the Bible, the word remember means to act upon. In true salvation all of your sin is forgiven. This is not a license to freely commit sin, because God will chasten, or discipline you for continued sin, even to death if necessary.

"He that hath the Son hath <u>life</u>; *and* he that hath not the Son of God hath not <u>life</u>." - 1 John 5:12

"For he that eateth and drinketh, eateth and drinketh judgment unto himself, if he discern not the body. For this cause many among you are weak and sickly, and not a few sleep." - 1 Corinthians 11:29-30

Live

Evil – Vile - Lie

Since Adam sinned all mankind is born in fallen a world, and all mankind is born with a sin nature. All of creation is under the curse that came when Adam brought sin into the world. The sin of man is evident throughout history with wars, racism, crimes, greed, corruption, addictions, sexual immorality, idolatry, false religions, pride, etc. If you <u>live</u>, you have part of your nature that is sinful, evil, vile and satanic. If you say you have never told a lie, you just did. You are charged by God to overcome this fallen

120

nature. You are not capable in your own power to achieve this. It is impossible for you to achieve it on your own. But God provided a way to overcome through Jesus. God is extraordinarily good! Even though there are those that lead apparent moral lives, and they think that they are good, they are not good. That is why you need God to obtain righteousness and overcome the world.

"Behold, I was shapen in iniquity; and in sin did my mother conceive me." - Psalms 51:5

"To open their eyes, *and* to turn *them* from darkness to light, and *from* the power of Satan unto God, that they may receive forgiveness of sins, and inheritance among them which are sanctified by faith that is in me." - Acts 26:18

"Nevertheless death reigned from Adam to Moses, even over them that had not sinned after the similitude of Adam's transgression, who is the figure of him that was to come." - Romans 5:14

"For as many as are of the works of the law are under a curse: for it is written, Cursed is every one who continueth not in all things that are written in the book of the law, to do them." - Galatians 3:10

"Christ redeemed us from the curse of the law, having become a curse for us; for it is written, Cursed is every one that hangeth on a tree:" - Galatians 3:13

"Now the just shall <u>live</u> by faith: but if *any man* draw back, my soul shall have no pleasure in him." - Hebrews 10:38

"In this was manifested the love of God toward us, because that God sent his only begotten Son into the world, that we might <u>live</u> through him." - 1 John 4:9

Last

Salt

Salt is a preservative and a purifier. Christians are supposed to be salt and light in the world. Christians have the responsibility to preserve truth and purity, and to represent the true character of God. God is love, but God also executes judgment against evil. It is human nature to want to be first rather than last. But the inspired Bible teaches that it is far more important to be a servant to others, than to be first for ourselves.

"and thou shalt make of it incense, a perfume after the art of the perfumer, seasoned with salt, pure *and* holy:" - Exodus 30:35

"Ye are the salt of the earth: but if the salt have lost its savor, wherewith shall it be salted? It is thenceforth good for nothing, but to be cast out and trodden under foot of men." - Matthew 5:13

"Salt is good: but if the salt have lost its saltness, wherewith will ye season it? Have salt in yourselves, and be at peace one with another." - Mark 9:50

M

Meekness

Knees – Seek(s)

The definition of the word meek may cause people to think that it is a flaw rather than a virtue. The Hebrew word for meek is *anaw*, meaning "in need, wretched, impoverished, and oppressed." When we hear the word meek, we think of weak, as in one who is easily brought to his knees; or one who is easy to trample over without much resistance. However, the definition of meekness, as seen in the Bible, is that of humility and kindness to our neighbors, and reverence for God. Meekness is a result of love, meaning it is an attribute of God. Some of the strongest people in the Bible are defined as being meek, like Moses, the Apostle Paul, and even the Lord Jesus.

Meekness is also a Fruit of the Spirit, and is the third characteristic that Jesus described in his teaching of the Beatitudes from his Sermon on the Mount. That should indicate how important this virtue is! He says the meek will be blessed and will inherit the earth. Why? Because meekness allows one to be prepared to do what Jesus commands, which is love your neighbor and love God. The meek don't seek revenge for insult or injury from those who wrong or oppress them. But instead they feel a sense of pity for them, and towards sinners in general, feeling inclined to love and help them with their character issues. Revenge is an attitude of get even, and it is prevalent and destructive. Jesus demonstrated this when He was on the cross, saying "Father, forgive them for they know not what they do." This is the true definition of meekness in action. He could have easily taken Himself down from the cross, but showed meekness by constraining His strength for our sake. Jesus reacted to insult, oppression, rejection, and condemnation with unconditional love for those who committed these things against Him.

The meek are also able to stay calm and are not quick to get angry with other people or with God. The meek humbly bow on their knees before God and willingly submit to Him. They will seek him and will be blessed for it. Meekness is also a cure for stress and anxiety, which allows room for joy to come in.

"Seek the Lord, all you meek of the earth, who have kept His ordinances; Seek righteousness, Seek meekness: it may be you shall be hid in the day of the Lord's anger." - Zephaniah 2:3

The meek shall eat and be satisfied: Those who seek the Lord shall praise Him: your heart shall live for ever. - Psalm 22:26

"The meek shall also increase their joy in the Lord, and the poor among men shall rejoice in the Holy One of Israel. - Isaiah 29:19

"Blessed are the <u>meek</u>: for they shall inherit the earth." - Matthew 5:5

Messiah

He - Is – I Am – Same

From the time that man sinned in the Garden of Eden, God promised His people a <u>Messiah</u>; One who would save them and reign over them. When the time was just right, God acted on this plan. The <u>Messiah</u> came to Earth in the form of a child, being born as a created being from the womb of one He created. Jesus existed long before anything was created. He was and **is** and **is** to come because He is part of the Godhead, Father, Son and Holy Spirit. Everything was created by Him and for Him. He is I Am. The prophesied Jewish <u>Messiah</u> is the same as the gentle Jesus. The <u>Messiah</u> was rejected nationally by Israel; therefore God placed the Jews, except for a remnant, in spiritual blindness. This condition has lasted to his very day, but it is not permanent. They have been in denial long enough, and they need to be true children of Abraham, "a friend of God" and the "father of faith." The "times of the Gentiles" will be brought to an end. This is not bad because the world will receive great blessings after Israel recognizes her <u>Messiah</u>. I see signs that God has already started the preparation for this transition of spiritual power from the Gentiles back to Israel. It is a privilege through prayer and giving, to be a part of this prophecy. It will happen with or without you. If you are on God's side you should gladly support Israel in ministry, particularly Messianic ministry, in Israel.

The Jewish people are amazed that Christians have taken their Old Testament all over the world. They are also amazed at our people numbers compared to theirs. Every true New Testament church in America, and the world, should have a passion for Israel. God separated the Jewish people for His purpose. Through them He produced prophets, the Old and New Testaments, the Apostles, the Church and most importantly the Jewish <u>Messiah</u>. The only Savior of the world, Jesus, was a Jew, while on earth. "And in

124

none other is there salvation: for neither is there any other name under heaven, that is given among men, wherein we must be saved." (Acts 4:12)   We have much to be thankful to Israel for, they gave us our Savior.

By God's grace we have been grafted into the kingdom inheritance. "The Messiah is "A light to lighten the Gentiles, and the glory of thy people Israel." (Luke 2:32) The Messiah is the "consolation of Israel." (Luke 2:25)

"and I will put enmity between thee and the woman, and between thy seed and her seed: he shall bruise thy head, and thou shalt bruise his heel." - Genesis 3:15

"Jesus said to them, 'Verily, verily, I say unto you, Before Abraham was, I Am.'" - John 8:58

"He findeth first his own brother Simon, and saith unto him, We have found the Messiah (which is, being interpreted, Christ)." - John 1:41

Ministers

Resist – Sin (s) - Insist

Insist means to stand upon or follow diligently, and how appropriate this is for ministers that have a calling from God. Ministers should stand firmly upon Scripture and insist on everyone's need for salvation; because all were separated from God by sin. First and foremost sin is an offense against a Holy God. Therefore ministers, as representatives of God, should resist sin. They should encourage people to have behavior that is based on what the Word of God says, because there are moral absolutes. Christian leaders should resist sin themselves, because they have a responsibility to correctly represent God's character to the best of their ability.   People expect to see a high standard of morality set by the people who have been chosen by God to minister to them.

When a spiritual leader sins, it may cause those who see this sin to be turned away from the church, or to think the sin is okay since a minister has committed it. That's why those who are in a position of power should resist sin, not only for themselves, but for the well being of others, the church, and the Kingdom.

"For after that in the wisdom of God the world by wisdom knew not God, it pleased God by the foolishness of preaching to save them that believe." - 1 Corinthians 1:21

"But now being made free from sin, and become servants to God, ye have your fruit unto holiness, and the end everlasting life" - Romans 6:22

Miracle

I – Am – Real – Clear

During the ministry of Jesus He performed many miracles, including those that fulfilled Messianic prophecy. Jesus said, "He that hath seen me, hath seen the Father." Jesus verified that He was the I Am in the Old Testament, and that He was real, because of the many miracles He performed. When Jesus cast out a demon from the one who was both deaf and blind it was clear that He was the expected Messiah.

"Insomuch that the multitude wondered, when they saw the dumb to speak, the maimed to be whole, the lame to walk, and the blind to see: and they glorified the God of Israel." - Matthew 15:31

"Then was brought unto him one possessed with a devil, blind, and dumb: and he healed him, insomuch that the blind and dumb both spake and saw." - Matthew 12:22

"And Jesus said unto them, I am the bread of life: he that cometh to me shall never hunger; and he that believeth on me shall never thirst." - John 6:35

"He answered and said, Whether he be a sinner *or no*, I know not: one thing I know, that, whereas I was blind, now I see." - John 9:25

"For the man was above forty years old, on whom this <u>miracle</u> of healing was showed." - Acts 4:22

Music(k)

Sum – Us

<u>Music</u> has always been described as a sort of universal language because just about anyone can understand the sound of an orchestra, a jazz quartet, or a solo classical guitarist. Furthermore, those who have become "fluent" in the language are able to read it and speak it. As with any other language, music has dialects, which are called genres. Classical, Jazz, Rock, Country, Blues, Eastern Indian, Celtic, and Klezmer are just a few of the many genres of music heard throughout the world. Each one is distinctive to its native people (A product of the wonderful diversity that God has created among man), but each of these distinct styles share the same roots (Melody, Harmony and Rhythm), just as each nation shares a common ancestor, Adam. And just as each man can choose to reject or accept God, each style of music can be used to praise or curse Him. He has created <u>music</u> for us, not only to enjoy and to express our desire to create (Man can create because he has been made like his Creator), but He expects us to use it to glorify Him. King David, as well as other men in Israel's history, knew this intimately. These musicians wrote, sang, and played songs to the Lord, giving back to Him with gifts and talents that were first given to them by God (See *Preeminence, Fruits*).

When studying the very basics of <u>music</u> (what is known as <u>Music</u> Theory), you can see God's fingerprints all over it. As seen in the Bible, God loves to use numbers and sums of numbers to

127

point back to Himself. Music is one of the most obvious cases in which we can see how individual numbers add up to create a sum that displays God's wisdom in creation. The following examples are meant only to show just that. Anything further would be delving into mysticism, which is not scriptural and can lead to false ideas about God.

Three: There are three parts to music. Melody, a series of notes played in succession and variance of notes. Harmony, the relative notes to a melody which are pleasant to the ear, and are used to make up chords. Rhythm, is the patterns within a song which govern the length of notes and give the song its form.

Harmony, one of these three parts of music, is based on the number three. A basic chord is made up of three notes, or a triad, which starts with the root, adds the third, and finally the fifth. These intervals can be major, minor, augmented or diminished. Three is a number representative of Divine Perfection. The musical triad is a prefect picture of the Godhead. The Holy Trinity, Father, Son, and Holy Spirit; three parts that are in such harmony that they are one. There are many threes seen in scripture aside from the Trinity. Jesus rose on the third day. His ministry lasted three years. The Earth was separated from the water on the Third day of Creation. The Seraphim proclaim "Holy, Holy, Holy!" three times at God's throne. There are many other scriptural references to three, as well. Outside of scripture, three is a prominent number in the things around us, and people around us. There are three Human abilities (Thought, Word, and Deed). There are three parts of the universe (Time, Space, and Matter). As with the Godhead, they exist together as one, but they also each have three parts of their own. Time: Past, Present, Future. Matter: Solid, Liquid, Gas. Matter: Depth, Width, Length.

Seven: There are seven notes in a musical scale (Major, Minor, Dorian, Phrygian and Aeolian are all types of scales called Modes, each with seven notes). A seven note scale is full, but not complete. It is missing four notes to make it chromatic (a total of eleven notes), and even then, it is not yet perfectly complete. The number seven biblically represents completion or fullness and can be seen several places in Scripture; Seven days in a week, Seven parables in Matthew, Seven seals and Seven Trumpets in

Revelation, Seven promises to the churches, and many other not-so-obvious Sevens and numbers divisible by seven.

Eight: An octave is the interval between ranges in <u>music</u>. Based on the seven note scale, where it is the end of a full scale, it notes the beginning of a new, but higher, range of notes, thus completing the scale. The number eight in the Bible represents New Beginnings. There were eight people on Noah's Ark, and circumcisions were performed on the eighth day. Eight is also synonymous with the number one, as seen in the example of the musical scale, and explains why this number is used for starting anew.

Eleven: There are eleven notes available in <u>music</u> (certain Eastern Indian genres uses a Carnatic scale, which includes microtones found slightly in between the twelve chromatic notes, making twenty-one available notes. Note that this number is divisible by seven). Played consecutively, they form a chromatic scale, with a twelfth note completing the scale (this note is the same note, eight, that completes a seven note scale). Eleven is the number of disorder and imperfection, and symbolizes something that is not yet full. Examples in Scripture include the state of the disciples after Judas committed suicide, leaving them incomplete at eleven. In Genesis, we see how Jacob's life becomes disorderly and somewhat chaotic after Joseph is sold into slavery, and the number of his children goes from a complete twelve to an incomplete eleven. Meanwhile, Joseph spends eleven years in the house of Potiphar, whose wife causes disorder for Joseph and causes him to be thrown into prison.

Twelve: There are twelve notes in a full chromatic scale, arranged in half-steps or semitones. The number twelve represents Perfection of Completion (In music, this is seen by filling in the missing four notes of a seven note scale and ending at the first note in the next octave, completing the chromatic, twelve note scale) , and also Perfection of Authority or Government. There are twelve months in a year, Twelve patriarchs, Twelve tribes of Israel, Twelve prophets of the Old Testament, Twelve legions of angels, Twelve Apostles, Twelve signs in the Hebrew Mazzorot (What eventually became the Zodiac. See *Constellations*), and Twelve foundations of the New Jerusalem.

"And David spake to the chief of the Levites to appoint their brethren to be the singers with instruments of <u>music</u>, psalteries and harps and cymbals, sounding, by lifting up the voice with joy."- 1 Chronicles 15:16

"And the priests waited on their offices: the Levites also with instruments of <u>music</u> of the LORD, which David the king had made to praise the LORD, because his mercy *endureth* for ever, when David praised by their ministry; and the priests sounded trumpets before them, and all Israel stood." - 2 Chronicles 7:6

"I will praise Thee, O LORD, with my whole heart; I will shew forth all Thy marvelous works. I will be glad and rejoice in Thee: I will sing praise to Thy Name, O Thou Most High." - Psalm 9:1-2

"Sing unto the LORD; for He hath done excellent things: this is known in ALL the earth." - Isaiah 12:5

"And they sung as it were a new song before the throne, and before the four beasts, and the elders: and no man could learn that song but the hundred and forty and four thousand, which were redeemed from the earth." - Revelation 14:3

"He hath made the earth by his power, he hath established the world by his wisdom, and hath stretched out the heaven by his understanding."- Jeremiah 51:15

"For by Him were all things created, that are in heaven, and that are in earth, visible and invisible, whether they be thrones, or dominions, or principalities, or powers: all things were created by Him, and for Him. And He is before all things, and by Him all things consist." - Colossians 1:16-17

N

Name

Man – Me

The word <u>name</u> contains man (woman) because everyone has a name, and that <u>name</u> is known by God. God has many <u>names</u>. These <u>names</u> are representative of qualities of God, and they help us to know more about God. Calling people by their name is a way of showing that you know them. People like to hear their <u>name</u>. Calling someone by their <u>name</u> also gives them honor and esteem. God values us so much that He has his own <u>names</u> for each of us in heaven. God also likes for us to know His <u>names</u> because He desires for us to know Him intimately. It is not all about me as it is said today, because it should always be more about God and less about us.

"And the man called his wife's <u>name</u> Eve; because she was the mother of all living." - Genesis 3:20

"But Peter said, Silver and gold have I none; but what I have, that give I thee. In the <u>name</u> of Jesus Christ of Nazareth, walk." - Acts 3:6

"He that overcometh, I will make him a pillar in the temple of my God, and he shall go out thence no more: and I will write upon him the <u>name</u> of my God, and the <u>name</u> of the city of my God, the new Jerusalem, which cometh down out of heaven from my God, and mine own new <u>name</u>." - Revelation 3:12

Nations

Saint - Sin

The Bible teaches the priesthood of the believer, so that all true believers have access to God. All believers are classified as saints. There will be saints in heaven from every nation on earth. Everyone that is not saved will be "without excuse." There will be no defense that my nation did not hear about or believe the prophets, the Bible, Jesus and the gospel. Every nation, Continent, and Island from America to Zante has demonstrated sin and departing from God. Nations are made up of people and people sin. In the book of Revelation, none of the seven churches that were named and described spiritually exist today. They were in Turkey; which is now primarily Muslim. When a nations' sin becomes full, God brings judgment. Unlike individuals, nations cannot be dealt with in eternity. Many believe that there are many nations today that are on a course for judgment and wrath. What do you think about your own nation?

"And in the fourth generation they shall come hither again: for the iniquity of the Amorite is not yet full." - Genesis 15:16

"if my people, who are called by my name, shall humble themselves, and pray, and seek my face, and turn from their wicked ways; then will I hear from heaven, and will forgive their sin, and will heal their land." - 2 Chronicles 7:14

"ye also, as living stones, are built up a spiritual house, to be a holy priesthood, to offer up spiritual sacrifices, acceptable to God through Jesus Christ." - 1 Peter 2:5

"Paul and Timothy, servants of Christ Jesus, to all the saints in Christ Jesus that are at Philippi, with the bishops and deacons:" - Philippians 1:1

"And they sing a new song, saying, Worthy art thou to take the book, and to open the seals thereof: for thou was slain, and didst purchase unto God with thy blood *men* of every tribe, and tongue, and people, and <u>nation</u>," - Revelation 5:9

Nature

Tune – Turn (return) - Art

    <u>Nature</u> gives us a macro and micro glimpse into God's <u>nature</u>. I appreciate <u>nature</u>, the science and the art, but it is better to love the Creator that the created. Turn means to rotate or revolve around, and our planet earth certainly does both of those. Tune can mean to bring into harmony, and God has certainly fine tuned <u>nature</u> throughout the universe. Man fell out of tune with God through sin. Everyone has a need to turn to God, and return to peace and harmony with God. The whole creation is in a fallen condition because of sin. There is no paradise or Garden of Eden anywhere on earth. Man may build a castle or mansion, but the curse still affects <u>nature</u> and everything that is there.

"The heavens declare the glory of God; And the firmament showeth his handiwork." - Psalms 19:1

"I will give thanks unto thee; For I am fearfully and wonderfully made: Wonderful are thy works; And that my soul knoweth right well." - Psalms 139:14

"And the peace of God, which passeth all understanding, shall guard your hearts and your thoughts in Christ Jesus." - Philippians 4:7

"For we know that the whole creation groaneth and travaileth in pain together until now." - Romans 8:22

Nothing

No - Thing

The Bible states in Genesis 1:1 that "God created ('ex nilo') the heaven and the earth." That verse is a summary statement and details follow. One of those details reveals that God made the creation of <u>nothing</u>. God created the universe "ex-nilo", meaning that He used no thing, but spoke everything into existence. This was explained in detail in section one, chapter two of this book.

"By the word of Jehovah were the heavens made, And all the host of them by the breath of his mouth." - Psalm 33:6

Numbers

Sum

What is the biggest <u>number</u> that you know? A google is 10^{99}; which is a one followed by ninety-nine zeros. A google is a sum that is greater than the <u>number</u> of stars in the universe, or the number of miles across the universe. The only thing can I think of that could be as large as or larger than 10^{99} is Jehovah's IQ.

"When thou takest the sum of the children of Israel, according to those that are <u>numbered</u> of them, then shall they give every man a ransom for his soul unto Jehovah, when thou <u>numberest</u> them; that there be no plague among them, when thou <u>numberest</u> them. - Exodus 30:12

O

Obedience

Be – Do – Bend

Why do you think that God would want us to practice obedience to His precepts and laws? He even says in the Bible that there is fun in sin for a season, so does He just want to take away our fun? God gave laws and moral values because He knows that obedience to His ways are best for strong families; which is the foundation for a strong society. Obedience is best for communities, best for individuals - both in the present and in eternity. And very importantly, obedience is necessary to properly reflect His image and reputation. Man was made in God's image, but when sin entered through Adam the natural man no longer reflected God's image.

When you have a spiritual birth (born again) you make the choice to "walk in the Spirit" practicing attributes of Christ. This includes obedience, because He was obedient unto death. You have the ability to reflect God's image through your life. This is not automatic, even for those that are saved. By being obedient to God, we let Him, through the power of His Spirit; show us how we should be and what we should do. By practicing obedience, we learn to bend to God's will because He knows what is best for us. Obedience is edified by faith, and rewarded by a growing and greater faith. When we have faith in God, we trust that He has the absolute best for us; and we know how to listen for His voice.

Obedience to God has a direct effect on just about everything in our lives. How would it be if murder was accepted in society and people could just kill anyone they felt like? Would you want to live in that environment? Hitler had a legal form of murder called genocide. Unfortunately, in America and many other nations, currently there is a legalized form of murder called abortion. All sin is an offense to God, but especially the shedding of innocent blood. This brings judgment and the wrath of God.

All of the laws God gave and instructions for righteous are beneficial for everyone.

Obedience determines how much He can use us, and how much He blesses us here on Earth, and with eternal rewards. It can also affect current and future generations. Adam and Eve's disobedience to God in the Garden of Eden caused every person who lived after them to be cursed by sin. If we do not do what God tells us, we may miss out on a huge blessing He has in store for us. Or we may suffer even worse consequences. Reflecting our own image to the world instead of Christ's is pride, which God hates.

Because of our fallen, sinful nature we can never be completely obedient to God in our flesh. But we should still strive to do God's will, and be who He calls us to be (Like Christ/Godly). Even though we may mess up, we cannot mess up God's plan. God may have someone picked out for a specific, important purpose, but if they disobey, God may choose to use someone else. A perfect example is King Saul. He disobeyed God's command, which led to his death, and God chose David to be the great King of Israel and to be the ancestral line for the Messiah.

"Every one that is proud in heart is an abomination to Jehovah:" - Proverbs 16:5

"Better is a little, with righteousness, Than great revenues with injustice." - Proverbs 16-8

"But ye are not in the flesh but in the Spirit, if so be that the Spirit of God dwelleth in you. But if any man hath not the Spirit of Christ, he is none of his." - Romans 8:9

"and being found in fashion as a man, he humbled himself, becoming obedient *even* unto death, yea, the death of the cross." - Philippians 2:8

Oil

Lo (Ph: Low) - Il (Ph: Ill)

Have you ever heard the statement that oil and water do not mix? That is true because oil is not water soluble, so it does not dissolve in water. The spiritual and the natural do not mix either. Oil was used in the Bible for anointing kings, priests and prophets. Jesus is all three and He was anointed with spikenard oil, which was very costly. I have anointing oil from Jerusalem that I order online from Abba Oil. The oil contains frankincense and myrrh. These were two of the gifts that the wise men brought to Jesus. I like to put on a little of this oil because if God passes by I feel that the smell will be pleasing to Him.

In scripture oil can represent the Holy Spirit. I believe having the "oil of gladness" means to be indwelt by the Holy Spirit. The Bible account given by Jesus about the ten virgins has oil as an essential part of the story. Only five were wise because they had the oil they needed when the bridegroom came. You will feel ill if you are caught low on oil like the five foolish virgins, because one day Jesus, the bridegroom will return for His bride.

"and thou shalt make it a holy anointing oil, a perfume compounded after the art of the perfumer: it shall be a holy anointing oil. And thou shalt anoint therewith the tent of meeting, and the ark of the testimony, and the table and all the vessels thereof, and the candlestick and the vessels thereof, and the altar of incense, and the altar of burnt-offering with all the vessels thereof, and the laver and the base thereof. And thou shalt sanctify them, that they may be most holy: whatsoever toucheth them shall be holy. And thou shalt anoint Aaron and his sons, and sanctify them, that they may minister unto me in the priest's office. And thou shalt speak unto the children of Israel, saying, This shall be a holy anointing oil unto me throughout your generations." - and thou shalt make it a holy anointing oil, a perfume compounded after the art of the perfumer: it shall be a holy anointing oil." - Exodus 25:31

"Then Samuel took the horn of oil, and anointed him in the midst of his brethren: and the Spirit of Jehovah came mightily upon David from that day forward. So Samuel rose up, and went to Ramah." - 1 Samuel 16:13

"Thou hast loved righteousness, and hated wickedness: Therefore God, thy God, hath anointed thee With the oil of gladness above thy fellows." - Psalms 45:7

"Jesus answered, Verily, verily, I say unto thee, Except one be born of water and the Spirit, he cannot enter into the kingdom of God!" - John 3:5

"Now the natural man receiveth not the things of the Spirit of God: for they are foolishness unto him; and he cannot know them, because they are spiritually judged." - 1 Corinthians 2:14

"Then shall the kingdom of heaven be likened unto ten virgins, who took their lamps, and went forth to meet the bridegroom. And five of them were foolish, and five were wise. For the foolish, when they took their lamps, took no oil with them: but the wise took oil in their vessels with their lamps. Now while the bridegroom tarried, they all slumbered and slept. But at midnight there is a cry, Behold, the bridegroom! Come ye forth to meet him. Then all those virgins arose, and trimmed their lamps. And the foolish said unto the wise, Give us of your oil; for our lamps are going out. But the wise answered, saying, Peradventure there will not be enough for us and you: go ye rather to them that sell, and buy for yourselves. And while they went away to buy, the bridegroom came; and they that were ready went in with him to the marriage feast: and the door was shut. Afterward came also the other virgins, saying, Lord, Lord, open to us. But he answered and said, Verily I say unto you, I know you not. Watch therefore, for ye know not the day nor the hour." – Matthew 25:1-13

Ordinary

Ordain(ed)

God has a knack for using, unexceptional, <u>ordinary</u> people for extraordinary purposes. One of the greatest all time preachers in America was Dwight L. Moody. Mr. D. L. Moody was a shoe salesman with a third grade education. He spoke at Oxford University in England, and astonished the listeners that were present. One doesn't have to go to seminary, have a DD, or PhD to know God, or to be able to spread the news of the Gospel. All born again believers have faith, at least one spiritual gift, direct access to God through prayer, and the privilege of receiving understanding from the Holy Spirit. Believers can be instruments through which God communicates to others.

There is formal ordination where a person is established by a specific organization for ministry. D. L. Moody was told no when he first went through the ordination process. He was told that he did not have the necessary qualities for the ministry. G. Campbell Morgan, one of England's greatest preachers, was also originally denied ordination and told he was not capable. Today, probably most or all of the Apostles would not look like good candidates for formal ordination.

Sometimes God just has fun with the standards for success that man values. Billy Sunday was a great baseball player. One day he was walking past a revival service, stopped and went in. The rest is history because he became the greatest evangelist in America during his day. The famous Ryman Auditorium in Nashville, Tennessee which is the original home of the Grand Ole Opry, was built by a riverboat captain. He went to a tent revival with some of his men to cause a disruption. Instead, he had a conversion and declared that the preacher would not stay in a tent. He raised $150,000 and the Ryman was built to hold revival meetings. Seeking God and growing through His Word allows us to be ordained by God. This enables us to be witnesses to lost souls, and to participate in the building of the Kingdom of God.

"But God has chosen the foolish things of the world to confound the wise; and God has chosen the weak things of the world to confound the things which are mighty." - 1 Corinthians 1:27

"Yea, even when I am old and grayheaded, O God, forsake me not, Until I have declared thy strength unto *the next* generation, Thy might to every one that is to come." - Psalm 71:18

P

Parables

Able – Real – Pearls – Pare - Par

Wisdom does not come as a result of man's searching; it is a gift from God. Wisdom does not need to explain every question. But it leads to a reverent awe of God and believing in the "Word." Wisdom is gifts of pearls from God. Parables are earthly stories that contain parallels to heaven. In the Bible, Jesus usually spoke to the multitudes in parables. Why parables? These parables contained pearls; fictional illustrations that had real truths hidden in them. Just as pearls are hidden inside of the shell, the valuable truths Jesus taught are hidden within these ordinary parables.

These truths were not for everyone to understand. Jesus had to pare, or remove the mystery for His disciples to be able to understand the meaning of the parable. The Bible provides us with the meaning of the parables, which puts us on par with the disciples that Jesus personally taught. Parables contain pearls of wisdom and truth brought to us by Jesus. Though most of the parables in the Bible don't paint a picture of life in the 21st century, they still have major value and are full of truth that still applies today.

"All these things spake Jesus in parables unto the multitudes; and without a parable spake he nothing unto them:" - Matthew 13:34

"And the disciples came, and said to him, 'Why do you speak to them in <u>parables</u>?' He answered, saying to them, 'Because it is given unto you to know the mysteries of the kingdom of heaven, but to them it is not given. For whosoever has, to him shall be given, and he shall have more abundance: but whosoever has not, from him shall be taken away even that which he has. Therefore I speak to them in parables: because though seeing they see not, and hearing they hear not, neither do they understand'." - Matthew 13:10-13

"And unto man he said, Behold, the fear of the Lord, that is wisdom; And to depart from evil is understanding." - Job 28:28

"And those are they that were sown upon the good ground; such as hear the word, and accept it, and bear fruit, thirtyfold, and sixtyfold, and a hundredfold." - Mark 4:20

Parents

Nest - Pear (Ph. - Pair) – Rent – Part

<u>Parents</u> naturally play a vital role in the proper raising of children; and it works best if they are a man and wife pair. Both the father and mother must do their part to teach their children about God as they raise them. Exposing the children to the teachings of Scripture, and sharing their own experiences with God should be regularly done. Children are supposed to grow up and leave the nest, because the <u>parents</u> only have them temporarily. They belong to God, not the <u>parents</u> who only rent them. Just as it is customary with anything that you rent, you are accountable for how you take care of something that is not your own. Statistics show that what children become as adults is determined more by who the parents are than by what they do for the children. These children could ultimately have families of their own, and produce your grandchildren. They carry on your name; and the greatest impact that you will make is determined by who you are. Are you

141

a godly father, mother, and family?

"Train up a child in the way he should go: and when he is old, he will not depart from it." - Proverbs 22:6

"But Jesus called them unto him, saying, Suffer the little children to come unto me, and forbid them not: for to such belongeth the kingdom of God." - Luke 18:16

"Children, obey your parents in the Lord: for this is right. Honour thy father and mother; which is the first commandment with promise; That it may be well with thee, and thou mayest live long on the earth. And, ye fathers, provoke not your children to wrath: but bring them up in the nurture and admonition of the Lord." - Ephesians 6:1-4

"The aged women likewise, that they be in behaviour as becometh holiness, not false accusers, not given to much wine, teachers of good things; That they may teach the young women to be sober, to love their husbands, to love their children, To be discreet, chaste, keepers at home, good, obedient to their own husbands, that the word of God be not blasphemed." - Titus 2:3-5

Patience

Pace – Peace –Pain

In the book of Acts, The Apostle Paul compared the Christian life to a race, and Jesus is the prize. There are no placements in this race, and we don't run to compete with each other. We run to finish the race. In Hebrews 12, it says we should run the race with patience, keeping our eyes on Jesus. Though the definition of patience has been obscured over the years to simply mean "waiting" without complaining, that's only part of what the word means. If you look in a dictionary, you will see that patience is defined as the ability to bear pain or trials without complaint, and to have peace and calmness in times of difficulty or inconvenience. Patience is a reflection of how well we trust the Lord. It is shown in our self control, our willingness to endure suffering and pain. It is also shown by having faith that God will deliver us, and our ability to wait for God's timing as opposed to our own.

Today's culture is all about urgency. Everything happens so fast, and we are so busy. Rushing here and there and having too much on our plate has not only become normal, but has almost become a mark of status. We keep ourselves connected to our work wherever we go with cell phones and laptops, while we should be keeping ourselves connected to God at all times. We even have fast food for people who need a quick bite to eat while they're on lunch break, just so they can get back to their busy day at the office.

Worship services have also become affected by this culture. People want to go to church and get it done and over with. We hurry through the service so we can beat the Methodists to the buffet, and get home to catch the kickoff of the NFL game. The Christian life should not be about rushing through the race to the finish line. If we do that, we will wear ourselves out, just as in a real race. Runners in a long race have to pace themselves and only sprint near the end. We should pace ourselves because the Christian run is life long. It is not a sprint; it is a marathon. We must finish well. In God's time the finish line will come, and we will eventually get there and cross it.

"Do you not know that they who run in a race all run, but one receives the prize? So run, that you may obtain the prize. And every man that strives for the prize shows self control in all things. Now they do it to obtain a corruptible crown; but we an incorruptible. So therefore I run, not as uncertainly; so I fight, not as one just beating the air: But I keep under my body, and bring it into subjection: lest that by any means, when I have preached to others, I myself should be a castaway." - 1 Corinthians 9:24-27

"Rest in the Lord, and wait patiently for him."- Psalm 37:7a

"For our citizenship is in heaven; whence also we wait for a Saviour, the Lord Jesus Christ:" - Philippians 3:20

"In your patience ye shall win your souls." - Luke 21:19

Perseverance

Race – Pace – Peace – Serve - Reverence - Verse

In the race of the Christian life that Paul talks about in Philippians, we not only need patience to reach the finish line, but perseverance, as well. These two virtues go hand in hand and work together to get us to the prize. Many times, Christians running the race may stumble due to sin, suffering, or complacency. They become discouraged and stop running, thinking that the finish line is too far away. Or they think that they can run the race without God's guidance; or that they simply don't deserve the prize because of failures. However, these things shouldn't keep us from finishing the race. If we keep our eye on the prize all the way to the end, we may stumble, but we will be able to get back up and keep running. Again, we should pace ourselves so that we don't get worn. But when we do get tired, we should rest in God and have peace in Him. When we suffer from the aches and pain that running such a long, hard race often causes us to have, we should trust God to heal us so that we may continue to run.

Our sins don't disqualify us from the race. We are born sinners, yet we are still able to enter the race at any time. God doesn't do background checks to see if we have any felonies, or have committed crimes in the past and not allow us to enter the race. Our past has been forgiven by the blood of Jesus. And we can run with joy, knowing that, if born again, we can serve him, no matter what sins we have committed or will commit in the future. This gives us a liberty in Christ: But this liberty is not a license to freely sin.

Thinking that you can win the race without God's help is a

144

sure fire way to stumble. But even then, you won't be disqualified. He will find a way to fix your eyes on the prize again and stay fixed on it to the end. In many children's sports, they tell the kids to "Believe in yourself!" This philosophy may work for kids playing tee-ball, but in the Christian race, we should believe in God and what He can do with us. We know that He is perfect and mighty, and we should show reverence for his sovereignty, power and love. To rely on yourself is a mistake because we are imperfect, weak, and sinful. Trust God to guide you and give you strength to complete His race to the end. Keep your eyes on the prize of Jesus, the Author and Finisher of your faith!

"I have fought the good fight, I have finished the course, I have kept the faith:" - 2 Timothy 4:7

"No servant can serve two masters: for either he will hate the one, and love the other; or else he will hold to one, and despise the other. Ye cannot serve God and mammon." - Luke 16:13

"with all prayer and supplication praying at all seasons in the Spirit, and watching thereunto in all perseverance and supplication for all the saints," - Ephesians 6:18

"And the peace of God, which passeth all understanding, shall guard your hearts and your thoughts in Christ Jesus." - Philippians 4:7

Philosophy

Phil (Ph: Full) – Los (Ph: loss)

Philosophy is defined as the love and pursuit of wisdom by intellectual means, and a view of reality based on logical reasoning and speculation. Man's wisdom is foolishness to God, and any philosophy without God is vain and lacking real wisdom. Many eastern religions are based on philosophical thought (Buddhism, Taoism, etc.), which are full of loss. This is because they do not know the saving grace of Jesus Christ; who is the one and only way to God the Father. "Without the shedding of blood there is no remission of sin."

The speculative philosophy of the Greeks opened up the minds of many to ideas on nature, creation, government, morality and ethics. And while they attempted to provide solutions and answers to all of these ideals; they were still full of loss because they are from man and not from God.

When this writer took a philosophy class in college, the Professor wrote on a paper, "you are an original thinker." Actually, I was a Christian thinker with some advantages over secular thinkers. Without Christ, there is loss, but with Him we are full and complete. Philosophy usually represents the pursuit of knowledge apart from God, which is what caused man to sin in the Garden of Eden in the beginning. And millions are still eating that fruit from the "Tree of Knowledge" to this day.

"Beware lest any man spoil you through philosophy and vain deceit, after the tradition of men, after the rudiments of the world, and not after Christ."- Colossians 2:8

Praise
Praise

Raise – Praer (Phonetically: Prayer)

When you give persons honest praise you raise them up. Sometimes if you have to deal with a negative issue it is wise to make a "praise sandwich." You start with praise and end with praise. In praise of someone you are expressing value for something about them. Authentic Christians are able to genuinely praise the Creator God because they know God through the Scripture and through a personal relationship. They can make honest statements of praise. The praise of God usually is in the beginning of prayer and is a prerequisite to real worship of the Almighty, Living and Holy God. The praise of God is a benefit to us, and it raises us and adds effectiveness to our prayer time.

"Enter into his gates with thanksgiving, And into his courts with praise: Give thanks unto him, and bless his name." - Psalms 100:4

Prayers (Use letter e twice)

Repay(s) – Ear – Prepare

Prayer is a privilege that gives believers direct access to the throne and the ear of God. The New Testament teaches the priesthood of the believer. So all authentic Christians have direct access, and do not need to go through anyone or anything else to access God. Prayer is an excellent way to prepare for a war or battle. George Washington believed in prayer and established the Chaplin Service for the US Military. Christians are in spiritual warfare, so prayer should be battle preparation.

Jesus is the High Priest, and He is our intercessor with God the Father. Prayer may be individual or corporate, like a church prayer group or prayer service. I have seen many answered prayers from both methods of prayer.

Christians should pray daily because prayer is a way to repay God for His grace toward us. Prayer should not just be for a life emergency, but rather a way of life. God also repays us for prayer because there is a reward associated with prayer. The prayer of a hypocrite does not get the reward. A hypocrite would be praying for recognition, not for contact with God. This would be a pretense. I have experienced amazing answers and accomplishments through prayer. Christians should love the privilege of prayer, and should pray in faith with the expectation of an answer.

"Jehovah is far from the wicked; But he heareth the prayer of the righteous." - Proverbs 15:29

"And when ye pray, ye shall not be as the hypocrites: for they love to stand and pray in the synagogues and in the corners of the

147

streets, that they may be seen of men. Verily I say unto you, They have received their reward." - Matthew 6:5

"For this cause we also, since the day we heard *it*, do not cease to pray and make request for you, that ye may be filled with the knowledge of his will in all spiritual wisdom and understanding," - Colossians 1:9

"Let us therefore draw near with boldness unto the throne of grace, that we may receive mercy, and may find grace to help *us* in time of need." - Hebrews 4:16

Provision

Vision - Son - Poor

Provision is an arrangement to meet needs. God is the Creator and the sustainer of the universe. All provision, both physical and spiritual, comes from God. There are common provisions and grace, like rain and sunlight that benefits everyone. You should have the vision to see that it is God that provides. The gift of salvation is a provision made by God, and Christ was "the Lamb that was slain before the foundation of the world."

Yes, God had made a provision to free mankind from the penalty of sin before He created Adam and Eve. Most people have a natural interest in wanting to live and have concern regarding death. Jesus defeated death, and this victory is offered as a free gift to all who will believe in the Son of God by faith. Those who are "poor on spirit" and have no hope, except in the provision of God, will be blessed citizens of the Kingdom.

"And he said, Hear now my words: if there be a prophet among you, I Jehovah will make myself known unto him in a vision, I will speak with him in a dream." - Numbers 12:6

"Cast thy burden upon Jehovah, and he will sustain thee: He will never suffer the righteous to be moved." - Psalms 55:22

148

"Then thou spakest in vision to thy saints, And saidst, I have laid help upon one that is mighty; I have exalted one chosen out of the people." - Psalms 89:19

"Where there is no vision, the people cast off restraint; But he that keepeth the law, happy is he." - Proverbs 29:18

"Blessed are the poor in spirit: for theirs is the kingdom of heaven." - Matthew 5:3

"And as they were coming down from the mountain, Jesus commanded them, saying, Tell the vision to no man, until the Son of man be risen from the dead." - Matthew 17:9

"But put ye on the Lord Jesus Christ, and make not <u>provision</u> for the flesh, to *fulfil* the lusts *thereof.*" - Romans 13:14

"and might deliver all them who through fear of death were all their lifetime subject to bondage." - Hebrews 2:15

"Death is swallowed up in victory. O death, where is thy victory? O death, where is thy sting?" - 1 Corinthians 15:54-55

Preachers

Hear – Shape - Reach

<u>Preachers</u> are people who are supposed to be called and ordained by God to reach lost souls and lead them to God the Father through the Lord Jesus Christ. They have spiritual gifts to super naturally equip them to hear from God and deliver inspired messages. This is not theory; I have personally witnessed this happen on multiple occasions. Ministers carefully shape messages from God with the aid of the Holy Spirit and Scripture. This allows their message to be understood and applied to the heart of those who hear it.

"For seeing that in the wisdom of God the world through its wisdom knew not God, it was God's good pleasure through the foolishness of the <u>preaching</u> to save them that believe." - 1 Corinthians 1:21

"Jesus saith unto him, I am the way, and the truth, and the life: no one cometh unto the Father, but by me." - John 14:6

"and how shall they <u>preach,</u> except they be sent? even as it is written, How beautiful are the feet of them that bring glad tidings of good things!" - Romans 10:15

Preeminence

Prime - Mine - Ripen

God is preeminent, meaning He is superior over everything. Because of this, He should be the prime focus of our worship, adoration, servitude, love, and sacrifice. All of these actions are forms of giving of ourselves, because anything we have received comes from God in the first place. God said to Job, "Who has first given to Me that I should repay him? Everything under Heaven is mine." God doesn't need these things from us since, as stated, everything already belongs to Him. But He delights in us giving back to Him through worship, love and service. Not only that, worshiping and serving God is for our own good. God designed it to be this way.

Jesus commands us to love God with everything that we are. We come to an understanding of true love by giving back to God. And since God is fully love, we come to understand and know Him better, as well. In return, we are blessed. When we receive the Holy Spirit as new believers, He brings us the Fruit of Love. Love brings forth all the other Fruits of the Spirit, because they are a result of love in action. So when we learn to love God fully and give him priority and worship, we mature like fruit will that will ripen on a tree. As these fruits from our life ripen more and more, the more we will have to give back to God. It becomes a cycle that draws us closer to God. Jesus also commands us to love our neighbors as we love ourselves. We learn to do this by loving God. As the Fruits of the Spirit ripen, it becomes easier and easier to follow this command.

"And you shall love the Lord thy God with all your heart, and with all your soul, and with all your mind, and with all your strength: this is the first commandment. And the second is this. You shall love your neighbour as yourself. There is none other commandment greater than these." - Mark 12:30-31

"But the fruit of the Spirit is love, joy, peace, longsuffering, kindness, goodness, faithfulness," - Galatians 5:22

"And he is the head of the body, the church: who is the beginning, the firstborn from the dead; that in all things he might have the preeminence." - Colossians 1:18

Pulpit

Pul (*Pull*) – Pit

"Hey, Preacher! Get up there and pull them out of the pit, Brother!"

"He brought me up also out of a horrible pit, out of the miry clay; And he set my feet upon a rock, and established my goings." - Psalm 40:2

"preach the word; be urgent in season, out of season; reprove, rebuke, exhort, with all longsuffering and teaching." - Timothy 4:2

Q

Qualified

Life – I – Lied - Die

You and I are not qualified to obtain righteousness on our own merit. No matter what we do, we are not deserving of God's love. Everything we receive from God is by grace because we are not deserving of it. If you are <u>qualified</u> you are worthy, and in heaven there will be a great voice saying, "Worthy is the Lamb." The Lamb laid down His life for us. Is your voice saying, "Worthy is the Lamb?" If it is not you need to ask why not.

"And Jehovah God formed man of the dust of the ground, and breathed into his nostrils the breath of life; and man became a living soul." - Genesis 2:7

"And he said unto him, I also am a prophet as thou art; and an angel spake unto me by the word of Jehovah, saying, Bring him back with thee into thy house, that he may eat bread and drink water. *But* he lied unto him." - 1 Kings 13:18

"Say unto them, As I live, saith the Lord Jehovah, I have no pleasure in the death of the wicked; but that the wicked turn from his way and live: turn ye, turn ye from your evil ways; for why will ye die, O house of Israel?

"saying with a great voice, Worthy is the Lamb that hath been slain to receive the power, and riches, and wisdom, and might and honor, and glory, and blessing." - Revelation 5:12

"For if, while we were enemies, we were reconciled to God through the death of his Son, much more, being reconciled, shall we be saved by his life;" - Romans 5:10

R

Rapture

Reap – Up

The Bible says that in the end times, those who were and are in Christ will be caught up to meet with Him in the air. First, He will take up those who are "dead in Christ," meaning those who are saved, but have died physically. Next, He will take up those who are in Him and are still alive. We as Christians are like a crop that has grown from seeds of faith. And the end times will find us ripe and ready for harvest. Jesus will reap the harvest of the earth during the rapture.

The exact day or hour of the rapture is not known. However, believers are supposed to recognize signs, just as we recognize seasons, as to when the time is near. The hope of His glorious return at any time, should remind believers to not get too attached to the things of this world. The possessions of this earthly life are temporary and insignificant compared to the eternity to come. One clue that the end should be approaching, is that in 1948 Israel was reestablished as a nation. The dispersion of the Jewish people and their return was prophesied about 2,500 years ago in Scripture. This important prophecy was fulfilled in exact detail and needed to take place before the end would come.

Israel is of special importance to God's end time plans for this planet. God weighs nations in the balances based on their treatment of this small unique nation. No nation or individual has any right to divide land that was given by God to this nation for an everlasting inheritance. If you are not a friend of Israel, you are probably not in a very good spiritual position for the Lord's return.

"For this we say unto you by the word of the Lord, that we which are alive in Christ and remain unto the coming of the Lord shall not prevent them which are asleep. For the Lord himself shall descend from heaven with a shout, with the voice of the archangel, and with the trumpet of God: and the dead in Christ shall rise first: Then we which are alive and remain shall be caught up together with them in the clouds, to meet the Lord in the air: and so shall we ever be with the Lord."-1 Thessalonians 4:15-17

"And I looked, and behold a white cloud, and upon the cloud one sat like unto the Son of man, having on His head a golden crown, and in His hand a sharp sickle. And another angel came out of the temple, crying with a loud voice to Him that sat on the cloud, 'Thrust in thy sickle, and reap: for the time is come for You to reap; for the harvest of the earth is ripe.' And He that sat on the cloud thrust in His sickle on the earth; and the earth was reaped." - Revelation 14:14-16

Rebellion

El (God) - Lion

Rebellion is resistance or defiance of authority. And since God is the supreme authority, defying God is the supreme rebellion. When Jesus Christ returns for His second advent, He will be the Lion of Judah. Rebellion will not fare very well, because He will rule with a rod of iron. There might still be sin, but there will not be any organized system of sin.

Satan led a rebellion in heaven, and one third of the angels followed him. The devil is in a spiritual battle with God, and he has brought tremendous death, destruction, and lies to this planet. The Devil led a rebellion in heaven that even one third of the angels joined. He is involved in rebellion on planet earth, and is looking for followers to devour. He has two very different approaches because Satan is both an "angel of light" and a "roaring lion."

His work and influence is very different depending of which of these two traits are in use. Hatred and persecution of Christians would clearly be the roaring lion. The angel of light would be more subtle, and could manifest in numerous ways. I along with many serious students of the Bible, share the opinion

154

that modern translations of the Bible fit this category. Satan could not eliminate the Bible even though he tried that throughout history. I have observed that a flood of copyrighted translations that omit important verses and change the meaning of dozens of verses, are well accepted.

Finally, this rebellious angel of enormous influence and power on planet earth, will eventually be removed by the Lion of Judah and the King of Kings. Satan will be cast into the lake of fire, and will no longer be the prince of this world. Please, Lord Jesus come quickly!

"An evil *man* seeketh only rebellion: therefore a cruel messenger shall be sent against him." - Proverbs 17:11

"Therefore thus saith the LORD; Behold, I will cast thee from off the face of the earth: this year thou shalt die, because thou hast taught rebellion against the LORD." - Jeremiah 28:16

"Hear, O heavens, and give ear, O earth: for the LORD hath spoken, I have nourished and brought up children, and they have rebelled against me." - Isaiah 1:2

"And no marvel; for Satan himself is transformed into an angel of light." – 2 Corinthians 11:14

"Be sober, be vigilant; because your adversary the devil, as a roaring lion, walketh about, seeking whom he may devour:" – 1 Peter 5:8

Reconcile

One - Circle

To reconcile is to make compatible or bring into harmony. Who better to reconcile us to God the Father, than the Son of God who brought the universe into existence! In Christ, whether Gentile or Jew, we are all made "one new man." By believing, we become a part of the family of faith. When we are <u>reconciled</u> unto God we are one faith, and an eternal circle of love for God in the presence of God.

"and through him to <u>reconcile</u> all things unto himself, having made peace through the blood of his cross; through him, *I say*, whether things upon the earth, or things in the heavens." - Colossians 1:20

Redeem

Reed (Ph. - Read) – Me

The Bible is a priceless account of God's <u>redeem</u>ing love. He promised redemption to Adam and Eve. He <u>redeem</u>ed the people of Israel from slavery in Egypt. And eventually fulfilled, through Jesus the Messiah, the Abrahamic Covenant to bless all nations. Scripture is God's inspired written Word. And it is the truth that reveals the true God. The God of Abraham, Isaac and Jacob is the true and living God.

Jesus is truth and in the Gospel of John, He is identified as the Word. Faith, the key to salvation, comes from hearing the Word of God. Every Christian, from the newly born-again, to the most seasoned ministers, needs the Holy Bible for correction, instruction, and guidance. Redemption is God's greatest gift, and it is received through a faith that comes from hearing the Word of God. The Bible is God's written word, and it is calling, "I am God's Word - read me, hear me in your heart, and love me!"

"So then faith *cometh* by hearing, and hearing by the word of God." - Romans 10:17

"for by grace have ye been saved through faith; and that not of yourselves, *it is* the gift of God;" - Ephesians 2:8

Reliant

Learn – Earn – El (God)

The more you learn about God the more you will rely on God. People can disappoint you, but God is completely reliable; so you can completely trust in God. The Bible teaches that God has some remarkable qualities that contribute to our being <u>reliant</u> on Him. God is unchangeable, all knowing, all powerful, merciful, gracious, and loving. Once you find God, He will earn your confidence and you will learn to love Him.

"Were not the Ethiopians and the Lubims a huge host, with very many chariots and horsemen? yet, because thou didst rely on the LORD, he delivered them into thine hand." - 2 Chronicles 16:8

"The God of my rock; in him will I trust: *he is* my shield, and the horn of my salvation, my high tower, and my refuge, my saviour; thou savest me from violence." - 2 Samuel 22:3

"The LORD *is* good, a strong hold in the day of trouble; and he knoweth them that trust in him." - Nahum 1:7

Religion

Lion – Legion – Lie - Gone

Uniting publicly with a Christian church is a profession of your faith or <u>religion</u>. Sometimes an individual will unite with a church for a reason other than their actually being an authentic believer. The church should only be for authentic Christians that profess faith in Jesus Christ, so a non-Christian should have to lie to gain membership. However, legions of churches are liberal and have gone so far from the faith that they will even allow a professing atheist to join. This policy is not biblically correct, and should not be found in Christian churches.

There is also a legion of false religions that are always works based, and will not lead you to saving faith. The first murder when Cain killed Able was over religion. Religion can be abused and misused. It can become more about business and money than about God. Do not let the failure of men through religion confuse you about God. Today, with many things that are done in the name of some religion or "deity", I understand why there are atheists that think all religion should be banned.

Jesus Christ, the Lion of Judah, is the head of the Christian church. True believers are the actual church: these are the body of Christ on earth. The church is the divine established institution for Christianity. The church has and does suffer persecution, has many divisions or denominations, and is certainly not perfect. In the book of Revelation, we find that churches had problems going back to the first century. Still, it is important for believers to assemble with and fellowship with other believers, and to support local churches. Some ritual and formal structure is necessary; however, I prefer a church that is more relational with God and less "religious." The Bible states that the church will prevail, and it has for twenty centuries because it is a supernatural institution.

Recently, I asked God what was His biggest fault with the church today? I got an immediate answer; which was a lack of passion. This seems to be the same as "lukewarm" in the church at Laodicea, the end of the age church as described in the book of Revelation. This means that we need passion driven churches and individuals with passion in the churches! What is your spiritual passion and what is the passion of your church? If you do not have an answer you might have a problem.

"How is it that ye do not understand that I spake *it* not to you concerning bread, that ye should beware of the leaven of the Pharisees and of the Sadducees?" - Matthew 16: 11

"And I say also unto thee, That thou art Peter, and upon this rock I will build my church; and the gates of hell shall not prevail against it." - Matthew 16:18

158

"I know thy works, that thou art neither cold nor hot: I would thou wert cold or hot. So then because thou art lukewarm, and neither cold nor hot, I will spue thee out of my mouth." - Revelation 3:15-16

Remain

Name – Near – Man – I am

During His first advent on earth Jesus did not have any title, property, wealth, or military victories. He was not a king or a conqueror. What He was is what He is, and that is the Christ, the Messiah, the only begotten Son of God. He is the King of Kings and Lord of Lords, and His name is above every name. No person that has ever lived has had more influence on events, and on the history of this planet than Jesus Christ.

How did a man of such low estate have such influence and have millions upon million believe in Him? It is only because He is exactly who He said that He is. Jesus is I am that I am. Jesus was God that became a man, so that He could be the atonement for the sins of the world. He is, and will always remain the second person of the eternal Godhead.

"Take my yoke upon you, and learn of me; for I am meek and lowly in heart: and ye shall find rest unto your souls. For my yoke *is* easy, and my burden is light." - Matthew 11:29-30

"Wherefore God also hath highly exalted him, and given him a name which is above every name:" - Philippians 2:9

"Let us draw near with a true heart in full assurance of faith, having our hearts sprinkled from an evil conscience, and our bodies washed with pure water." - Hebrews 10:22

"Who is a liar but he that denieth that Jesus is the Christ? He is antichrist, that denieth the Father and the Son. Who is a liar but he that denieth that Jesus is the Christ? He is antichrist, that denieth the Father and the Son. Whosoever denieth the Son, the same hath not the Father: *(but) he that acknowledgeth the Son hath the Father also*. Let that therefore abide in you, which ye have heard from the beginning. If that which ye have heard from the beginning shall remain in you, ye also shall continue in the Son, and in the Father." - 1 John 2:22-24

Resurrection

Risen – Sure – Erect

As Jesus was risen after three days and three nights in the tomb, so are authentic Christians sure to physically stand erect before God. The risen Saviour is a claim that is unique to Christianity. Because of the tremendous evidence for the resurrection of Jesus, believers have a blessed assurance and hope that they also will be raised from the grave.

"For unto you is born this day in the city of David a Saviour, which is Christ the Lord." - Luke 2:11

"Jesus said unto her, I am the resurrection, and the life: he that believeth in me, though he were dead, yet shall he live:" - John 11:25

"In a moment, in the twinkling of an eye, at the last trump: for the trumpet shall sound, and the dead shall be raised incorruptible, and we shall be changed." - 1 Corinthians 15:52

Revelations

Alert – Listen – See – Israel - Seal

The last chapter in the Book of Daniel, in the Old Testament, prophesies that near the end of time there will be a tremendous increase in knowledge and in transportation. In the

160

last fifty years knowledge has increased by more than it had in the previous 5,000 years. Transportation went from horse & buggy to automobiles, airplanes, jet airplanes and space in just a few generations. This alone is a major announcement relating to the twentieth and twenty-first Century. This, and a number of other biblical prophecies, have been fulfilled just since I was born. This is an exciting spiritual time.

Conditions that are described as being present as the end nears, are observable now. These include, but are not limited to, the increase of earthquakes and wars. One in five nations presently is involved at some level in war. There is war that is unseen, but it is above the earthly wars. There is spiritual warfare between light and darkness, between God and Satan. This battle will increase as the end nears, and it will have tremendous effects on planet earth. Israel is prominent in end time events, and is a key to understanding the "signs of the times." As a nation, Israel, is still secular and not accepting of Jesus, their Messiah. But that will change. And God's purposes for Israel will be fulfilled.

Revelation, the last Book of the Bible, is an amazing picture of end times events, and of the tribulation that will affect the entire planet. It is a book that reveals a victorious Jesus Christ. I would summarize Revelation in two words: "Jesus wins." There is a lot of encouragement and hope for believers; but a grim picture for spiritual powers, nations, false religion, and individuals on the wrong side of the battle. There is no neutrality; everyone is on one side or the other.

This amazing book written by the Apostle John provides an alert, so believers will have understanding for preparation and appropriate response. John is witness to seven seals opened by the "Lamb of God." The Apostle John is able to see the future. It would be wise to listen to the prophets, especially the prophecy of John as the end approaches. Are you ready for the Lord's return? If your answer is no, the Lord would love an opportunity to help you to become ready. "Ask and ye shall receive."

"All ye inhabitants of the world, and dwellers on the earth, see ye, when he lifteth up an ensign on the mountains; and when he bloweth a trumpet, hear ye" - Isaiah 18:3

"And they that be wise shall shine as the brightness of the firmament; and they that turn many to righteousness as the stars for ever and ever. But thou, O Daniel, shut up the words, and seal the book, *even* to the time of the end: many shall run to and fro, and knowledge shall be increased." - Daniel 12:3-4

"The Revelation of Jesus Christ, which God gave unto him, to shew unto his servants things which must shortly come to pass; and he sent and signified *it* by his angel unto his servant John:" - Revelation 1:1

Reward

Ward - War - Draw

God's word does promise a reward to believers for laboring together with God to build on the foundation that was laid: which is Jesus Christ. Reward is one of four motivations for Christian service (the other three are gratitude, compulsion and fear). God wants to draw us near and have us follow Him. The advantage for doing this is a richer spiritual life now, and a reward in heaven. Believers are supposed to be more concerned about the kingdom of God than building treasure on earth. You cannot take your treasure here with you when you die, but you can "pay it forward." That way you can build up a reward in heaven. Those that do not think that heaven would interest them have no idea of the treasures and rewards that will be received by faithful followers of Jesus.

Christians are children of God. That makes us like children under a guardian or court appointed ward, because we are under God's protection and care. No one of us deserves God's love, and no one can earn God's love. His priceless unconditional love is given by grace. For our sins to be completely forgiven, and for us to be allowed to spend eternity in heaven in God's presence; is far more than any of us merit. So, even though I like the privilege of building up a treasure on the other side, I know that this too is by God's grace.

I know how excited I was to be saved. Heavenly rewards

162

were the farthest thing from my mind. However, as the years go by and I am aware of spiritual contributions, I think more about <u>reward</u>s. It will be interesting in heaven to see how God's accounting system works when it comes to <u>reward</u>s. I feel that there are many ways to earn eternal rewards, and I know that prayer is one of them. I believe a prayer partnership with God is very powerful. The more you know God the more you appreciate God. And I want to know God. Little knowledge of God usually produces little interest in God.

I believe that <u>reward</u>s could include positions, titles, mansions, travel, and personal transportation vehicles to use on streets of gold. However, I believe that the greatest <u>reward</u> would be to be close to God, like the twenty-four elders sitting around the throne of God. I see that as the ultimate <u>reward</u>. The <u>reward</u> of heaven is great beyond our understanding. Unfortunately many trade eternity for this brief time in a sinful world. It is so sad that many sell the opportunity for an eternal inheritance cheap: really cheap. It is far better to be poor on earth and rich in heaven, than vice-versa.

Spiritual warfare is a reality and there is no neutrality with God. Being a soldier and fighting in this war on God's side will bring a <u>reward</u>. The other option will bring a <u>reward</u> that you definitely would not want. Instructing individuals in becoming human bombs, or being a suicide bomb participant is the wrong side of the war. Fighting against Christianity in America, or any other nation is the wrong side of the war. Persecuting Christians is the wrong side of the war. Trying to divide or eliminate Israel is the wrong side of the war. If you are on the wrong side you need to repent – change your mind.

"The LORD recompense thy work, and a full <u>reward</u> be given thee of the LORD God of Israel, under whose wings thou art come to trust." - Ruth 2:12

"Behold, the Lord GOD will come with strong *hand*, and his arm shall rule for him: behold, his <u>reward</u> *is* with him, and his work before him." - Isaiah 40:10

"He that receiveth a prophet in the name of a prophet shall receive a prophet's <u>reward</u>; and he that receiveth a righteous man in the name of a righteous man shall receive a righteous man's <u>reward</u>." - Matthew 10:41

"Rejoice ye in that day, and leap for joy: for, behold, your <u>reward</u> *is* great in heaven:" - Luke 6:23

"For where your treasure is, there will your heart be also." - Luke 12:34

"And round about the throne *were* four and twenty seats: and upon the seats I saw four and twenty elders sitting, clothed in white raiment; and they had on their heads crowns of gold." - Revelation 4:4

Righteousness

Right - In - His - Sight

 <u>Righteousness</u> involves restoring or setting right. So how is this done between mankind and God? No person on earth is righteous before God in their natural condition. All are sinners and unable to meet God's standard for <u>righteousness</u>. Many think, without a Scriptural basis, that if they do enough good then God will accept them. Good works is not the method to obtain <u>righteousness</u> before God. Without <u>righteousness</u> no one can be in God's glorified presence. So, if not by works, how does anyone become righteous? Justification or <u>righteousness</u> has to be imputed to you by God, and it is not done by works or by divine clemency.
 There is one way to God, and anyone trying to come by any other method is rejecting God's salvation plan. You are saved by believing in God's perfect Passover Lamb, Jesus the Christ. Salvation or <u>righteousness</u> is a gift that you receive through faith. To enter heaven you will have to be right in His sight.

"And he believed in the LORD; and he counted it to him for righteousness." - Genesis 15:6

"There is a way that seemeth right unto a man, but the end thereof *are* the ways of death." - Proverbs 16:25

"Jesus saith unto him, I am the way, the truth, and the life: no man cometh unto the Father, but by me." - John 14:6

"Even as David also describeth the blessedness of the man, unto whom God imputeth righteousness without works," - Romans 4:6

"What shall we say then? That the Gentiles, which followed not after righteousness, have attained to righteousness, even the righteousness which is of faith." - Romans 9:30

"For by grace are ye saved through faith; and that not of yourselves: *it is* the gift of God:" - Ephesians 2:8

S

Saints

Ain't - Stain – Sin

The New Testament Scriptures reveal that all believers in this present age are saints. To be a saint means to be set apart to God. Sometimes people who are believers do not behave like they are a pure and godly saint. This does not change their position of sainthood if they are true believers. A saint ain't got any stain from sin because they are clean by the covenant sacrifice of Jesus.

"He will keep the feet of his saints, and the wicked shall be silent in darkness; for by strength shall no man prevail." - 1 Samuel 2:9

"Gather my saints together unto me; those that have made a covenant with me by sacrifice." - Psalms 50:5

"Unto the church of God which is at Corinth, to them that are sanctified in Christ Jesus, called *to be* saints, with all that in every place call upon the name of Jesus Christ our Lord, both theirs and ours:" - 1 Corinthians 1:2

"Paul and Timotheus, the servants of Jesus Christ, to all the saints in Christ Jesus which are at Philippi, with the bishops and deacons:" - Philippians 1:1

"And he gave some, apostles; and some, prophets; and some, evangelists; and some, pastors and teachers; For the perfecting of the saints, for the work of the ministry, for the edifying of the body of Christ:" - Ephesians 4:11-12

"When he shall come to be glorified in his saints, and to be admired in all them that believe (because our testimony among you was believed) in that day." - 2 Thessalonians 1:10

"And Enoch also, the seventh from Adam, prophesied of these, saying, Behold, the Lord cometh with ten thousands of his saints," - Jude 1:14

Salvation

Lost – Sin – Son - Nails - Stain — Slain

Our graceful and merciful God loved us so much that He sent His only son for our salvation. We who were stained with sin drove nails into the hands and feet of the one who was blameless. He that was slain is the blameless Passover Lamb, and the covenant sacrifice. That is why there is a new covenant and a New Testament. We are in a lost condition without that sacrifice applied to us. He forgives us for the sin against Him by everyone who accepts this sacrifice. By His blood the stain of sin is covered

166

and removed. The hymn states, "His perfect salvation, His wonderful love. I'll shout it with millions on high."

Salvation sets us free from bondage to sin. And we are able to enter into the presence of God and to personally know Him. The more you know God, the more you want to know God. Those who know God little have little interest in knowing God. This is a benefit and the purpose of salvation, not only that we will be able to live eternally after death, but that we will be able to live eternally with God. After salvation the opportunity is there to know more and more about God. Because of the magnitude and complexity of God, the saved will need eternity to get to know Him fully. God wants us to know Him.

"The LORD liveth; and blessed *be* my rock; and exalted be the God of the rock of my salvation." - 2 Samuel 22:47

"Jesus answered them, Verily, verily, I say unto you, Whosoever committeth sin is the servant of sin. And the servant abideth not in the house for ever: *but* the Son abideth ever. If the Son therefore shall make you free, ye shall be free indeed." - John 34-36

"But God commendeth his love toward us, in that, while we were yet sinners, Christ died for us." - Romans 5:8

"For the grace of God that bringeth salvation hath appeared to all men" - Titus 2:11

"How shall we escape, if we neglect so great salvation; which at the first began to be spoken by the Lord, and was confirmed unto us by them that heard *him*;" - Hebrews 2:3

Sanctified

Saint - Set– Aside – Distance

The blood of Jesus washes away all of our sins, making us

clean. The word <u>sanctified</u> as seen in the Old Testament comes from the Hebrew word Qadash, meaning to make clean. By Jesus' sacrifice for us, we have been made Holy in God's sight and set aside to be used by Him for His purposes. Though no one but Jesus was ever perfected, or will ever be perfect in the flesh and on this side of death, but we should strive for that Christ like perfection.

Believers are <u>sanctified</u> by Christ's blood, meaning that we will be continually going through a sanctification process to make us more spiritual. This means that we are to distance ourselves from the world because being too attracted to the world removes us from God's leading. There are spiritual expectations of saints, and to serve the Living God is advantageous, but it is impossible to win in a fight against God. If a saint does not distance themselves enough from the world you can be sure that God knows how to get their attention.

"To open their eyes, and to turn them from darkness to light, and from the power of Satan to the power of God, that they may receive forgiveness of sins, and inheritance among them who are <u>sanctified</u> by faith that is in Me."- Acts 26:18

"And such sinners were some of you: but now you are washed, and you are <u>sanctified</u>, and you are justified in the name of the Lord Jesus, and by the Spirit of our God." - 1 Corinthians 6:11

"Ye adulterers and adulteresses, know ye not that the friendship of the world is enmity with God? whosoever therefore will be a friend of the world is the enemy of God." - James 4:4

Sanctuary

Satan

A <u>sanctuary</u> is a place set aside to worship God. This would include Christian churches, but it especially applies to the Jewish Temple at Jerusalem. The last Temple there was destroyed

168

by the Roman Army in 70 AD. Jesus had prophesied the destruction of the Temple. According to Scripture it must be rebuilt, because it will be defiled by the anti-Christ (empowered by Satan) in the great tribulation three and one-half years before the Battle of Armageddon. This event is called the "abomination of desolations." Satan is always trying to enter or influence the worship in the <u>sanctuary</u>. Satan desires to "be like the most High" and receive worship.

"I (Satan) will ascend above the heights of the clouds; I will be like the most High." - Isaiah 14:14

"But when ye shall see the abomination of desolation, spoken of by Daniel the prophet, standing where it ought not, (let him that readeth understand,) then let them that be in Judaea flee to the mountains:" - Mark 13:14

Scripture

Ure (Ph. - Your) – Script – Cite - Picture

The Holy Bible is God's written word and it is your script. The script has some things that are the same for everyone and it has others that are just for you. It is about God's will and plan for you. Just as ignorance of the law is not a legal excuse, neither are you excused if you do not know your script. You are responsible to search the <u>Scriptures</u> and respond as it gives guidance to your life. Bible <u>Scripture</u> is a vital part of a growing and maturing Christian life.

God's written word was produced by forty men over a period of about 1,500 years, and it came by divine inspiration. It is a priceless and timeless book that is absolutely astonishing. It reveals the true God, and answers the four major questions any religion must answer. The Bible gives consistent, logical explanations, and also includes hundreds of accurate prophecies. Proving that only God knows the future.

<u>Scripture</u> is the best source of revelation about a complex

and mysterious God. Fortunately, God has removed much of the mystery about Him for those that read <u>Scripture</u> in prayer for understanding. <u>Scripture</u> paints a marvelous picture for us of God's attributes and character; and through the written word God reveals Himself in the Son. We should use the Bible to become godly and Christ-like, so that the Bible becomes a picture of our lives, as well.

The Bible is truth, and once you find real truth there is just nothing else that can compare. You would never give it up. Believers should be prepared to cite the Bible as their authoritative source for truth and absolute values. If the Bible says it, then that settles it. Our responsibility is not to interpret <u>Scripture,</u> but rather to understand it and find the script there that God has for us.

"And beginning at Moses and all the prophets, he expounded unto them in all the <u>scriptures</u> the things concerning himself." - Luke 24:27

"Jesus saith unto him, Have I been so long time with you, and yet hast thou not known me, Philip? he that hath <u>seen</u> <u>me</u> hath seen the Father; and how sayest thou *then*, Shew us the Father?" - John 14:9

Secular

Curse – Use - Lure

Secular means those things that are not spiritual or sacred. Whether or not a person is spiritual or secular makes a big difference in their view of reality. Do you have a Christian world view, or a secular world view? Many believers see secularists as having an incorrect view of reality and walking in darkness. Those lacking true spirituality are at a disadvantage because things like the origin of life, the meaning of life, their purpose, and destiny are viewed incorrectly. They would not even realize that because of sin the whole world is under a curse, and that everyone has a fallen nature. Yes, a person's view of the world affects their life, and the lives of others in many ways. An example would be research that

170

shows Christians give more to all types of charity than non-Christians.

Some organizations exist to advance God's purposes and kingdom, and unfortunately others exist for exclusively contrary secular goals. Many secularists are known as secular humanists. This means that they think that man is the measure of all things. They start from the assumption that there is no real god, so they have their own gods. The Pharaoh of Egypt resisted God and the last of the plagues killed the entire first born population, including his son. Pharaoh was linked to the sun god.

If your god is the sun, the moon or any god other than the God of the Bible you might not be secular, but still have a serious spiritual problem. Like Pharaoh, all secular persons eventually lose their fight against the Almighty.

Worldly, secular things may not necessarily be bad in and of themselves. Yet, they can lure us away from godly thoughts and behavior. The world has many temptations, and is always trying to encroach on or replace the spiritual realm. Worldly attractions have no use to us spiritually, and can even end up being a curse. If you love this world too much you will be more secular than spiritual, and the spiritual is superior to the physical.

God is a spirit and should be worshipped in spirit and in truth. Christians are in the world, but not of the world. We are merely pilgrims that are passing through because our citizenship is actually in heaven in the presence of God.

"He that giveth unto the poor shall not lack: but he that hideth his eyes shall have many a curse." - Proverbs 28:27

"Then the magicians said unto Pharaoh, This is the finger of God: and Pharaoh's heart was hardened, and he hearkened not unto them; as the LORD had said." - Exodus 8:19

"But I say unto you, Love your enemies, bless them that curse you, do good to them that hate you, and pray for them which despitefully use you, and persecute you;" - Matthew 5:44

"Ye are of *your* father the devil, and the lusts of your father ye will do. He was a <u>murderer</u> from the beginning, and abode not in the truth, because there is no truth in him. When he speaketh a lie, he speaketh of his own: for he is a liar, and the father of it." - John 8:44

"And lead (lure) us not into temptation, but deliver us from evil: For thine is the kingdom, and the power, and the glory, for ever. Amen." - Matthew 6:13

"In whom the god of this world hath blinded the minds of them which believe not, lest the light of the glorious gospel of Christ, who is the image of God, should shine unto them." - 2 Corinthians 4:4

"Charge them that are rich in this world, that they be not highminded, nor trust in uncertain riches, but in the living God, who giveth us richly all things to enjoy;" - Timothy 6:17

"Teaching us that, denying ungodliness and worldly lusts, we should live soberly, righteously, and godly, in this present world;" - Titus 2:12

"God *is* a Spirit: and they that <u>worship</u> him must worship *him* in spirit and in truth." - John 4:24

"Love not the <u>world</u>, neither the things *that are* in the world. If any man love the world, the love of the Father is not in him." - 1 John 2:15

Serpent

Repent – See - Step - Tree

In the Garden of Eden, Satan used the serpent to deceive Eve into eating the fruit of the Tree of Knowledge of Good and Evil. Satan told her "your eyes shall be opened and ye shall be as gods, knowing good and evil." After she and Adam ate the fruit, they could see that they were naked, and they were ashamed. Public nakedness is a sin because sin is passed on through the genitals through reproduction. Since the serpent did this, God cursed the serpent, saying he would crawl on his belly and eat dust.

The seed of Eve would step on and bruise his head, and he would bruise his heel. This verse in the third chapter of Genesis was prophesying the virgin birth and the outcome of battle between God and Satan. The bruise to Satan's head, and bruise the seed of woman's heel was carried out on a tree in Jerusalem that was used to make a cross.

He also cursed the woman with labor pains, and a desire to control her husband instead of a willingness to accept his leadership role. God cursed the man with ground that would be hard to cultivate and would bring forth thorns. The sin carried a death sentence. Spiritual separation from God and physical death – they would return to dust. Because they were tempted in the garden by the Serpent, we now have sin, and we must strive to repent from choosing evil and get back in good standing with God. If you do not think that mankind needs to change their mind about evil, just look at the world today.

"Christ hath redeemed us from the curse of the law, being made a curse for us: for it is written, Cursed *is* every one that hangeth on a tree:" - Galatians 3:13

Sinner

Risen

The Greek philosophers thought that the body was bad; and at death the spirit, which was good, was freed from the body. They believed that after death you would remain as a spirit thereafter. Spirits lacking a body are very weak. The Hindu religion teaches that you are reincarnated after you die, and the womb, sweet or sour, that you enter is based on your deeds in this life. This wacky, pagan, works based belief system allows for extreme social injustice. There are 260 million Dalits, or untouchables, in India that live in abject poverty. How convenient this belief system is for those in the higher classes.

Well, what is the truth about existence after death? Jesus Christ had a physical resurrection three days (72 hours) after His death and burial. Believers will also receive a new physical resurrection body. This body will be incorruptible and will be glorified. Our lives in our current body are temporary because of sin. God will not allow immortality in a sinful body. As Christians and sinners our hope is in the risen savior.

"And as they came down from the mountain, he charged them that they should tell no man what things they had seen, till the Son of man were risen from the dead." - Mark 9:9

Song

Son

The Bible says a lot about song. Song and the new song is about the Son, the Lord Jesus Christ. There is nothing more important to sing about here or in heaven than the Son. The Son got the victory when on Calvary He said, "it is finished." The 144,000 that sing in heaven before the very throne of God are all Jewish. They are twelve thousand from each of the twelve tribes of Israel. If you thought God was finished with Israel, or that the church replaced Israel you had better read the Bible again.

"And he hath put a new song in my mouth, *even* praise unto our God: many shall see *it*, and fear, and shall trust in the LORD." - Psalms 40:3

"O sing unto the LORD a new song; for he hath done marvelous things: his right hand, and his holy arm, hath gotten him the victory." - Psalms 98:1

"And they sung a new <u>song</u>, saying, Thou art worthy to take the book, and to open the seals thereof: for thou wast slain, and hast redeemed us to God by thy blood out of every kindred, and tongue, and people, and nation;" - Revelation 5:9

"And they sung as it were a new <u>song</u> before the throne, and before the four beasts, and the elders: and no man could learn that <u>song</u> but the hundred *and* forty *and* four thousand, which were redeemed from the earth." - Revelation 14:3

"And I heard the number of them which were sealed: *and there were* sealed an hundred *and* forty *and* four thousand of all the tribes of the children of Israel. Of the tribe of Juda *were* sealed twelve thousand. Of the tribe of Reuben *were* sealed twelve thousand. Of the tribe of Gad *were* sealed twelve thousand. Of the tribe of Aser *were* sealed twelve thousand. Of the tribe of Napthali *were* sealed twelve thousand. Of the tribe of Manasseh *were* sealed twelve thousand. Of the tribe of Simeon *were* sealed twelve thousand. Of the tribe of Levi *were* sealed twelve thousand. Of the tribe of Issachar *were* sealed twelve thousand. Of the tribe of Zebulun *were* sealed twelve thousand. Of the tribe of Joseph *were* sealed twelve thousand. Of the tribe of Benjamin *were* sealed twelve thousand." - Revelation 7:4-8

Sound

Son – Sun

Where could this enormous universe have come from? Modern science supports that it did not always exist, but rather had a beginning. Could God speak everything into existence? The claim made by God in His Bible is, that everything was spoken into existence by Almighty God. Where there is speaking there is <u>sound</u>. Scripture is clear that God alone is responsible for all that exists. This means that the Son spoke the universe into existence, including our sun. (More about this topic in section three).

"In the beginning God created the heaven and the earth." - Genesis 1:1

"All things were made by him (Son); and without him was not any thing made that was made." - John 1:3

"For by him were all things created, that are in heaven, and that are in earth, visible and invisible, whether *they be* thrones, or dominions, or principalities, or powers: all things were created by him, and for him: And he is before all things, and by him all things consist." - Colossians 1:16

"For this they willingly are ignorant of, that by the word of God the heavens were of old, and the earth standing out of the water and in the water:" - 2 Peter 3:5

"In a moment, in the twinkling of an eye, at the last trump: for the trumpet shall <u>sound,</u> and the dead shall be raised incorruptible, and we shall be changed." - 1 Corinthians 15:52

Spirit

Tips – Stir

Jesus Christ not only gives us the gift of salvation, but also the gift of the Holy <u>Spirit</u> that He called the Comforter. Both Jesus and the Holy <u>Spirit</u> are gifts from the Father, and they are one with Him. At the time of salvation believers are sealed with the Holy <u>Spirit,</u> and He remains with them forever. The Holy <u>Spirit</u> inside of us makes our body a temple, and gives us 24/7 access to God the Father. The presence of the Comforter also gives God a means in which to communicate with us, to teach us, and to guide us. Learn to listen to the Holy <u>Spirit,</u> because He is the mind and purpose of God. The <u>Spirit</u> not only guides us in our walk, and conveys God's thoughts to us, but He gives us tips for the Christian life. He teaches us how to walk, how to talk, and how to be like Christ.

When God wants us to listen, He will stir the <u>Spirit</u> up so that we will take notice. This can be through reading Scripture and coming across a verse that applies to a situation we are facing at the time, through prayer and God's answer to that prayer, or through a sudden thought that makes us stop and listen closely for direction. Personal experiences in our walk with God improve our ability to discern that God is speaking to us. I personally have found that a whisper is serious and important. The importance of the Holy <u>Spirit</u> is often underrated, but it's important to know that He is vital to our growing relationship with God.

"The <u>Spirit</u> of the Lord *is* upon me, because he hath anointed me to preach the gospel to the poor; he hath sent me to heal the brokenhearted, to preach deliverance to the captives, and recovering of sight to the blind, to set at liberty them that are bruised," - Luke 4:18

"If ye then, being evil, know how to give good gifts unto your children: how much more shall *your* heavenly Father give the Holy <u>Spirit</u> to them that ask him? - Luke 11:13

"But when they shall lead *you*, and deliver you up, take no thought beforehand what ye shall speak, neither do ye premeditate: but whatsoever shall be given you in that hour, that speak ye: for it is not ye that speak, but the Holy Ghost." - Mark 13:11

"Jesus answered, Verily, verily, I say unto thee, Except a man be born of water and *of* the <u>Spirit</u>, he cannot enter into the kingdom of God. That which is born of the flesh is flesh; and that which is born of the <u>Spirit</u> is <u>spirit</u>." - John 3:5-6

"And I will pray the Father, and he shall give you another Comforter, that he may abide with you for ever;" - John 14:16

"But when the Comforter is come, whom I will send unto you from the Father, *even* the <u>Spirit</u> of truth, which proceedeth from the Father, he shall testify of me:" - John 15:26

"And it shall come to pass in the last days, saith God, I will pour out of my <u>Spirit</u> upon all flesh: and your sons and your daughters shall prophesy, and your young men shall see visions, and your old men shall dream dreams:" - Acts 2:17

"God *is* a <u>Spirit</u>: and they that worship him must worship *him* in spirit and in truth." - John 4:24

"Wherefore I put thee in remembrance that thou stir up the gift of God, which is in thee by the putting on of my hands. For God hath not given us the <u>spirit</u> of fear; but of power, and of love, and of a sound mind." - 2 Timothy 1:6-7

Study

Duty - Us

The most important duty for us regarding learning is to <u>study</u> the Word of God. Early public education in America included verses from the Bible as an integral part of classroom teaching. Even the alphabet was learned by tying each letter to a Bible verse. "In Adam's fall we sinned all." If a person with a Doctor of Philosophy degree did not <u>study</u> the Bible, I believe by God's standard they would be considered a learning failure.

The freedom of religion amendment in the Bill of Rights of the U.S. Constitution was a restriction on Congress preventing the government from interfering with religion. Now we are told that it restricts us by separating church and state. Since the founding Fathers clearly intended only to restrict government, what a blatant lie is being told to the American people.

"Having the understanding darkened, being alienated from the life of God through the ignorance that is in them, because of the blindness of their heart:" - Ephesians 4:18

"Study to shew thyself approved unto God, a workman that needeth not to be ashamed, rightly dividing the word of truth." - 2 Timothy 2:15

Suffering

Fire – Urn – Rise – Us – Use - Sin – Refine -

After the fall of mankind in the Garden of Eden many changes occurred that cause suffering. There are diseases, disasters, wars, accidents, famines, aging, death, and many difficulties and challenges. I am persuaded that in this life everyone has to deal with adversity to some degree or another. We are not in a perfect world – that is reserved for the next life in heaven. A huge amount of suffering has its origin is sin and man's inhumanity to man. Suffering provides opportunities for character building, and can help us grow stronger by overcoming unfavorable situations. Sometimes <u>suffering</u> brings repentance, and turning to God. A contrite heart and a broken spirit could be just what you need. Better to suffer a little while here than be in the eternal fire.

God allows <u>suffering</u> to happen. The book of Job is the "instruction manual" for dealing with <u>suffering</u>. Satan stated that the only reason Job feared and respected God was because of all the blessings that he enjoyed. Satan stated that Job would curse God if he lost his processions and blessings. God allowed Satan to bring severe suffering unto Job. Satan destroyed everything that was dear to Job, including physical sufferings, bringing him close to death. However, Job never turned from God, and later God blessed Job with even more than he had before. God's victory over Satan through Job was very important because that is an accusation that Satan can no longer use against any of us.

I recently saw a book in an airport book store that said that the Bible cannot explain <u>suffering</u>. I disagree, but I will say that unspiritual people do not have the ability to properly understand suffering. Moses chose to suffer affliction with the people of God rather than the pleasure of sin for a season. That is your Bible answer. The man who wrote the first five books of the Bible chose suffering with God over the Palace of Egypt. There are two ff's in the words difference and suffering. God is the difference because without God suffering could not be explained. Without God suffering would not make any sense. The scripture even tells believers to suffer for his sake.

So how does this apply in our lives today? How do we deal with suffering? It's simple. We maintain strong faith in God, realizing that he is the Supreme power in the universe, and God will not bring us more suffering than we can endure. Suffering is an opportunity for us to build character. If we have faith during times of suffering, God will use it to shape and mold us into what He wants us to be in order for Him to use us for Kingdom purposes. He is the Potter, and we are the clay. He may want to shape you into a beautiful urn, so as you grow in your spiritual walk, He will mold you into the perfect piece of pottery for his purposes. Satan may bring the fire of suffering, but God will use that for His good. Like a kiln which a potter uses to harden the clay, making the urn tougher than it was when it was only soft clay. Furthermore, when a potter wants to make a piece of pottery more beautiful, he will add a coat of glaze and fire it again. Trusting God throughout our hard times will make us even more beautiful each time. God will refine you like silver and gold. God will use this process will build godly character.

Jesus' suffering is a prime example by which to handle hard times that Satan may bring upon us. He was tortured and beaten and nailed to a cross on Calvary Hill in Jerusalem. Satan probably celebrated thinking that he had taken care of that problem. Though Satan thought he was victorious, what he didn't know that just three days later Jesus would rise and be victorious over death. As it turned out the crucifixion of Christ was the most important victory for God and us that will ever occur. Jesus trusted His Father, and once again the Sovereign God prevailed over the evil purposes of Satan. When we put our trust in God and our faith in Jesus, no amount of suffering can ultimately defeat us, even to the point of death, because we will rise to live eternally.

"If I must need glory, I will glory of the things which concern mine infirmities." - 2 Corinthians 11:30

"Take, my brethren, the prophets, who have spoken in the name of the Lord, for an example of suffering affliction, and of patience." - James 5:10

"Even as Sodom and Gomorrah, and the cities about them in like manner, giving themselves over to fornication, and going after strange flesh, are set forth for an example, suffering the vengeance of eternal fire." - Jude 1:7

"And I will bring the third part through the fire, and will refine them as silver is refined, and will try them as gold is tried: they shall call on my name, and I will hear them: I will say, It *is* my people: and they shall say, The LORD *is* my God." - Zechariah 13:9

T

Temptations

Eat – Sin - Potent – Pain – Test - Point– Son

Temptations are anything that allures or entices us into immorality or sin. Satan is called in Scripture "the Tempter," and no doubt this adversary is potent in his efforts to lead into temptations. Satan, as a serpent, tempted Eve to eat the fruit God had forbidden; and Adam willfully followed Eve and ate as well. This was the original sin for mankind, and from that moment sin and pain entered the world to become a reality of life. Other sources of temptations, besides Satan, include attractions of this world and pride, greed, envy, flesh, lust, etc.

When I was a young teenage boy an older female second cousin invited me to go to the drive-in theater. This cousin had a reputation of being very "wild", and no doubt immorality would have been planned for the evening. My parents were usually lenient on my choices of activities, but this time my father was very adamant that I could not go. This shows us another side of temptation: God providing me a way out of temptation. The heavenly Father is also in the business of keeping us from temptations or evil. This protection may have happened in our lives many times without us even knowing it.

God is also in the business, not of tempting us, but of testing us. David passed a major test by not killing King Saul when he had the opportunity. He would not kill God's anointed. This test demonstrated something very important – God was more important to David than being King. I know that I had this same test many years ago. So I suspect that this type of test, God being first, might be a common one for God to use. Do you know of any spiritual tests that you might have passed or failed?

God sent His Son, who was also tempted by Satan, to set us free from the bondage of sin. And though sinless, He bore the pain of the cross for our sakes. The Holy Spirit, who dwells in the body of believers, will lead and point us away from temptation and sin. The reality is that even those who are born again still have a sin nature and are not sinless. Believers should agree with God that righteousness should be preferred over sin. Believers are subject to being chastened by God when they sin. Also, God established the church, which gives us other believers to keep us accountable and encouraged so that we are able to better resist temptations. Christians should make the effort to restore a fellow believer who has been tempted to sin, but a warning in Galatians says to be watchful in such cases, *"Lest thou also be tempted."*

"Now the serpent was more subtle than any beast of the field which the LORD God had made. And he said unto the woman, Ye, hath God said, Ye shall not Eat of every tree of the garden? And the woman said unto the serpent, We may Eat of the fruit of the trees of the garden: But of the fruit of the tree which is in the midst of the garden, God hath said, Ye shall not Eat of it, neither shall ye touch it, lest ye die. And the serpent said unto the woman, Ye shall not surely die: For God doth know that in the day ye Eat thereof, then your eyes shall be opened, and ye shall be as gods, knowing good and evil. And when the woman saw that the tree was good for food, and that it was pleasant to the eyes, and a tree to be desired to make one wise, she took of the fruit thereof, and did Eat, and gave also unto her husband with her; and he did Eat. And the eyes of them both were opened, and they knew that they were naked; and they sewed fig leaves together, and made themselves aprons. And they heard the voice of the LORD God walking in the garden in the cool of the day: and Adam and his wife hid themselves from the presence of the LORD God amongst the trees of the garden. And the LORD God called unto Adam, and said unto him, Where art thou? And he said, I heard thy voice in the garden, and I was afraid, because I was naked; and I hid myself. And he said, Who told thee that thou wast naked? Hast thou Eaten of the tree, whereof I commanded thee that thou shouldest not Eat? And the man said, The woman whom thou gavest to be with me, she gave me of the tree, and I did Eat. And the LORD God said unto the woman, What is this that thou hast done? And the woman said, The serpent beguiled me, and I did Eat." - Genesis 3:1-13

"Then was Jesus led up of the Spirit into the wilderness to be tempted of the devil. And when He had fasted forty days and forty nights, He was afterward an hungred. And when the tempter came to Him, He said, If Thou be the Son of God, command that these stones be made bread. But He answered and said, It is written, Man shall not live by bread alone, but by every word that proceedeth out of the mouth of God. Then the devil taketh Him up into the holy city, and setteth Him on a pinnacle of the temple, And saith unto Him, If Thou be the Son of God, cast thyself down: for it is written, He shall give his angels charge concerning thee: and in their hands they shall bear thee up, lest at any time thou dash thy foot against a stone. Jesus said unto him, It is written again, Thou shalt not tempt the Lord thy God. Again, the devil taketh Him up into an exceeding high mountain, and sheweth Him all the kingdoms of the world, and the glory of them; And saith unto Him, All these things will I give Thee, if Thou wilt fall down and worship me. Then saith Jesus unto him, Get thee hence, Satan: for it is written, Thou shalt worship the Lord thy God, and him only shalt thou serve. Then the devil leaveth Him, and, behold, angels came and ministered unto Him." - Matthew 4:1-11

"Behold, this day thine eyes have seen how that the LORD had delivered thee to day into mine hand in the cave: and *some* bade *me* kill thee: but *mine eye* spared thee; and I said, I will not put forth mine hand against my lord; for he *is* the LORD'S anointed." - 1 Samuel 24:10

"And it shall come to pass, if ye shall hearken diligently unto my commandments which I command you this day, to love the LORD your God, and to serve him with all your heart and with all your soul," - Deuteronomy 11:13

"And lead us not into temptation, but deliver us from evil: For thine is the kingdom, and the power, and the glory, for ever. Amen." - Matthew 16:13

"For all that *is* in the world, the lust of the flesh, and the lust of the eyes, and the pride of life, is not of the Father, but is of the world." - 1 John 2:16

"Watch and pray, that ye enter not into temptation: the spirit indeed *is* willing, but the flesh *is* weak." - Matthew 26:41

"Brethren, if a man be overtaken in a fault, ye which are spiritual, restore such an one in the spirit of meekness; considering thyself, lest thou also be tempted." - Galations 6:1

"Blessed *is* the man that endureth temptation: for when he is tried, he shall receive the crown of life, which the Lord hath promised to them that love him." - James 1:12

Temperance

Act - Repent –Trap - Tame

Christianity is a faith that primarily teaches moderation rather than abstinence. Temperance is defined as moderation and self-restraint in actions, thoughts, and emotions. Examples of moderation could include eating, drinking, spending, amusement, etc. The supernatural Fruit of the Spirit gives one the potential to have self control; yet it's the Spirit Himself who points a heart and mind away from wrongful desires and emotions. This part of the Fruit of the Spirit is a book-end of sorts (the other being love) which holds the Fruit as a whole together. It's difficult to have love, joy, peace, longsuffering, kindness, goodness, faithfulness and gentleness without <u>temperance</u>. And likewise, it is impossible to have any of these without love. If <u>temperance</u> is completely accomplished by self, it would fail because self is flesh and flesh is weak.

Before salvation, and before the Spirit, we are left vulnerable to sin because <u>temperance</u> does not come naturally. Individuals without the Spirit are in a trap, unable to get out of the habits of excess: ill emotions, unclean thoughts, and a bad temper. The Holy Spirit will tame the heart and soul so that we are better able to control them. Even still, we are unable to control everything our flesh desires, and we must repent (examine our thoughts and actions and see beneficial changes) daily.

"But the fruit of the Spirit is love, joy, peace, longsuffering, gentleness, goodness, faith, Meekness, <u>temperance</u>: against such there is no law." - Galatians 5:22-23

Testament

Meant - Test - Man – Ten

In the Bible <u>testament</u> is another word for covenant. Biblically, a covenant is a solemn promise by God to man, usually containing requirements for man to fulfill. The covenant requiring males to be circumcised on their eighth day is an example of this type of covenant. God is always faithful, but God knows that man is a covenant breaker. Fortunately, there are covenants that God will keep regardless of what man does or does not do. An example, God made a covenant with Noah that the rainbow would be a sign that the earth would never be destroyed by water again. More importantly, the covenant of salvation by grace through faith has no test that will reverse this covenant, once it has been received by saving faith.

Many covenants are meant to test man. God tested Abraham with the sacrifice of his son Isaac. In which, Abraham was ready to faithfully follow through until the Lord stopped him and made a covenant with him there, calling him faithful. Later, God allowed the nations that Joshua had not driven out of the Land to remain and to test Israel, to see whether they would keep God's commands and ways in the midst of turmoil.

In both Old and New Testaments faith in God was the test, and salvation has always come by faith. "Abraham's faith was counted for righteousness." The Law of Moses, the Ten Commandments (or Torah), was a standard of righteousness that God gave to the Jewish people. Man is imperfect, has a sin nature, and no individual has ever met this standard, with the exception of Jesus. You are not able to obtain salvation from good works or from the law. God's requirement to be justified by the law is 100% compliance. If you make 99.9% then you still have failed. The law is the schoolmaster showing that you are indeed a sinner in need of God's grace.

Jesus came as both God and man, God incarnate, and fulfilled the precepts and law of God. He demonstrated the proper balance between faith, law, and works. God wants His Word in our heart and His law written on our hearts. Through our faith we live in a relationship with God. And obedience should flow from a renewed heart and spirit which, is why it is written "The just shall live by faith."

186

"This *is* my covenant, which ye shall keep, between me and you and thy seed after thee; Every man child among you shall be circumcised." - Genesis 17:10

"And it came to pass after these things, that God did tempt (test) Abraham, and said unto him, Abraham: and he said, Behold, here I am. And he said, Take now thy son, thine only son Isaac, whom thou lovest, and get thee into the land of Moriah; and offer him there for a burnt offering upon one of the mountains which I will tell thee of." - Genesis 22:1-2

And said, By myself have I sworn, saith the LORD, for because thou hast done this thing, and hast not withheld thy son, thine only *son*: That in blessing I will bless thee, and in multiplying I will multiply thy seed as the stars of the heaven, and as the sand which *is* upon the sea shore; and thy seed shall possess the gate of his enemies; And in thy seed shall all the nations of the earth be blessed; because thou hast obeyed my voice." - Genesis 17-18

"Then said the LORD unto Moses, Behold, I will rain bread from heaven for you; and the people shall go out and gather a certain rate every day, that I may prove them, whether they will walk in my law, or no." - Exodus 16:4

"The fining pot is for silver, and the furnace for gold: but the LORD trieth (tests) the hearts." - Proverbs 17:3

"That whosoever believeth in him should not perish, but have eternal life." - John 3:15

"But that no man is justified by the law in the sight of God, *it is* evident: for, The just shall live by <u>faith</u>." - Galatians 3:11

"For by grace are ye saved through faith; and that not of yourselves: *it is* the gift of God:" - Ephesians 2:8

Time

Mite – Tie – Me

Sixty seconds from now, a minute will have passed, and in sixty minutes, an hour will have done the same. What can you accomplish in an hour, or a day? How many years did you wait for something you prayed for before God answered that prayer? How much longer before Jesus returns to reign? We, as humans, wonder these things because we live in time and space. It drives our lives because we have schedules and deadlines. We have become trained to the tune of *"Westminster Quarters"*, and to whatever number of bell chimes follows telling us it's time to do something important. We hurry and hurry because time is fleeting, and you can't get time back once it's gone. And it's been this way since man learned how to measure minutes, hours, and days.

But God works outside of the limits of time and space. A century is but a mite to Him, and eternity has no calendar. God created time for us, even though He may not need to measure time for Himself. He knew in all his wisdom that, however much we tend to give too much value to it, we would need it. It's important for us to know seasons for crops and harvest, days of the week for worship, work, and rest, and days of the year for feasts and Biblical holy days; which are mostly ignored today by churches.

Though God exists outside of time and space, He works inside time for us to be able to understand Him. His creation process took six days, and He gave Himself a seventh for rest. Do you think the Sovereign God of the Universe needed six days to create all that exists? Or does a God who is all powerful need a day of rest? It's clearly not for Him that He did it this way. He did it to establish the week as a period of time for you and me. His wisdom provided for only six days of work at a time before a day of rest and spiritual renewal. He showed us what the seventh day is for Shabbat (שבת). Shabbat is rooted in the Hebrew word shavat, meaning to rest, cease, or stop working; and where we also get the word Sabbatical, which is a needed time off from work. Shabbat is a day that God created for us to rest, but how many Christians keep the day for what it was intended? Shabbat is the day to rest and to worship the Creator of the Universe.

God also chooses specific timing to do His works, to show us His sovereignty and wisdom, and to usually tie events together so that we see it as no coincidence. This is easy to see when studying the fulfillment of the Old Testament by Jesus' renewed covenant of the latter testament Scriptures. For example, the nativity story that we all know as "Christmas" did not happen on the 25th of December. This date has no value whatsoever to the story of the Messiah. He was born during the Biblical feast of Sukkot (סכות) also called "Feast of Tabernacles", "Feast of Nations", and "Season of Our Joy." While Christmas (Christ Mass) was set up by Constantine to be concurrent with the pagan observance of the winter solstice, this was not the true day of Christ's birth. The true timing God chose in bringing his Son into the world, during Sukkot, holds much more significance and ties in perfectly with Jewish tradition seen in the Old Testament, which was set up by God Himself. John 1:14 chooses the Greek word Skenoo   which means "Tabernacle", thus Jesus came to Tabernacle with us during the Feast of Tabernacles. In the Nativity account of Luke, we see in chapter 2 verse 10, *"And the angel said unto them, Fear not: for, behold, I bring you good tidings of Great Joy which shall be to All."* This ties in correctly with Sukkot being called "Season of our Joy" and "Feast of Nations." Galatians describes the nativity story as occurring in "fullness of time", which God knew to be the correct time even before the universe was brought into existence.

Spiritual awareness is required for one to see and understand the timing of God. An event in a believer's life that is a clear act of the Father, done in His perfect timing, may seem like but a coincidence to an unbeliever. But a believer, seeing with spiritual eyes, will realize that God was involved and that He is glorified. These writers have had more personal experiences of this type with our God than we could count.

"Six days thou shalt do thy work, and on the seventh day thou shalt rest: that thine ox and thine ass may rest, and the son of thy handmaid, and the stranger, may be refreshed." - Exodus 23:12

"Now I say, That the Heir, as long as He is a child, differeth nothing from a servant, though He be Lord of all; But is under tutors and governors until the time appointed of the Father. Even so we, when we were children, were in bondage under the elements of the world: But when the fulness of the <u>Time</u> was come, God sent forth His Son, made of a woman, made under the law, To redeem them that were under the law, that we might receive the adoption of sons. And because ye are sons, God hath sent forth the Spirit of his Son into your hearts, crying, Abba, Father. Wherefore thou art no more a servant, but a son; and if a son, then an heir of God through Christ." - Galatians 4:1-7

"To every thing there is a season, and a <u>time</u> to every purpose under the heaven" - Ecclesiastes 3:1

"When they therefore were come together, they asked of Him, saying, Lord, wilt thou at this <u>time</u> restore again the kingdom to Israel? And He said unto them, It is not for you to know the <u>times</u> or the seasons, which the Father hath put in his own power. But ye shall receive power, after that the Holy Ghost is come upon you: and ye shall be witnesses unto me both in Jerusalem, and in all Judaea, and in Samaria, and unto the uttermost part of the earth. And, Thou, Lord, in the beginning hast laid the foundation of the earth; and the heavens are the works of thine hands: They shall perish; but thou remainest; and they all shall wax old as doth a garment; And as a vesture shalt thou fold them up, and they shall be changed: but thou art the same, and thy years shall not fail." - Hebrews 1:10-12

"Praise be to the LORD, the God of Israel, from everlasting to everlasting. Amen and Amen." - Psalm 41:13

Transgressions

Atone – Risen – Season – Sin – Sinners - Son

Transgressions are the violation of a law or command. From a theological standpoint, this means any command that God gives, which when broken down all fall under the Ten Commandments or laws of Moses (Torah). These ten are changed to two by Jesus, but these are inclusive in that the ten fall under the two commands that Jesus gave (Love God, and Love your Neighbor). The Bible proclaims that we are all equal in that all are sinners, and fall short of the standard that Gods requires for righteousness.

Yes, we are all born into sin and deserve nothing more than eternity apart from God for our transgressions, since God requires perfect righteousness. Self-righteousness gets you nowhere as far as heaven is concerned. Fortunately, He is a gracious and loving God that wants us to enter an eternal relationship with Him. He is aware that no man can live without breaking His commands. Therefore, He sent His Son to die for our sins. The blood of Jesus is the only sacrifice that can atone for our transgressions against Him. Just as He was risen from the grave after taking our sins upon Himself, those who are covered by His blood will also rise to live eternally with God on high. A sinner's righteousness is only possible when God the Father sees the righteousness of His Son that has been imputed to them.

Though sins may be forgiven, and we have a changed heart and the Holy Spirit to lead us away from the inclination to sin; we still may go through a season of sin on occasion due to the flesh we dwell in. Flesh which will be left behind when we are risen in Christ at death, being made perfect in Spirit.

"For all have sinned, and come short of the glory of God;" - Romans 3:23

"Remember not the sins of my youth, nor my transgressions: according to thy mercy remember thou me for thy goodness' sake, O LORD." - Psalm 25:7

"Wash me thoroughly from mine iniquity, and cleanse me from my sin. For I acknowledge my Transgressions: and my sin is ever before me. Against thee, thee only, have I sinned, and done this evil in thy sight: that thou mightest be justified when thou speakest, and be clear when thou judgest." - Psalm 51:2-4

"But He was wounded for our Transgressions, He was bruised for our iniquities: the chastisement of our peace was upon Him; and with His stripes we are healed." - Isaiah 53:5

"For when we were yet without strength, in due time Christ died for the ungodly. For scarcely for a righteous man will one die: yet peradventure for a good man some would even dare to die. But God commendeth his love toward us, in that, while we were yet sinners, Christ died for us. Much more then, being now justified by his blood, we shall be saved from wrath through him. For if, when we were enemies, we were reconciled to God by the death of his Son, much more, being reconciled, we shall be saved by his life. And not only so, but we also joy in God through our Lord Jesus Christ, by whom we have now received the atonement. Wherefore, as by one man sin entered into the world, and death by sin; and so death passed upon all men, for that all have sinned: (For until the law sin was in the world: but sin is not imputed when there is no law. Nevertheless death reigned from Adam to Moses, even over them that had not sinned after the similitude of Adam's transgression, who is the figure of him that was to come. But not as the offence, so also is the free gift. For if through the offence of one many be dead, much more the grace of God, and the gift by grace, which is by one man, Jesus Christ, hath abounded unto many. And not as it was by one that sinned, so is the gift: for the judgment was by one to condemnation, but the free gift is of many offences unto justification. For if by one man's offence death reigned by one; much more they which receive abundance of grace and of the gift of righteousness shall reign in life by one, Jesus Christ.) Therefore as by the offence of one judgment came upon all men to condemnation; even so by the righteousness of one the free gift came upon all men unto justification of life. For as by one man's disobedience many were made sinners, so by the obedience of one shall many be made righteous. Moreover the law entered, that the offence might abound. But where Sin abounded, grace did much more abound: That as sin hath reigned unto death, even so might grace reign through righteousness unto eternal life by Jesus Christ our Lord." - Romans 5:6-21

Truths

Trust – Hurts - Ruth

God wants you to trust in His <u>truth</u> and experience His goodness. God's word is filled with His <u>truths</u>. But, we live in a world full of people who try to discredit these <u>truths</u> with ridiculous theories and ideals. There has been a seemingly annual attack recently on Christian beliefs by the over-hyping of Gnostic accounts, such as The Gospel of Judas and fictional works like *The Da Vinci Code*, as well as attempts by a movie producer to try and prove that Jesus and His family are in a tomb in the suburbs of Jerusalem. These fallacies contradict Scripture and mislead individuals away from the sound <u>truths</u> that God revealed to us in His holy scriptures.

In order to defend ourselves from being caught up in the lies of the world, we must study Scripture and learn how the Bible works and fits together as a whole. Even our modern church is filled with subtle lies that have become part of our Christian 'tradition', such as Christmas and Easter (see "Time"). While some of these may seem like "white lies" and are essentially harmless, the <u>truth</u> is much more powerful and meaningful. Bible prophecy states there will be a Christian falling away or apostasy in the end times. Do not make the mistake of judging God by the behavior of professing Christians or the state of Christianity. The sacrifice of truth and sound doctrine to avoid controversy and to produce fast growing mega churches is a questionable modern trend. People might let you down, but the rock of our salvation is faithful, trustworthy, unchanging, caring, and a constant source of strength.

It has never been necessary for one to know that Passover was the correct time when Jesus was crucified, and that He died on a Wednesday and not on "Good" Friday. The important thing has always been that He died for our sins, and physically rose again to claim victory over death. This is the one great truth that causes millions of people to put their faith in Jesus. He is the truth, and we must trust in Him to receive eternal life.

There is something about truth that once you find it you will never give it up. The best secular life does not compare to the priceless experience of truth. Ruth was a Gentile woman that put her trust in the God of Israel as her God. Boaz became her kinsman redeemer, and she was grafted into the lineage that produced Jesus Christ: the kinsman redeemer for the whole human race. Ruth found truth. God is always presenting new truths to His children.

There is an old saying, "The Truth hurts." But, actually true truth will set you free. God has complete freedom, as He chose to create the universe. Mankind was made in God's image, and likeness and freedom is one of those characteristics we should have in common with God. If you are in bondage to sin and are under the curse of death you are not really free. God has a great plan for you that involves the truth in His Word.

"He shall cover thee with His feathers, and under His wings shalt thou Trust: His Truth shall be thy shield and buckler." - Psalm 91:4

"Come unto me, all ye that labour and are heavy laden, and I will give you rest." - Matthew 11:28

"And ye shall know the truth, and the truth shall make you free." - John 8:32

"Jesus saith unto him, I am the way, the truth, and the life: no man cometh unto the Father, but by me." - John 14:6

"Pilate therefore said unto him, Art thou a king then? Jesus answered, Thou sayest that I am a king. To this end was I born, and for this cause came I into the world, that I should bear witness unto the truth. Every one that is of the truth heareth my voice." - John 18: 37

194

U

Understand

Stand - Under

God's ways are not man's ways, and God's thoughts are higher than man's thoughts. Compared to God and apart from God, all men lack the understanding of that which is really important. Man cannot reach up to God; God had to come down to man. To really understand yourself and life you have to stand under the God that created you.

"All *this, said David,* the LORD made me understand in writing by *his* hand upon me, *even* all the works of this pattern." - 1 Chronicles 28:19

"The LORD looked down from heaven upon the children of men, to see if there were any that did understand, *and* seek God." - Psalms 14:2

"Who can understand *his* errors? cleanse thou me from secret *faults.*" - Psalms 19:12

"Many shall be purified, and made white, and tried; but the wicked shall do wickedly: and none of the wicked shall understand; but the wise shall understand." - Daniel 12:10

"And in them is fulfilled the prophecy of Esaias, which saith, By hearing ye shall hear, and shall not understand; and seeing ye shall see, and shall not perceive:" - Matthew 13:14

Universe

Uni (one/first) - Verse – Sun - Rise

I have one word for those that promote evolution, which is an *evil* *notion*, and that word is <u>universe</u>. The <u>universe</u> exists because of one verse, and it is the first verse in the Bible. This first Bible verse is a summary statement, and what follows are many details.

This verse answers one of two main questions, "From where did everything originate?" By plainly stating that matter did have a beginning time. And yes, evolution is not only false, but it is evil. Those that promote this feeble theory would be better served to seek God and eternal life.

Fortunately, there have been evolution scientists that did see the light and have become strong defenders of the Genesis creation account. One such well-known scientist that comes to mind is the published author Dr. Henry Morris. His doctorate in paleontology provided an academic evolution background. He became a creation apologetics (defender) author. If you do not believe this author, please read a book or two written by Dr. Henry Morris.

Scientists state that our sun is a star and one of the trillions of stars in the <u>universe</u>. However, this theory of stars may not be correct because Scripture states that the sun and stars were made separately. Planet earth has the sun for the day because the Son of God is the spiritual light of the world. Just as we can count on the **sun** to always rise, so are we able to count on the risen Son of God for strength and salvation.

"In the beginning God (Elohim) created the heaven and the earth." - Genesis 1:1

"And this is the condemnation, that light is come into the world, and men loved darkness rather than light, because their deeds were evil." - John 3:19

"Then spake Jesus again unto them, saying, I am the light of the world: he that followeth me shall not walk in darkness, but shall have the light of life." - John 8:12

V

Verse

Serve

Jesus explained to His disciples that to be great meant to have a heart to serve others, and to esteem others as greater than ourselves. Jesus left the glory of heaven and came to earth, as the meek and lowly Lamb of God. Have you personally gotten to know this servant of God that thought it not wrong to be equal with God?

"Take my yoke upon you, and learn of me; for I am meek and lowly in heart: and ye shall find rest unto your souls." - Matthew 11:29

"The next day John seeth Jesus coming unto him, and saith, Behold the Lamb of God, which taketh away the sin of the world." - John 1:29

"*Let* nothing *be done* through strife or vainglory; but in lowliness of mind let each esteem other better than themselves." - Philippians 2:3

"Who, being in the form of God, thought it not robbery to be equal with God:" - Philippians 2:6

Veil

Evil – Lie – Live

Veils are used to cover, conceal, protect, or separate. What is being covered can be evil, or can be good. In "Song of Solomon", for example, the writer tells his beloved how, "your eyes behind your <u>veil</u> are like doves" and "your temples behind your <u>veil</u> are like the halves of pomegranates" thus focusing on the beauty that is hidden behind the veil and yet to be uncovered. "Song of Solomon" is a book that parallels the love relationship with the Messiah and his bride, the church.

The Holy of Holies, which was located in the Temple, was separated by a thick <u>veil</u>. The privilege of entering and being where God was present was only allowed once a year, and only by the High Priest. The priest had to follow procedures and take special care to be "clean" before entering, or he would be struck dead. At the end of Jesus' crucifixion, the <u>veil</u> in the temple was torn from top to bottom. This demonstrates that God is now accessible for all those who believe in salvation through Jesus.

Through Jesus' sacrifice, it is now possible to enter the presence of God and live not worrying about being struck down; because His blood has covered our sins and made us righteous in the sight of the Father. When Christ comes to dwell in our hearts following salvation, He gives us direct spiritual access to the throne of God the Father. Christ is the High Priest that is being an intercessor between us and the Father.

There is a similar <u>veil</u> that covers the eyes of Israel, as well. 2 Corinthians speaks of a <u>veil</u> that represents a blindness covering the eyes and hearts of the Jewish people when the Old Covenant is read. And the Apostle Paul (Rabi Saul) refers back to Moses, who wore a <u>veil</u> over his face to keep the Israelites from seeing the glory of God shining from his face. According to the book of Romans, this <u>veil</u> has been used to cover the eyes of Israel for the sake of the Gentiles. However, God promises the <u>veil</u> will be lifted once the fullness of the Gentiles has come; and the people of Israel will know their Messiah.

A remnant has always been saved. But nationally, Israel, is still in unbelief and spiritual blindness. It is important to the whole world for Israel to recognize the Messiah and to be restored to being "the servant of God", so they can spiritually lead the world. Thankfully, I see signs that are encouraging that this is close to happening. Israel, the only covenant nation on earth, is of extreme importance to God. This little nation, by God's grace, has produced the Prophets, the Messiah, the Apostles, the entire Bible and the Church. Stay tuned, there is a lot more to come from Israel.

Just as the Bible uses <u>veils</u> to cover a beautiful thing, it can also be used to cover something evil. False prophets and false teachers can <u>veil</u> the truth with lies. Ezekiel writes of false prophets and prophetesses within the land who lie to the people of Israel. They say that the words they speak are from God. The Lord tells Ezekiel that their <u>veils</u> will be ripped from their faces, and that the people will be saved from their trickery.

"Seeing then that we have such hope, we use great plainness of speech: And not as Moses, which put a <u>veil</u> over his face, that the children of Israel could not stedfastly look to the end of that which is abolished: But their minds were blinded: for until this day remaineth the same <u>veil</u> untaken away in the reading of the old testament; which <u>veil</u> is done away in Christ. But even unto this day, when Moses is read, the <u>veil</u> is upon their heart. Nevertheless when it shall turn to the Lord, the <u>veil</u> shall be taken away." - 2 Corinthians 3:12-16

"For I would not, brethren, that ye should be ignorant of this mystery, lest ye should be wise in your own conceits; that blindness in part is happened to Israel, until the fullness of the Gentiles be come in. And so all Israel shall be saved: as it is written, There shall come out of Zion the Deliverer, and shall turn away ungodliness from Jacob: For this is my covenant unto them, when I shall take away their sins." - Romans 11:25-27

"To wit, the prophets of Israel which prophesy concerning Jerusalem, and which see visions of peace for her, and there is no peace, saith the Lord GOD. Likewise, thou son of man, set thy face against the daughters of thy people, which prophesy out of their own heart; and prophesy thou against them, And say, Thus saith the Lord GOD; Woe to the women that sew pillows to all armholes, and make kerchiefs (veils) upon the head of every stature to hunt souls! Will ye hunt the souls of my people, and will ye save the souls alive that come unto you? And will ye pollute me among my people for handfuls of barley and for pieces of bread, to slay the souls that should not die, and to save the souls alive that should not live, by your lying to my people that hear your lies? Wherefore thus saith the Lord God; Behold, I am against your pillows, wherewith ye there hunt the souls to make them fly, and I will tear them from your arms, and will let the souls go, even the souls that ye hunt to make them fly. Your kerchiefs (veils) also will I tear, and deliver my people out of your hand, and they shall be no more in your hand to be hunted; and ye shall know that I am the LORD. Because with lies ye have made the heart of the righteous sad, whom I have not made sad; and strengthened the hands of the wicked, that he should not return from his wicked way, by promising him life: Therefore ye shall see no more vanity, nor divine divinations: for I will deliver my people out of your hand: and ye shall know that I am the LORD." - Ezekiel 13:16-23

Victory

City – Cry

The greatest victory that ever took place or ever will take place happened in a city. It happens to be the city that God views as the center of the world. That city is Jerusalem. And the victory was over sin, death, and hell when Christ gave out the cry "It is finished." Our faith in Him as our Saviour through His sacrifice is our victory.

"The words of the Preacher, the son of David, king in Jerusalem." - Ecclesiastes 1:1

"Then the moon shall be confounded, and the sun ashamed, when the LORD of hosts shall reign in mount Zion, and in Jerusalem, and before his ancients gloriously." - Isaiah 24:23

"When Jesus therefore had received the vinegar, he said, It is finished: and he bowed his head, and gave up the ghost." - John 19:30

"O death, where *is* thy sting? O grave, where *is* thy <u>victory</u>?" - 1 Corinthians 15:55

"For whatsoever is born of God overcometh the world: and this is the <u>victory</u> that overcometh the world, *even* our faith." - 1 John 5:4

"Him that overcometh will I make a pillar in the temple of my God, and he shall go no more out: and I will write upon him the name of my God, and the name of the city of my God, *which is* new Jerusalem, which cometh down out of heaven from my God: and *I will write upon him* my new name." - Revelation 3:12

Vile

Live

One of the biggest roadblocks for the spiritually lost are doubts that they can ever truly be saved because of a sinful past. But it's clear from reading the Gospels of the New Testament writers that anyone can be saved from sin. We are all sinners, and fall short of the glory of God, says the Bible. Jesus made himself a sacrifice, so that His blood would atone for our sins forever. One could be a <u>vile</u> sinner, spending most of his life as a murderer, thief, adulterer, idolater, and enemy of God. He could suddenly find the grace of God that will let him live eternally, forgiven and clean. But there's more to it than just saying that you believe. One has to truly believe in their heart that Jesus died for their sins.

So how does a new believer really know that they are saved? Because when they truly believe, their heart changes and their actions change. They start to live what they believe. The commandments of God are no longer a burden, and love (for God, others, and self) comes more naturally, thanks to the guidance of the Holy Spirit. Thus, it becomes obvious to oneself when they are truly saved.

Paul is a perfect example of a <u>vile</u> sinner who was persecuting Christians, including murdering some of them. He found the grace of God through Jesus on the road to Damascus. He zealously persecuted believers, yet he became a chosen Apostle and one of the greatest writers of the New Testament. Though a former Pharisee (trained in the Torah or law), Paul became the one to take the gospel to the Gentiles. This Jewish man became a man of faith in Jesus, and is one whom Christians around the world learn from and admire. *"The Vilest offender who truly believes, That moment, from Jesus, a pardon receives"*

"Purge me with hyssop, and I shall be clean: wash me, and I shall be whiter than snow." - Psalms 51:7

"For the <u>vile</u> person will speak villany, and his heart will work iniquity, to practice hypocrisy, and to utter error against the LORD, to make empty the soul of the hungry, and he will cause the drink of the thirsty to fail." - Isaiah 32:6

"Who shall change our <u>vile</u> body, that it may be fashioned like unto his glorious body, according to the working whereby he is able even to subdue all things unto himself." - Philippians 3:21

Vision

I & I (phonetically - two eyes) – Son – Is – Sion (Zion) – On

Jesus healed a man that had been blind from birth. When the former blind man was questioned by religious leaders he said, "I was blind, now I see." Everyone that is born again is able to make that same statement. Spiritually we need to see the Son with our two eyes. See Jesus and say yes!

The Son's <u>vision</u> is on Zion; which is the Apple of God's eye. Israel and Jerusalem are central to God's ultimate plan for redemption and the establishment of His Kingdom on earth. All Christians should share this <u>vision</u> and support Israel, especially they should support Messianic (Jesus is the Messiah) Ministry.

"If ye had known me, ye should have known my Father also: and from henceforth ye know him, and have seen him." - John 14:7

"If I had not done among them the works which none other man did, they had not had sin: but now have they both seen and hated both me and my Father." - John 15:24

W

Weather

Water – Awe – Wet – Earth – War - Wrath

Two thirds of planet earth is covered by water, which includes oceans, seas, rivers and lakes. Even through there are still some deserts, the Earth has been blessed to be a very wet planet. Ever since I took ninth grade science, I have been in awe of water; because it has some amazing characteristics. It is actually lighter than air, so why is it mostly in the form of a liquid (on Earth it is always also in solid and vapor form)? It is a dipolar molecule, so the molecules are attracted to each other and bond together. If water (H_2O) did not have this quality, it would not be in liquid or solid form. Also, water has the very unusual characteristic of expanding when it freezes instead of contracting. If it did not do this then ice would go to the bottom of lakes and rivers, and they would eventually freeze solid. Without water having these two special characteristics it would mean that this wonderful planet Earth would not be able to support life. This was by design, not accident. We should all be in awe of God who designed and created this amazing planet.

Our physical bodies are two-thirds water. And water is important spiritually, as well as physically, because of the rainbow, water baptism, and Jesus saying that He is the Living Water. The rainbow is a sign of a covenant God made with Noah that the world would not be destroyed by water again. Baptism by immersion is symbolic of being buried with Christ and risen as He was buried and raised from the dead. And "living water" is symbolic of receiving salvation and spiritual blessings from Jesus that will flow from you to others.

The Dead Sea has water flowing into it, but there is no way for water to flow out. It is in a desert area and the trench is probably the deepest on earth. At the northern end the water is 1,200 feet deep. The high temperatures there cause rapid evaporation that leaves minerals making the water seven times denser than ocean water. That is why it is highly concentrated with minerals and it is poisonous to drink. These Dead Sea minerals have economic value. Christians are not supposed to be stagnant like the Dead Sea, but rather have a spiritual flow like the river that brought the water to the Garden of Eden.

Weather can have a wide range of characteristics anywhere from calm and benign, to a tornado or hurricane. These changes in weather can have a huge impact including the outcome of a battle or war. The first battle of the American Revolutionary war was at Harlem Heights, New York. General Washington had his forces in the hills and there was no way to retreat. A tremendous storm of unusual strength and duration hit the area. The British general, not knowing the artillery capacity of the American colonists, made a decision during this storm to leave and go to Nova Scotia. The historian, James Flexner, said that had the storm not arrived and the battle continued the American Continental Army would have been easily defeated. I see evidence of the intervention of God on behalf of Washington and his army, throughout this eight year war that ended British rule in America.

God is able to use weather to bring wrath and judgment. Hurricane Katrina, that did such extensive damage to New Orleans and the Gulf coast area, was God's justifiable wrath against

America. Several days before this "natural" disaster occurred, I told my wife that God would soon be bringing a disaster to America. I based this on the heavy influence by the United States on Israel to give up the Gaza Strip (gauze –wound, strip – take away). I knew from a g-mail that this would happen, even though Scripture gives a serious warning against anyone dividing the land of Israel. The Prime Minister's name was the clue – Sharon (share own). I sent a letter to the Prime Minister nine months before the pullout stating that I knew it would take place.

I had been very involved with the Gaza issue for about a year before Hurricane Katrina hit. I knew that this hurricane was not going to be typical, because it was going to bring God's wrath and judgment. God was fully justified to demonstrate His displeasure with our country. Gaza was the main issue, but New Orleans had a very immoral parade scheduled for Monday, and this city had a long reputation for crime and sin. Also, by hitting the Gulf Coast and affecting the price of oil, this disaster was felt throughout this entire country. It was a judgment on America and a message for Americans. It was a time for salvation through judgment, but most churches and individuals missed the message and opportunity.

On Saturday night the hurricane was a category five and headed straight for New Orleans. I am sure that many people were praying. I did an intercessory prayer stating that God's wrath was justified, but I asked for mercy anyway. I knew a lot about this situation since I had been involved for a year, and felt that I was in a position to make an effective prayer. After praying, I sensed that God was going to do something, but I did not know what. This was especially puzzling since I knew that God's judgment was an appropriate response for the Gaza giveaway. When I got up on Sunday morning I turned on the television and the very first thing I heard was, "the meteorologists are scratching their heads because a puff of warm air changed Hurricane Katrina from a 5 to a 4, and caused it to hit below New Orleans." Well, I knew where that air had come from. This hurricane caused the greatest disaster in the history of America, and yet there was mercy because the death toll could have been tens of thousands higher. Somebody's prayer was heard and answered. Make no mistake God can bring judgment through the <u>weather</u>.

What about all the fuss over global warming? Is <u>weather</u> controlled by God or can man have an influence? *USA Today* had an article by Susan Page stating that a poll taken in 46 countries and Palestinian territories identified environmental problems such as increasing global warming as the world's greatest threat. The only problem here is that the earth's temperature is directly related to Sun spot activity. When Sun spots increase, the temperature goes up, and when they decrease temperature goes down. The correct answer is that God, not man, controls the weather on planet earth. Planet has plan in the word and control of the weather was part of that plan!

"And a river went out of Eden to water the garden; and from thence it was parted, and became into four heads." - Genesis 2:10

"And said unto me, Behold, I will make thee fruitful, and multiply thee, and I will make of thee a multitude of people; and will give this land to thy seed after thee *for* an everlasting possession." - Genesis 48:4

"Be strong and of a good courage: for unto this people shalt thou divide for an inheritance the land, which I sware unto their fathers to give them." - Joshua 1:6

"Riches profit not in the day of wrath: but righteousness delivereth from death." - Proverbs 11:4

"Jesus answered and said unto her, If thou knewest the gift of God, and who it is that saith to thee, Give me to drink; thou wouldest have asked of him, and he would have given thee living water.

"He that believeth on me, as the scripture hath said, out of his belly shall flow rivers of living water." - John 7:38

"And he arose, and rebuked the wind, and said unto the sea, Peace, be still. And the wind ceased, and there was a great calm." - Mark 4:39

"For the wrath of God is revealed from heaven against all ungodliness and unrighteousness of men, who hold the truth in unrighteousness;" - Romans 1:18

"This is he that came by water and blood, *even* Jesus Christ; not by water only, but by water and blood. And it is the Spirit that beareth witness, because the Spirit is truth." - 1 John 5:6

"And he said unto me, It is done. I am Alpha and Omega, the beginning and the end. I will give unto him that is athirst of the fountain of the water of life freely." - Revelation 21:6

"And the Spirit and the bride say, Come. And let him that heareth say, Come. And let him that is athirst come. And whosoever will, let him take the water of life freely." - Revelation 22:17

Well

El (God) - We

We are never really <u>well</u> without God.

"If thou doest <u>well</u>, shalt thou not be accepted? and if thou doest not <u>well</u>, sin lieth at the door. And unto thee *shall be* his desire, and thou shalt rule over him." - Genesis 4:7

"Let the elders that rule <u>well</u> be counted worthy of double honour, especially they who labour in the word and doctrine." - 1 Timothy 5:17

Wickedness

Sick – Die – Sin – Wide

Because man has a sin nature <u>wickedness</u> is wide spread in the earth. Many choose the wide way that leads them to destruction. Many get sick and die because of the <u>wickedness</u> of man. Many like to say that man is basically good, but that both contradicts scripture and observed history.

"And GOD saw that the <u>wickedness</u> of man *was* great in the earth, and *that* every imagination of the thoughts of his heart *was* only evil continually." - Genesis 6:5

"The soul that sinneth, it shall die. The son shall not bear the iniquity of the father, neither shall the father bear the iniquity of the son: the righteousness of the righteous shall be upon him, and the <u>wickedness</u> of the wicked shall be upon him." - Ezekiel 18:20

"Again, when the wicked *man* turneth away from his <u>wickedness</u> that he hath committed, and doeth that which is lawful and right, he shall save his soul alive." - Ezekiel 18:27

"Enter ye in at the strait gate: for *wide is* the gate, and broad *is* the way, that leadeth to destruction, and many there be which go in thereat:" - Matthew 7:13

Wisdom

Sow - Dim - *"Sounds like "We Is Dumb"*

Reading Scripture will allow the Spirit to sow seeds of <u>wisdom</u> within us, so that we may (1 Corinthians 2:4) bear fruit to further the Kingdom. However, if your <u>wisdom</u> comes from the things of the world, you'll be just another dim wit! Man's knowledge compared to God's is foolishness, so <u>wisdom</u> that is from man and not from Scripture is flawed. God is all knowing, and real <u>wisdom</u> is from God. Without God we is dumb!

"Folly *is* joy to *him that is* destitute of <u>wisdom</u>: but a man of understanding walketh uprightly." - Proverbs 15:21

"And when he was come into his own country, he taught them in their synagogue, insomuch that they were astonished, and said, Whence hath this *man* this <u>wisdom</u>, and *these* mighty works?" - Matthew 13:54

"For Christ sent me not to baptize, but to preach the gospel: not with <u>wisdom</u> of words, lest the cross of Christ should have no effect. For the preaching of the cross is just foolishness to those who are dying; but to us who are saved it is the power of God. For it is written, 'I will destroy the wisdom of the wise, and will bring to nothing the understanding of the prudent.' Where is the wise? Where is the scribe? Where is the disputer of this world? Has God not made foolish the <u>wisdom</u> of this world? For seeing that in the <u>wisdom</u> of God, the world by it's <u>wisdom</u> did not know God, it pleased God by the foolishness of preaching to save them that believe."- 1 Corinthians 1:17-21

"And my speech and my preaching *was* not with enticing words of man's <u>wisdom</u>, but in demonstration of the Spirit and of power:" - 1 Corinthians 2:4

Withstand

Stand – With

Crisis and suffering are a part of life, and spiritual warfare is ever present in the world around us. No one, even Jesus Christ, was immune from it. But when we stand with God, we can <u>withstand</u> trials. There might still be pain and hurt. But there will also be a special joy and peace that only the Holy Spirit can provide, giving us a huge advantage in tough situations.

God is our armor of defense, and our sword of offense. He protects us from evil, and He fights it off as well. It would be unwise for a man to run into battle in just his boxers, waving a plastic sword. Without God, that is what people do. And without His word we have no defense, we have no sword, and we will never withstand the attacks of the offender.

"And said, O LORD God of our fathers, *art* not thou God in heaven? and rulest *not* thou over all the kingdoms of the heathen? and in thine hand *is there not* power and might, so that none is able to withstand thee?" - 2 Chronicles 20:6

"For we wrestle not against flesh and blood, but against principalities, against powers, against the rulers of the darkness of this world, against spiritual wickedness in high places. Wherefore take unto you the whole armor of God, that you may be able to withstand in the evil day, and having done all, to stand. Stand therefore, having your loins girt about with truth, and having on the breastplate of righteousness; And your feet shod with the preparation of the gospel of peace; Above all, taking the shield of faith, wherewith you shall be able to quench all the fiery darts of the wicked. And take the helmet of salvation, and the sword of the Spirit, which is the word of God: Praying always With all prayer and supplication in the Spirit, and watching there unto with all perseverance and supplication for all saints; " - Ephesians 6:12-18

"And the peace of God, which passeth all understanding, shall keep your hearts and minds through Christ Jesus." - Philippians 4:7

Witness

News – New – Sent - Win

As Christians, it is our duty to lead the lost to a new life in Christ. We become a witness to others of the gospel or good news. When a Christian plants a seed of faith in a lost person's soul, the hope is for that seed to grow into a vine rooted in Christ, that will someday bear the fruit that carries the very same seed by which they were saved. The common term used by professing Christians who lead others to Christ, is to win souls to Jesus. Jesus' disciples were the first witnesses. They were sent by Jesus to tell the world of the good news of His death, burial, and resurrection. Likewise, we as Christians are sent by God to share the good news and to win souls to Jesus.

"And Pharaoh sent, and called for Moses and Aaron, and said unto them, I have sinned this time: the LORD *is* righteous, and I and my people *are* wicked." - Exodus 9:27

"And this gospel of the kingdom shall be preached in all the world for a <u>witness</u> unto all nations; and then shall the end come." - Matthew 24:14

"And these are they which are sown on good ground; such as hear the word, and receive *it*, and bring forth fruit, some thirtyfold, some sixty, and some an hundred." - Mark 4:20

"I am the true vine, and my Father is the vinedresser. Every branch in me that bears no fruit he takes away: and every branch that bears fruit, he prunes it, that it may bring forth more fruit" - John 15:1-2

"And they said, Cornelius the centurion, a just man, and one that feareth God, and of good report among all the nation of the Jews, was warned from God by an holy angel to send for thee into his house, and to hear words of thee." - Acts 10:22

"And how shall they preach, except they be sent? as it is written, How beautiful are the feet of them that preach the gospel of peace, and bring glad tidings of good things!" - Romans 10:15

"And sent Timotheus, our brother, and minister of God, and our fellow labourer in the gospel of Christ, to establish you, and to comfort you concerning your faith:" - 1 Thessalonians 3:2

"Remember that Jesus Christ of the seed of David was raised from the dead according to my gospel:" - 2 Timothy 2:8

Words

Dor (Ph. - Door) – Sword – Sow - Rod

Jesus, the second person of the Godhead, is called the Word. This tells me that words are probably rather significant to God. The Holy Bible is the inspired, inerrant Word of God; and Scripture says that God will preserve His Word to all generations.

Today, there are many translations or versions of the Bible, but I prefer the King James Version (KJV) for several reasons. Firstly, it definitely meets the requirement of being powerful and sharper than a two edged sword, which indicates an anointing on the writers. This translation and the writing of Shakespeare are the highest quality writing ever produced in the English language. Secondly, it has proven itself effective over a long period of time – several centuries. Thirdly, the KJV is in the public domain (no copywriter royalties or permission to use is needed,) and it is not influenced by Wall Street. Fourthly, it is translated primarily from the Textus Receptus manuscript. I am suspect of later discovered manuscripts, like Alexandrian, used for "modern" translations. And lastly, I have found the word choices by the KJV translation scholars to be reliable and best when tested by Gmail.

For those that think the KJV is too hard to read, please understand that it starts at the fifth grade reading level with Genesis, and ends at the eighth grade level with Revelation. Centuries have proven that people best understand the Bible in their common language; therefore I do not feel that knowledge of Latin, Greek or Hebrew is at all necessary for biblical understanding. I realize that knowledge of these languages may benefit Christian scholars; but I am convinced that for most of us foreign language is not necessary and can even be confusing. When Governor Pilate put "KING OF THE JEWS" in three languages on the sign on the cross, it was so that everyone could read it in their own language. When someone tells you what the

Greek means, they usually have made a choice based on their own bias. I have confidence in the KJV, to provide the understanding to convert the soul, and to provide the instruction that will bring a close personal relationship with God. Amen.

Jesus taught a parable about a sower that when out to sow his seed. The seed is the Word of God and all believers should sow this seed. When the Word of God lands on good ground (hearts) and is kept, it brings forth fruit for the Kingdom.

There will be a "second coming" of Jesus Christ, and it will be quite different from His coming as a Lamb to be sacrificed for our sins. He will establish His earthly Kingdom and rule the nations with a rod of iron from Jerusalem. Christians are supposed to "watch and pray" for His coming, and not be taken by surprise. Many will not be expecting it, or be prepared when the Lord returns.

When will this event occur? No man knows the day or hour; however Christians are supposed to see the signs that will be evidence that this could happen soon. It could not have happened until after Israel was a nation once again. That happened in May 1948, and was the fulfillment of a 2,500 year old prophecy. These signs of His coming are very evident today, so I believe that this could happen in the life time of most that are living today. Are you watching and praying?

"So shall my <u>word</u> be that goeth forth out of my mouth: it shall not return unto me void, but it shall accomplish that which I please, and it shall prosper *in the thing* whereto I sent it." - Isaiah 55:11

"And I will make them one nation in the land upon the mountains of Israel; and one king shall be king to them all: and they shall be no more two nations, neither shall they be divided into two kingdoms any more at all:" - Ezekiel 37:22

"Verily, verily, I say unto you, He that entereth not by the door into the sheepfold, but climbeth up some other way, the same is a thief and a robber. But he that entereth in by the door is the shepherd of the sheep." - John 10:1-2

213

"I am the door: by me if any man enter in, he shall be saved, and shall go in and out, and find pasture." - John 10:9

"Now the parable is this: The seed is the <u>word</u> of God." - Luke 8:11

"Heaven and earth shall pass away: but my <u>words</u> shall not pass away." - Luke 21:33

"And a superscription also was written over him in letters of Greek, and Latin, and Hebrew, THIS IS THE KING OF THE JEWS." - Luke 23:38

"Behold, I stand at the door, and knock: if any man hear my voice, and open the door, I will come in to him, and will sup with him, and he with me." - Revelation 3:20

"And I will scatter you among the heathen, and will draw out a sword after you: and your land shall be desolate, and your cities waste." - Leviticus 26:33

"For the word of God *is* quick, and powerful, and sharper than any two edged sword, piercing even to the dividing asunder of soul and spirit, and of the joints and marrow, and *is* a discerner of the thoughts and intents of the heart." - Hebrews 4:12

"And he had in his right hand seven stars: and out of his mouth went a sharp two-edged sword: and his countenance *was* as the sun shineth in his strength." - Revelation 1:16

"Thou shalt break them with a rod of iron; thou shalt dash them in pieces like a potter's vessel." - Psalms 2:9

"Yea, though I walk through the valley of the shadow of death, I will fear no evil: for thou *art* with me; thy rod and thy staff they comfort me." - Psalms 23:4

"That then the LORD thy God will turn thy captivity, and have compassion upon thee, and will return and gather thee from all the nations, whither the LORD thy God hath scattered thee." - Deuteronomy 30:3

"Then shall the kingdom of heaven be likened unto ten virgins, which took their lamps, and went forth to meet the bridegroom. And five of them were wise, and five *were* foolish. They that *were* foolish took their lamps, and took no oil with them: But the wise took oil in their vessels with their lamps. While the bridegroom tarried, they all slumbered and slept. And at midnight there was a cry made, Behold, the bridegroom cometh; go ye out to meet him. Then all those virgins arose, and trimmed their lamps. And the foolish said unto the wise, Give us of your oil; for our lamps are gone out. But the wise answered, saying, *Not so*; lest there be not enough for us and you: but go ye rather to them that sell, and buy for yourselves. And while they went to buy, the bridegroom came; and they that were ready went in with him to the marriage: and the door was shut. Afterward came also the other virgins, saying, Lord, Lord, open to us. But he answered and said, Verily I say unto you, I know you not. Watch therefore, for ye know neither the day nor the hour wherein the Son of man cometh." - Matthew 1-13

"Watch ye therefore, and pray always, that ye may be accounted worthy to escape all these things that shall come to pass, and to stand before the Son of man." - Luke 21:36

"And out of his mouth goeth a sharp sword, that with it he should smite the nations: and he shall rule them with a rod of iron: and he treadeth the winepress of the fierceness and wrath of Almighty God." - Revelation 19:15

World

Lord – Word

The reason we are allowed to live in this <u>world</u> is because it has the Lord in it and the Word. The Lord Jesus Christ came and lived a sinless life in an imperfect <u>world</u>. He faced the temptations that we face, and set the example for us to follow. We also have truth revealed in the Word of God. But is that enough? There's the blood of Jesus that covers sins. There's the Word of God, which is the foundation of faith, and it provides instruction in righteousness and a blessed hope.

In this <u>world</u> we face disappointments, disease, death, suffering, war, crime, lies, false religions, greed, corruption, temptations, and evil. The Bible says that we are in the world, but not of the world. We are not supposed to love this <u>world</u> too much, and are not to expect to be too accepted by the <u>world</u>. This is the same <u>world</u> that rejected its Creator, Jesus Christ. The <u>world</u> is worldly and not friendly to the things of God. A born again believer is just a pilgrim here, because we are a citizen of heaven. As authentic Christians we are aware that we only live is this <u>world</u> temporarily, and that our permanent address is in heaven.

All those that have the spiritual birth are sealed with the Holy Spirit at that time of regeneration. The Holy Spirit is the key to being able to follow the Lord, and to love and understand the word; so that we can be on Earth and not be so <u>world</u>ly. He is the link between the two, enabling us to be more like the Lord and understanding the word. Living a spirit filled life in relationship with God is a far superior experience to an ordinary secular life. A spiritual life will help us get the best out of our time in this <u>world</u>.

The Bible states "For where your treasure is, there will your heart be also." (Matthew 6:21) We can not "take it with us" when we die, but we can "pay it forward." In heaven there are no sins on our record, but there is record of works that will determine a reward. Why would anyone place their focus on building up temporary wealth, when an eternal treasure is a promise? I think a reasonable accumulation of wealth in this <u>world</u> is prudent, but our love should be for God and not for money. We should want to have far greater asset value on the other side than on this side. Where is your heart and treasure?

One problem is that wealth tends to make wealthy people "self reliant." They might trust more in their own resources instead of on God. I truly would not trade places with a billionaire if they were not born again. God owns everything, and that is why you are not allowed to take anything with you at death. It stays here because it is not actually yours. Certainly there are individuals that have great wealth that are also spiritual and not worldly. They would understand that money and material processions are not eternal.

The most important commandments in the Bible are "Love the Lord God with all your heart, soul, mind, and strength" and "Love your neighbor as yourself." Unfortunately, most of the inhabitants of this world are not going to value or practice those ideal absolutes. Scripture reveals that conditions in the world will get worse and worse before the end comes, and the Lord returns. The end times events and conditions are observable today. Many prophecies have been fulfilled since I was born in 1943.

This once great nation was founded on Christian beliefs, laws, and principles. America showed the world the economic benefits of freedom along a large middle class. America was a leader in spreading the Gospel around the globe. Today, America is slipping more and more away from God. Now this nation produces eighty percent of the world's pornography. Now this nation has the distinction of spreading pornography around the globe. Pornography does not even have a "sin" tax like tobacco and alcohol. Are our leaders asleep? There have been fifty million "legal" abortions in America making this land polluted with innocent blood. The disregard for the sanctity of human life is the world, and a violation a God's will. In World War II, seventy-five percent of all the children in Britain were in Sunday School. Today, only four percent of the people in Britain go to church. Britain is the mother and America is the daughter. And we are not far behind in abandoning God and slipping further into worldly materialism and decadence.

217

"And shed innocent blood, *even* the blood of their sons and of their daughters, whom they sacrificed unto the idols of Canaan: and the land was polluted with blood." - Psalm 106:38

"Their feet run to evil, and they make haste to shed innocent blood: their thoughts *are* thoughts of iniquity; wasting and destruction *are* in their paths." - Isaiah 59:7

"And that which fell among thorns are they, which, when they have heard, go forth, and are choked with cares and riches and pleasures of *this* life, and bring no fruit to perfection." - Luke 8:14

"And he answering said, Thou shalt love the Lord thy God with all thy heart, and with all thy soul, and with all thy strength, and with all thy mind; and thy neighbour as thyself." - Luke 10:27

"I have given them thy Word; and the world hath hated them, because they are not of the world, even as I am not of the world. I pray not that thou shouldest take them out of the world, but that thou shouldest keep them from the evil." - John 17:14-15

"Ye adulterers and adulteresses, know ye not that the friendship of the world is enmity with God? whosoever therefore will be a friend of the world is the enemy of God." - James 4:4

Worshiping

Who - Is – Show – Sing – Worship (Ph: War ship)

Why should we worship God? Is it because He needs for us to worship him? An emphatic no! In fact, it's us who needs to worship Him. We benefit enormously from worship. It brings us close to God, and equips us for spiritual battle. That is why worship sounds like war ship. The word worship comes from the Anglo-Saxon word worthship, meaning worthy. "Let them praise the name of the LORD: for his name alone is excellent; his glory *is* above the earth and heaven." (Ps.148:13)

Real worship requires knowledge of the true God. When you know the creator God you know that God alone is worthy of worship. No created being should ever be exalted to receive worship. Worship is the way of acknowledging who He is in all of His glory and power. He is the all powerful, all knowing, all present, and eternal God. Worship is us giving back love straight from our hearts, for the love, grace and mercy that He regularly shows to us. God is not impressed with vain repetitions. Love is the heart of worship, and true worship is from the heart, soul, and spirit of the worshipper.

So, if worship is directed towards God, why is it us who are on the needing end of it, and not God? It's because God doesn't need anything. He created the universe, and because of the three persons of the Godhead, He has love and fellowship! But we do need Him, and everything we do in worship benefits us. Through worship we get to know God better and learn to hear His voice. Through worship, we acknowledge the fact that we do need Him, and in return, He provides. Through worship, we show that we are obedient to Him, which allows us to be used by Him. Through worship, we are saying "You are our protector and defender, and our sword and our armor. You are like a great war ship that defends us from the enemy!" It also shows that we fear (fear, awe, respect) the Lord, and we know that He is sovereign and greater than any other force or power.

Therefore, when we sing, pray, study God's word, and fellowship with others, we are obediently worshiping God. Even recognizing the beauty of a sunset or colors and patterns in the sky and attributing it's splendor to God, is a form of worship.

"You alone are the LORD; You have made heaven, The heaven of heavens, with all their host, The earth and everything on it, The seas and all that is in them, And You preserve them all. The host of heaven worships You." - Nehemiah 9:6

"The LORD is my strength and my shield; my heart trusted in him, and I am helped: therefore my heart greatly rejoiceth; and with my song will I praise him." - Psalm 28:7

"God is a Spirit: and they that worship him must worship him in spirit and in truth." - John 4:24

X

There are no X words in Scripture in English and therefore no hologram message from any word that starts with this twenty-fourth letter of the English alphabet. The Greek work Xulon means Book of Life, but I do not do Greek GMAIL.

Y

Yeshua

Shu (Ph. - Shoe) - Yes
Hebrew:
יֵשׁוּעַ – Yeshua
שׁוּעַ – Shua – A desperate cry for help
שַׁי – Shai – A gift

Jesus is the English name for Joshua, which was the Greek name for Yeshua. Yeshua was the actual name that Christ would have been known as in the land of Israel. Today, this is the name that is used for Christ in Messianic Congregations, and by a very small number of other Christians. Messianic congregations primarily consist of Jewish members that are believers in the Messiah or Yeshua. There are more Jews coming to faith in Yeshua now than at any other time.

The Book of Ruth was written about 3,000 years ago during the reign of David. Ruth was a Moabitess woman. She was a Gentile that was rescued from childlessness and poverty by Boaz, the Jewish kinsman-redeemer. This book of the Bible is an exciting account of romantic love between a Jew and a Gentile. Ruth epitomizes godly womanhood, beauty, devotion, gratitude, and spiritual sensitivity. Ruth's commitment to Naomi, her poverty stricken mother-in-law, and Naomi's God was rewarded. Ruth was blessed by the love of a wealthy husband, the joy of motherhood, and became a member of the Messianic lineage.

Therefore, her redemption was not just physical, but also spiritual. Boaz was a type of <u>Yesuha</u>, the kinsman-redeemer that would arrive a thousand years later and redeem man from sin. Boaz had to take off his shoe and give it to make his redemption official. As Ruth was so profoundly needy when she was redeemed by Boaz, so are all sinners profoundly in need of the Redeemer. Seek truth and say yes to the Redeemer.

The Hebrew word for Salvation is Yeshuah ישועה This is Yeshua's (Jesus) name with an extra letter at the end (ה). So in the word Salvation, we not only have the name of Messiah, but also Lamb – שה (Seh) but also the word for Work (Spiritual work) –עשה (Aseh). From a Jewish perspective, this is defined as a Positive Command. Jesus came to show us how to do good works (his whole public ministry was filled with these works). Also, on the word Shua – שוע which is a desperate cry for help, the Modern Hebrew dictionary defines it also as "to cry out to, to implore; *to need desperately.*" We all have a desperate need Jesus or Yeshua for our salvation.

"Then went Boaz up to the gate, and sat him down there: and, behold, the kinsman of whom Boaz spake came by; unto whom he said, Ho, such a one! turn aside, sit down here. And he turned aside, and sat down. And he took ten men of the elders of the city, and said, Sit ye down here. And they sat down. And he said unto the kinsman, Naomi, that is come again out of the country of Moab, selleth a parcel of land, which *was* our brother Elimelech's: And I thought to advertise thee, saying, Buy *it* before the inhabitants, and before the elders of my people. If thou wilt redeem *it*, redeem *it*: but if thou wilt not redeem *it, then* tell me, that I may know: for *there is* none to redeem *it* beside thee; and I *am* after thee. And he said, I will redeem *it*. Then said Boaz, What day thou buyest the field of the hand of Naomi, thou must buy *it* also of Ruth the Moabitess, the wife of the dead, to raise up the name of the dead upon his inheritance. And the kinsman said, I cannot redeem *it* for myself, lest I mar mine own inheritance: redeem thou my right to thyself; for I cannot redeem *it*. Now this *was the manner* in former time in Israel concerning redeeming and concerning changing, for to confirm all things; a man plucked off his shoe, and gave *it* to his neighbour: and this *was* a testimony in Israel. Therefore the kinsman said unto Boaz, Buy *it* for thee. So he drew off his shoe. And Boaz said unto the elders, and *unto* all the people, Ye *are* witnesses this day, that I have bought all that *was* Elimelech's, and all that *was* Chilion's and Mahlon's, of the hand of Naomi. Moreover Ruth the Moabitess, the wife of Mahlon, have I purchased to be my wife, to raise up the name of the dead upon his inheritance, that the name of the dead be not cut off from among his brethren, and from the gate of his place: ye *are* witnesses this day. And all the people that *were* in the gate, and the elders, said, *We are* witnesses. The LORD make the woman that is come into thine house like Rachel and like Leah, which two did build the house of Israel: and do thou worthily in Ephratah, and be famous in Bethlehem: And let thy house be like the house of Pharez, whom Tamar bare unto Judah, of the seed which the LORD shall give thee of this young woman. So Boaz took Ruth, and she was his wife: and when he went in unto her, the LORD gave her conception, and she bare a son. And the women said unto Naomi, Blessed *be* the LORD, which hath not left thee this day without a kinsman, that his name may be famous in Israel. And he shall be unto thee a restorer of *thy* life, and a nourisher of thine old age: for thy daughter in law, which loveth thee, which is better to thee than seven sons, hath born him. And Naomi took the child, and laid it in her bosom, and became nurse unto it. And the women her neighbours gave it a name, saying, There is a son born to Naomi; and they called his name Obed: he *is* the father of Jesse, the father of David" - Ruth 4:1-17.

"For I know *that* my redeemer liveth, and *that* he shall stand at the latter *day* upon the earth:" - Job 19:25

"Thus saith the LORD, thy redeemer, and he that formed thee from the womb, I *am* the LORD that maketh all *things*; that stretcheth forth the heavens alone; that spreadeth abroad the earth by myself;" - Isaiah 44:24

"For thy Maker *is* thine husband; the LORD of hosts *is* his name; and thy Redeemer the Holy One of Israel; The God of the whole earth shall he be called." - Isaiah 54:5

"And when these things begin to come to pass, then look up, and lift up your heads; for your redemption draweth nigh." - Luke 21:28

Z

Zion

I (Ph. – Eye) – On

Because I care about the God of Abraham, Isaac, and Jacob, I keep a close watch and a close eye on <u>Zion</u>. Israel is the apple of God's eye, so He is keeping a close watch on Jerusalem, or <u>Zion</u> the Capital city. Israel is the only covenant nation on earth, and this small nation will receive divine protection when their existence is jeopardized by enemies. Israel was reestablished as a nation in 1948, and this event fulfilled a 2,500 year old prophecy to the letter.

<u>Zion</u> is an enigma because it has no river, no port, or no major industry, and yet it is highly valued by a majority of the worlds' population as represented by their religions. This ancient city has spiritual significance, first for the Jews, second for the Christians, and third for the Muslims. These three groups represent over three billion followers. It is a very important key to end time events, and is a truly important place. Even a casual

observer of the news will recognize that the Middle East is prominent in reported activity.

Following the Battle of Armageddon that will occur near Jerusalem, Yeshua will be crowned King of Israel. His earthly throne will be a continuation of the Davidic monarchy, and Yeshua will rule the entire world from Zion.

There is on going spiritual warfare, and this will increase as the end approaches. Always above the physical battle that you can see, there is a spiritual battle that mortal eyes cannot see. As a student of eschatology, I am aware of the tremendous attacks that Israel will experience prior to the Messiah becoming King.

The land of Zion is part of an eternal inheritance of the Jewish people. I love America, but I am convinced that Israel is of far greater importance even than the USA. Satan is God's enemy, and Israel and Zion is the prime target that he wants to conquer. Now is the time to join sides, and the right side will support Zion. "For Zion's sake will I not hold my peace, and for Jerusalem's sake I will not rest." Isaiah 62:1

At this late hour, all believers should support the Holy Land with prayer, and financial support, especially to Messianic congregations. Just as Paul told the early churches to provide financially for the church at Jerusalem (Zion), we should do the same today. Churches and individual believers have a stake in this nation, and need to show God where you stand. Already the blessings that the world has received through God's chosen people is unequalled by any other nation or people in history. I am assured by Scripture that more great spiritual blessings are yet to come from Zion!

"Nevertheless David took the strong hold of Zion: the same *is* the city of David." - 2 Samuel 5:7

"Oh that the salvation of Israel *were come* out of Zion! when the LORD bringeth back the captivity of his people, Jacob shall rejoice, *and* Israel shall be glad." - Psalms 14:7

"Do good in thy good pleasure unto Zion: build thou the walls of Jerusalem." - Psalms 51:18

"Remember thy congregation, *which* thou hast purchased of old; the rod of thine inheritance, *which* thou hast redeemed; this mount Zion, wherein thou hast dwelt." - Psalms 74:2

"Behold, he that keepeth Israel shall neither slumber nor sleep." - Psalm 121:4

"For thus saith the LORD of hosts; After the glory hath he sent me unto the nations which spoiled you: for he that toucheth you toucheth the apple of his eye." - Zechariah 2:8

"And it shall come to pass, *that he that is* left in Zion, and *he that* remaineth in Jerusalem, shall be called holy, *even* every one that is written among the living in Jerusalem:" - Isaiah 4:3

"Thy watchmen shall lift up the voice; with the voice together shall they sing: for they shall see eye to eye, when the LORD shall bring again Zion." - Isaiah 52:8

Summary of Gmail Word Count by Letter

A – 11	B - 10	C - 13	D – 11
E - 7	F - 7	G - 6	H – 5
I - 8	J – 5	K - 2	L – 5
M - 5	N - 5	O - 3	P – 12
Q - 1	R - 11	S - 13	T – 6
U - 2	V - 4	W - 8	X – 0
Y - 1	Z - 1	Total =	162

SECTION THREE

CHAPTER ONE

THE MIRACLE OF SPIRITUAL BIRTH . . .

The following is my personal testimony about the conversion experience that I had over twenty-five years ago. You are not a Christian because you were raised that way, because you belong to a church, or because you have a high standard of morality. You are only a Christian if you have had the supernatural experience of being spiritually born again. "Jesus answered and said unto him, Verily, verily, I say unto thee, Except a man be born again, he cannot see the kingdom of God." (John 3:3)

You are not a Christian because you think that this would provide you with a nice lifestyle. If the teachings of Jesus are not true, then Christians should be pitied above all people, because we would have used our life for a false cause. However, the Apostles, and countless thousands of Christians from every corner of the planet have followed the faith, even to death when that was necessary.

Becoming a member of God's family is supernatural and similar to getting Gmail because God, the Holy Spirit, must draw you and give you the faith that is life saving. "For by grace are ye saved through faith; and that not of yourselves: *it is* the gift of God." Therefore, true spirituality is a profound and supernatural experience. Once you have true faith in God I am convinced that you will never lose it.

> "Nor height, nor depth, nor any other creature, shall
> be able to separate us from the love of God, which
> is in Christ Jesus our Lord." - Romans 8:39

The two thieves on crosses along with Jesus reviled him. One of them, as the day progressed, went through a change, "And Jesus said unto him, Verily I say unto thee, To day shalt thou be with me in paradise." I believe that this criminal experienced five things, in this order: <u>reviled</u> God, <u>recognized</u> God, <u>repented</u> (changed his mind) to God, <u>responded</u> (called out to God - public proclamation of the change that had happened) and was <u>regenerated</u> by God (new birth) and inherited the promises of God. None of this was by works, but by grace. I experienced that same pattern and I feel that all non-believers revile God and also experience the following four steps in the pattern to receive eternal life and live in paradise or heaven. Without the cross there is no gospel message. Where are you in the salvation steps?

Once you truly believe, you may be disappointed by people, churches, and even yourself, but not by God. Through genuine faith you believe in God with your head and more importantly your heart. The heart represents the center and essence of your soul; of who you are. True Christians are convinced by supernatural faith, as well as empirical evidence and experience, that truth is found in the person of Jesus Christ, the only begotten Son of God the Father.

One day when I was a young boy around age eight, I was walking down the street within a few blocks of my home (in the 1940's kids had more freedom to play throughout their neighborhood and I had extensive freedom of this kind.) I saw an older man sitting on a front porch with a Bible in his lap and our eyes connected. I immediately had the thought that some day that book was going to be very important to me. It was impacting enough that I never forgot the experience. In reflection, I think that it might have been an angel, because he seemed to know me. If it had been an angel no one else would have even seem him. Did this indicate that God knew I would be called to write a book about the Bible over fifty years later?

My parents required pretty regular Sunday school and worship service attendance for me, but many times they did not attend themselves. I do not remember discussions about God from my parents or from any of my many relatives. I know I must have been taught to pray because there is a photo of me praying as a young boy. I do not remember hearing family accounts of answered prayer, etc. There was a Bible in the home, but I did not see it read. I had heard that I had a great grandmother that read the Bible daily. There was neither a library of Christian books nor any Christian radio. There was no evidence of a passion for God. I had a grandfather who started life in Ireland. He went to church every Sunday, but he did not talk to me about God. He took a food basket to someone needy every Sunday afternoon. He was a believer and helped many families. He has now been with the Lord for over fifty years and my father followed him at the age of eighty-six.

At age eleven I was baptized with my whole immediate family. This was not believer's baptism because I was told we were getting baptized. That type of baptism just gets you wet. Later, the pastor of this church called me into his office and brought up about me going into the ministry. He said that when I spoke in front of the church that everyone in the church sat up and listened. He said they did not even do that for him. At that time I had not given a thought to ministry.

Once, around age twelve, while sitting in a Sunday school class, I wanted to know so badly if what they were telling me about Jesus was true. I felt like every cell in my body wanted to know if He was really God. I just was not able to know if it was true or not. I just could not take the teachers word and I was not able to believe.

When I was in high school, I did not become popular until my senior year, and this next account was a year or two before that. I was attending a Presbyterian church that was liberal; therefore the environment was as confusing as convicting. They had a youth group and I was given an assignment to present a lesson on the parable of the talents. The lesson was going over the allotted time and Sara Jane, who was a very popular girl in my high school said, "Don't stop."

There was a church leader there and because of the impact of this lesson I was added to the church Evangelistic Committee. I was amused because all of the other members were adults and had important positions in the church. I never attended a meeting or went on a visitation. Unfortunately, this church did not draw me toward believing because I felt that the teaching was not truth and not consistent.

At age twenty-one my immediate supervisor at work was a committed soul-winner. Later he became a pastor. He was the most convincing Christian I had ever met, and I was around him regularly. After months of his witnessing I made a decision that I would become a Christian and I prayed the sinner's prayer. The problem with that was I had made the <u>response</u> where I needed the step of <u>recognition</u>. It was premature because I responded before I had truly recognized God. We do the recognizing and following that we have a natural responding through faith. Then, God in His way and in His time shows that we are indeed regenerated. For the man on the cross the process took hours, but he found out he was saved immediately after he called out to Jesus.

I have known only a few individuals that wake up lost and get through the salvation process or steps in one day. My personal experience and observation is that for most it takes longer than a day and trying to hasten the process can be detrimental rather than beneficial.

I think get saved fast and selling of response is one of the biggest errors of modern evangelism. The model did not come from the Bible. Jesus did not ask the thief to make a response. No one asked me either when I had my real conversion. It came naturally from following the process of the other steps. The pray and get saved or give your life message has been so prevalent I wonder how many have others have made the same subtle premature substitution of response when they should be completing prior steps; especially the real recognition of God.

I thought that I was a true Christian and I did "Christian things." I did not drink alcohol, rejected sexual advances from young women, and read the Bible daily. I put up a good front, but in reality I had some confusion, doubts, and unhappiness. I prayed every night, but was not aware of any prayers answered. I did not consciously experience God. Still, I had some influence on others because they saw something that they felt that they did not have. In reality, I did not have it either.

This brief period of my life as a practicing Christian became extremely difficult for me. I knew the Bible taught about

Satan sifting a person and I felt like that had happened to me. I felt loneliness with an intensity that I had never known. I had tried Christianity and it did not work for me. I had experienced more difficulty and unhappiness than I had ever known. Since I had not been a true believer I became secular and skeptical, not wanting anything to do with God, religion, and certainly not church. If a person is not really born again Christian I would not recommend just being a Christian or giving Christianity a try.

A very secular life was my condition for the next seventeen years, but I was experiencing a life that I really enjoyed. I was physically fit (could easily run 10 miles without stopping), I owned a successful insurance agency, which provided an excellent income with ease. I owned my home, had friends and a good social life, I dated attractive women, and I had a very promising career in politics. A Christian would say I was blessed.

I thought that I had a great life, and I did except that spiritually I was lost. That means that if you die in that condition you go to the place that was prepared for Satan and his angels. That is eternal separation from God in the "lake of fire." But, if God was not relevant then who cares? I certainly did not. I was thirty-eight years old and had a good hedonist lifestyle. I did revile God.

The Bible uses the term self-will. Unfortunately, it is man's nature to want to be on the throne himself, and not answer to a higher authority. Now I know if you are born again it is the best life. A spiritual life is a better life than any secular life; even that of a popular celebrity, king, or billionaire. Actually, your eternal life inheritance begins here on earth after you have saving faith. You inherit an 'abundant life' and it is different and I have now experienced that life in countless ways.

I have an analytical mind, and I was contemplating the question, what is life? I realized that we were more than a mass of trillions of cells. Our life was more than that. I remembered the Bible verse about, "What did it profit a man if he gained the whole world and lost his soul?" I had analytically determined that we must have a soul, and realized that I agreed with the Bible. I think that gave me pause, but did not produce any action on my part.

Not too long after that I was in a *secular* book store with a close friend, and he started to say something about a rack of books. He caught himself and stopped and just dropped the subject. Had I known this book, *Late Great Planet Earth* by Hal Lindsey was a Christian book, I would not have gone near it. But I did not know and I was curious about this paperback book, because for some reason my friend did not want to tell me something he knew about it. I went back by myself and bought a copy.

I started reading this book and I could not stop. This was a book about prophecy concerning the last days. I realized that if the Bible was able to accurately describe events hundreds or even thousands of years in advance, that I might have made a serious mistake about God. As stated in Scripture, "work out your own salvation with fear and trembling." (Philippians 2:12)

I immediately went to church on Sunday. I picked a nondenominational church with a reputation for being conservative and Bible believing. The attendance there was about 1,000 on Sunday mornings. I do not think I missed a Sunday for an entire year. The Sunday school class that I was in had a teacher that had been teaching for twenty-nine years. It was a fairly large class and there were some members of this class that held leadership positions in the church. I only listened; I did not feel worthy or knowledgeable enough to contribute so I did not talk during the class lesson.

Right after I began attending the class, they started studying through the book of Revelation. After *Late Great Planet Earth* and the book of Revelation, I had gotten a baptism in prophecy and end time events. This gave me an interest in Eschatology, so I continued to study and follow material relating to the end times from then to the present. I am jumping ahead here, but in April 2001 I had an expectation. I verbalized to a Sunday school class, that in the near future something momentous might take place on earth. When I saw 9-11 unfold on television, I felt that this was the end time event I was expecting.

The "Day of the Lord" is fast approaching. This is a period of judgment on the whole earth. Lot was vexed in his soul daily prior to judgment coming upon Sodom and Gomorrah. Do events taking place locally and around the world today vex your soul? Are you able to be thankful that God has the power and the will to one day bring judgment and correct all the sin, injustice, corruption, and false religion on planet earth? Are you ready?

The pastor in this Bible church I attended used the KJV and was a tremendous expository preacher. The Scriptures were presented in a way that I felt clearly demonstrated that the Bible could only have come through God's inspiration. The truth and power of the Word astonished me and humbled me. I had no choice but to believe. Faith this time was easy for me because I realized that the Bible is the word of God (not including modern translations) and I believed it all. That has not changed in over twenty-five years. "Faith cometh by hearing, and hearing by the word of God." (Romans 10:17)

However, I did not have an understanding of the gospel, and I was confused about salvation. In the final days leading up to Christ's arrival in Jerusalem and His crucifixion, He gave His sternest of messages. One of these statements made me think that I was "not worthy of the Kingdom of God," and that I could not be saved. I certainly did not feel at all worthy or deserving of inheriting an eternal life in the presence of God.

I realized that "Who was I to question the God that was intelligent enough to design and create this universe?" I did not want to be condemned to Hell, but if God determined that was where I belonged, then I needed to accept it. God must know what He is doing and I needed to accept my destiny. I was motivated to pursue God and to learn all I could about God. I reasoned that since I would be separated from God after death, that this life was the only chance I was going to have to learn about Him. Heaven or hell did not matter. I just pursed God with passion and determination. I went to church because they knew a lot about God. You will not learn all you should learn about God without church.

In my earlier religious experience I was focused on me and only a little focused on God. This time it was very different because I was insignificant and irrelevant. I pursued God with determination. It was all about God, and by God's grace I rapidly gained biblical and spiritual knowledge. God had allowed me into the reality of truth and that experience is very special. Once you find truth you know that there is nothing else that satisfies the same way. So, I continued my quest to know about God, and little did I know that I was going to be able to know God - to really know God. That close relationship did not begin for me until a little over a year after I had returned to church. The Bible states, "But seek ye first the kingdom of God, and his righteousness; and all these things shall be added unto you." (Matthew 6:33)

God deals with us individually, so we all have testimonies that are unique. The experience is not exactly the same for everyone. I had learned a lot at this church, but I did not feel that I fit in well. I later found out that because they required a committee interview and approval for membership, that only about 400 of the thousand attending were actually members. They were serious committed Christians, but I think there was some attitude of elitism, and a need for members to fit their Christian view or mold.

When I left, I immediately changed to another church and unfortunately, it had very weak preaching. But I had some great experiences while there. Shortly after I left the first church, and through a connection from the first church, I was invited to join a home Bible study that was made up of doctors, lawyers, and their wives. This group had some seasoned Christians, and this was a real spiritual blessing for me. It was unusual that I would have this privilege, and it was the beginning of my starting to experience God some on a personal basis. My spiritual confidence began to grow and I became more outspoken in Sunday school. I, in fact, was a believer and a child of God.

I had experienced God enough by this time that I felt my faith in God was very strong. It did not seem to me that others in this second church experienced faith in the same way that I now enjoyed. This church had a picnic that I attended and I decided that I wanted to do something during this picnic to demonstrate faith. I made it a prayer request. One event was an uncooked egg toss contest. I got a partner and went next to last. I asked where the mark was for the current longest toss. I had my partner start there and I kept telling him to go back farther. I had him continue backing up until his distance from me was several times the current record. It was a really long distance. Someone observed that is too far to throw the egg underhanded. I said, "You are right." I drew back and threw the egg over handed like a baseball, as high and far as I could. It went right to my partner's hands and he caught the egg without it breaking. People were astonished! A lawyer realized what he had seen, and he said that he had not really been a Christian. He made a profession of faith and told me he would never forget the experience. I do think it was miraculous.

After about half a year I left this second church, because I just could not tolerate such a weak worship experience. I went to another church, but only stayed for a few months because I realized that I was in disagreement with too much of their doctrine (dogma). There were some people there that I did like very much and the young pastor became a friend while I was there. He regularly came by my office.

Earlier, I mentioned that I had encouragement in politics and had been referred to as 'a rising star.' I won the primary my first try, and barely lost in the general election to serve in the state legislature. I was invited to a 'political' party a few weeks after the election. I noticed that I was the only candidate there that had lost in the last election. The highest elected official to attend was the Chief Justice of the State Supreme Court. When he arrived, everyone stood, and when I left, he stood for me. These people knew protocol, and I saw how surprised they were to see this Chief Justice stand for a non-elected official.

I experienced profound accomplishments during my campaign for elected office. One person told me that political action committees did not know what to do with me because I was the only candidate that gave an intelligent answer to every question. I received many endorsements and gave some speeches that impressed veteran politicians. In looking back, I think that God may have allowed me this success to set up a test for me. God does not tempt us, but He will test us. I was certain that I would win if I ran for office again, but I chose God instead.

I saw politics as a great temptation for me. There is something about having power that is addictive. I experienced enough from winning the primary to know that this could really get in your blood. Politics could be both very rewarding and very consuming. For me, as a young believer in Jesus, I felt that I could not be in politics and grow spiritually. I decided that the real power was with God, and political power was only a sort of illusion. I chose to continue to pursue God rather than return to politics. I am very glad I made that choice. The right God is always the right choice.

I think that this may have been a crossroads decision for me. Not affecting my salvation, but my future of having increasing power with God. The Bible says you cannot serve God and money, and I was not going to be able to serve God and politics. I do not mean to say that some individuals cannot serve both. I know they can if they are able to put God above their political career. Pontius Pilot failed. He tried hard, but finally gave into the pressure from the Jewish leaders and the crowd when his standing with Caesar was threatened.

King David demonstrated clearly that he put God above the throne of Israel; however his predecessor King Saul did not. How strong could America have become if all politicians would have put God first throughout their political life? It seems that today politics is a lot less about serving, and a lot more about personal interests. Elected and appointed officials may not have considered God or do not believe, but this will happen anyway. One day they will stand before Almighty God, and they will be held accountable for every official action they have made.

The church that I chose next was a good fit for me for the next several years. It was a conservative, Bible believing (KJV only in the pulpit), preaching church that was growing on a regular basis. The pastor was an authority on spiritual gifts and he was intrigued by the gifts that he knew I had demonstrated. For those that do not know, every believer receives at least one spiritual gift at the time of their salvation. The gift(s) you receive are chosen by God for the benefit of the church. You do not lose them until death, because they are not needed on the other side. It is important to use your gift(s) for God's Kingdom, as long as you have that opportunity. I find gifts to be humbling because they increase your responsibility. How do we know how well our accomplishments please God based on all we had been given?

I served this church and eventually held various leadership positions. I ushered, did some teaching, served on committees, chaired a committee, etc. The whole church knew that I had

235

spiritual gifts. I could connect with God in a way that I could demonstrate to others. I found God to be very accessible, especially when the request was in line with His will and purposes. I had some profound experiences with God during this period and was able to understand exactly how God designed the New Testament church to function. It is a supernatural organization with Christ as the head.

I stated that in my religious experience years earlier, I was not aware of any answered prayer. I remember just one prayer that I believe God answered years later. God knows our hearts, and I did pray earnestly that I would not be a false teacher. I am a person that is persuasive, and I usually am able to convince others to my point of view. I remembered how people in the church would listen to me even when I was a young boy.

When I was in my early twenties, I knew that I lacked a lot of spiritual understanding and I did not want to mislead others. After becoming a believer, I received spiritual gifts equipping with me discernment, the ability to recognize sound doctrine from doctrine that was not sound or correct. That is a prayer that would probably be good for many religious leaders to pray – especially legalists and liberals.

The legalists want to add one or more plusses to "grace through faith," and some want to add to the Ten Commandments. Many of these professing Christians are probably saved, but not representing the gospel accurately. I do not understand how anyone that has experienced grace would not understand it. On the other hand, I do not know how anyone that has not experienced grace could understand it. One point that I want to make for those with legalist tendencies is that liberty is not license. God is long suffering, gracious and loving, but there is accountability with the God that is a "consuming fire."

The liberals are upset by the fundamentals of the faith. They will accept about any belief position except conservative Christianity. They do not even like the question, "do you know where you will go when you die? They do not respect the Bible as the authentic, inspired, sacred Word of God. Most would not take Genesis as historic and literal. Some are even very conservative in their lifestyle, but their theology is liberal. They do not seem to be able to recognize truth as truth. Some years ago, I was talking with a young Jewish lady who had attended a very liberal divinity school. I asked her why she went there. She said that she was looking for answers. I told her that she would not have found them there. She did not disagree.

One day during my time of membership at this church, I was sitting in the state cultural center building watching a free movie. About two-thirds of the way through the movie I had the feeling that I needed to get up and go home. This was not logical, and I was enjoying the movie. I walked outside and saw a mixed race gang of four young men severely beating a young white male that was slightly built. I started walking right toward them. I just felt that God was going to let me win. I thought it might be with supernatural strength like Sampson. I was wrong about that, but right that God would allow me to prevail. God used a technique that He has recorded using at times in the Bible. When they saw one person coming after them they immediately stopped, and then ran in four different directions. I wanted to go after at least one of them, but the victim was unconscious and bloody. I knew I needed to help him first.

Months later, a detective came to my office for insurance. I brought up this incidence, and he explained that he had solved the crime. The detective said it was a totally unprovoked attack. He said that all four assailants had been convicted, and were now serving time in prison. He told me the victim had been beaten so badly that the next day he was still not coherent. I relay this account to share an example of a demonstration of faith. Faith is evidence of things unseen. I could not see God there, but felt that it was He that brought me out of that movie. If I had not been a Christian, I would not have been able to go toward this gang unarmed. If David had not been a believer with faith and a personal relationship with God, he would not have been able to challenge and defeat Goliath.

My last year at this church was disappointing because of some things I saw. Also, I strongly disagreed with the pastor every Sunday during the invitation saying, "Make a total commitment and be saved." The gospel is grace through faith, and not by works. I did not really understand, but I felt that God wanted me to sell my business and leave the state. That is what I did, and that is when I left this church that had been so meaningful to me for a long time. I can understand Abraham having to leave and go to a new country. It was not an easy experience, but it did not shake my faith.

I went to northern Georgia, and spent a few weeks (rent free) in a new vacation home that was owned by a married couple that had been insurance clients. I loved the area and visited several churches and had many spiritual discussions with those that I would meet. It was from this area that I later got the comment from one of those people I had met. A 70 year man that became a Christian, said, "Around here you are known as John the Baptist."

The next phase was confusing, because I just was not able to decide on a new location and begin to get established. It took three years for that to happen and many different experiences occurred during this time; including becoming a grandfather for the first time. I was a young grandfather, and looked even younger. At the hospital the staff would not believe that I was the grandfather, and not the father.

I did have a mystical experience a few months after I started my transition to life in a new place. I was going through Nashville, Tennessee on Interstate 65. It was evening and I saw that the next exit had a Sheraton Hotel. After I exited the interstate I recognized the exit as belonging to the only family I knew in Nashville. I thought if I can find their house, I probably would get to visit and get a free room for the night. I did find their house and stay; but not before spending a little time looking and driving around the area where they lived. One street that I drove on while looking for them is where I ended up living about four years later. I met my future wife in a Cracker Barrel restaurant three years later, and she lived on that street. Was that God's way to show that he knew my future? I think that it was.

When I met my future wife she was not a Christian, and as she says she was a "happy heathen." I called her for a date about a week and a half after we met; she told her best friend that she knew something had to be wrong with me. And she said that she hoped it was not that I was religious. At dinner, I ordered a glass of wine and she thought this is a good sign. Later, I brought up the subject of God. She thought, "I knew it." I saw God building her faith, but did not want to say too much. After she became a believer, I saw her quickly begin to enjoy a close relationship with God. I knew that I had experienced this for years, but I marveled at her personal relationship with God. She became spiritually empowered and loved church and Bible studies.

I want to share an experience we had early in our relationship. We were visiting out of state at the home of friends that I had known for many years. The family matriarch, now a widow, told me after I became a Christian that she had prayed for me for years. During this visit there were some theology conversations because everyone there was a professing believer. This was Saturday, and that night when I prayed I asked God which church I should visit the next day, my old church or this old and dear friend's church. The next morning I overslept and it was too late to go to either church. During this period in my life, I was used to getting prayers answered, and I was disappointed that God had not answered this one. I actually silently fussed at God – "I wanted to go to church and You did not awaken me."

Later, my wife and I were having lunch at a restaurant in a small town, located between where the two churches are that I had prayed about. I saw an older retired pastor that had attended my former church. This was a man that I really liked and respected. I asked him for his opinion about us going to my old church for a visit. He did not recommend that I go back to the old church. He said it had really gone down after I left, but he highly recommended a new church in a rural area about ten miles from where we were having lunch. When he told me the pastor's name, I recognized it, and I knew he had been the pastor at the city church where my friend was a member for years. When I went back to the table, the acoustics, or something, had carried our conversation to our table, so my wife heard it all. She said we needed to go to that church.

We spent the afternoon visiting with my daughter and her husband. I was getting tired and was not dressed well for church, but agreed that God wanted us to go to the Church in the Valley. So, we drove there and arrived before the Sunday evening service started. I was surprised that the church was full for an evening service. It was an excellent sermon and a good one for my wife, because her church experience was one of works and not one of grace. Even so, I was disappointed because I was expecting something really special from God.

The pastor was at the back of the church and was greeting everyone as they left. I shook his hand and said that I knew a lady that was a member of his previous church. I told him who, and he said, "No, she is a member here." I was just stunned because she had not said a word about this new church. Also, it was at least a 30 minute drive from her home and she did not drive. He saw I might not believe him so he told me her vacation schedule. My wife had a big laugh, "God played a joke on you and I got see it." God actually had answered my prayer. I did not realize how complicated the prayer was, because I did not know about the church change. I did learn a lesson. I do not think I have not complained about an unanswered prayer since.

This pilgrim's spiritual journey has been a varied and interesting adventure. I have experienced the joy of everything from a mission trip to Brazil, to coaching church league basketball. I am very skilled at coaching at this level; which has gotten pretty competitive. I loved coaching young men along with teaching them about God. My wife and I have had countless personal experiences with God and answered prayers. We had learned to hear God and see the God's providence at work many, many times.

Years ago, we realized that many professing Christians were not aware of these same kinds of experiences. There were times that if we tried to share an experience of this type we were looked at like we were aliens. We came to the conclusion that Christ had many disciples, but only a few inner circle disciples. "Many are called, but few are chosen." We decided that some of our experiences were for us only and that we should not share this information with others. This book has been an exception, because I think that the evidence presented in *Amazing* for revelation and inspiration should be obvious. We have found that all churches are not equal in this regard. Some have more understanding about a personal relationship with God, and are more receptive regarding sharing experiencing God.

The powerful Hurricane Katrina was America's greatest natural disaster. Was this destructive force a random act of nature or was it a purposeful act of God? This is an account of my experience relating to this event. I have a strong interest in Israel because I have a strong interest in God. Israel is the only covenant nation on earth, and it is of primary importance in this final phase of history. Is there a connection between a Hurricane in America and Israel?

The Bible has a strong warning against dividing the land that God gave the Jews for an inheritance. Many Evangelical and Messianic believers were very upset that plans called for the Gaza Strip to be turned over to the Palestinians. I was one of those that were very concerned, and I wrote a letter to Prime Minister, Ariel Sharon, making a case that this not be done. Days after I sent the letter, my wife got a Gmail on the Prime Minister's name; Sharon – share own. He was in fact going to give away land that Israel owned. I sent another letter nine months before Gaza was turned over by the Prime Minister to the Palestinians. In this letter, I indicated that I knew the Gaza giveaway would take place. It was not right, but it was going to occur. I advised a Messianic ministry in Israel to calm down about this because it would happen. The American governments "Road Map for Peace" put a lot of pressure on Israel to give up this the Gaza Strip. (Gmail – Gaza - sounds like gauze that you put on a wound; strip – strip away).

A few days before Katrina, I told my wife that God was soon going to bring a judgment on America because of our role in the Gaza giveaway. I had been spiritually concerned and involved with this issue for a year. While Katrina was out in the ocean, but getting quite strong, I told my wife that this hurricane was the judgment event that I was expecting. The night before it hit land (Saturday or Sunday), I knew the situation was serious and I made an intercessory prayer. I agreed with God that this nation had gone against His warning about Israel and that we deserved to suffer judgment. I pleaded for mercy in the midst of His judgment. The night before the hurricane was to reach the coast, when I went to bed, the hurricane was a category five and heading straight toward New Orleans. I felt that God was going to do something special, but I did not know what it would be.

The next morning when I woke up, I turned on the television and the first thing I heard was, "the meteorologists are scratching their heads because a puff of warm air that they do not know where it came from changed Hurricane Katrina from a five to a four and moved it below New Orleans." I believe I know the source of that warm air. I believe that prayer(s) brought mercy to New Orleans residents. I am glad that I was one of those that had prayed on their behalf.

As bad as it was, do you have any idea what the death and destruction would have been if New Orleans had gotten a direct hit category five? Destruction and death would have been total. I would say that God did show mercy in the midst of judgment. We knew that Rita; that came after Katrina, also involved judgment because the letters for Rita are in Katrina. The reports from Israel about the refugees from Gaza, and the news reports about the refugees from New Orleans had many remarkable similarities. God showed mercy, but still made a direct hit that was felt all over America. We all paid when we went to the gas pump, and many of us made financial contributions for relief. Also, it was costly for our government in both money and reputation.

I have heard the question, "Was New Orleans reputation for sin, for corruption, and for the scheduled gay parade responsible for this tremendous destruction?" I do not think that this was the cause, but probably was the reason that this area was targeted. The primary cause was ignoring God's word regarding dividing the land of Israel; that is a bad idea for any nation or any person. Actually, the progression of sexual immorality that started in the early 1960's is not judgment, but rather the evidence of judgment on America.

Several days before Prime Minister Sharon had the massive stroke; I had heard from God that he was finished politically. I did not know any details, and I do not know why God gave me that information. Yes, I do think the timing of his loss of power was the result of his Gaza decision. He was a great field general, and I admired and respected this man. The Gaza situation provides a good lesson for America, other nations, and other political leaders. That is why I included this account; and I do have a love for intercessory prayer. I highly recommend not dividing Israel, and

242

also recommend earnestly making intercessory prayers for this covenant nation.

The question that you should consider is whether there is a connection between 9-11, Katrina, Rita, earthquakes (the tsunami that killed over 120,000 people), droughts, floods, destructive tornados, plagues, famine, the Iraq War, Iran developing nuclear weapon capability, importance of oil, economic uncertainty, increasing anti-Semitism, etc. I am persuaded that the seventh millennium began in April 2001, and we are in the judgment period that is the "Day of the Lord." Time for serving the living God, Maker of Heaven and Earth, is quickly running out. Now is the time for salvation.

There have been numerous Bible prophecies fulfilled just since I was born. This is a time of many spiritual opportunities. It is a bad time to be secular, because the problems of this world will continue and increase until the return of the Lord. Evil will increase and spiritual blessings and power will increase. A biblical world view, based on knowing that God will prevail and be victorious, is an encouragement in difficult and challenging times.

In heaven there will be people from every color, language, and nation on earth. I pray that faith will increase and especially all those that read this book will be among those joyous millions in God's Kingdom. Amen.

CHAPTER TWO
THE LITTLE NATION OF ISRAEL

The following words (2) will be used in this chapter: Israel, and Revelations.

The Bible states that God made a covenant with Abraham.

> *"Now the Lord had said unto Abram, Get thee out of thy country, and from thy kindred, and from thy father's house, unto a land that I will shew thee: And I will make of thee a great nation, and I will bless thee, and make thy name great; and thou shalt be a blessing; And I will bless them that bless thee, and curse him that curseth thee; and in thee shall all families of the earth be blessed:* - Genesis 12:1-3

This visit to Abraham by God occurred about 4,000 years ago, probably in an area near the Persian Gulf. The questions are, "Did God keep this covenant?" "Did a nation come from Abraham?" "Have all the families of the earth been spiritually blessed by Abraham's seed?"

Yes, many nations came from Abraham; but the great nation from God's perspective is Israel. This little nation was predestined by Almighty God to bring divine blessing to the entire world. ISRAEL was named this because God *is real*. The true God is the God of Abraham, Isaac, and Jacob. The nation of Israel was to be a blessing to both Jew and Gentile. This means Jews and the inhabitants all other nations of this world. What did God give to the entire world from this little nation?

The contributions have turned out to be by far the most important in human history. They are as follows: Prophets (spoke divine revelation), Old and New Testaments (inspired word of God), Yeshua (actual Hebrew name) or Jesus (God's son that was fully man and fully God), and the Church (the body of Christ which are the true believers). God's plan for divine spiritual blessing to the entire human race was brought forth through this

244

covenant with Abraham. This people group fulfilled this promise to Abraham through a crucified (sacrificial Lamb of God) and resurrected Messiah. Direct words of the Messiah:

> *"Ye worship ye know not what: we know what we worship: for salvation is of the Jews."* John 4:22

To qualify, your lineage would have to go back to one of the original 70 descendents of Abraham that entered into Egypt. I am thankful for Israel and to God, for His wisdom in providing a way through this nation, ISRAEL, to reconcile people from all nations to Himself.

> *"After this I beheld, and, lo, a great multitude, which no man could number, of all nations, and kindreds, and people, and tongues, stood before the throne, and before the Lamb, clothed with white robes, and palms in their hands; And cried with a loud voice, saying, Salvation to our God which sitteth upon the throne, and unto the Lamb."* Revelation 7:9, 10

I pray that you will be at this tremendous event from your nation, and that you will take part with this great multitude that have been so blessed through the covenant made many centuries ago with Abraham. You might be surprised to know that the letters for the word *Israel* is contained in the word REVELATIONS. That should be a clue that Israel is definitely important; especially as the end approaches. Thank God for Israel!

The current rabbinic system is at its heart in rebellion against Yeshua, the Messiah and second person of the Godhead. Though it does have many areas of wisdom and truth it misses the heart of God's revelation and His only way of salvation. Yeshua did say, "Think not that I come to destroy, the law, or the prophets: I am not come to destroy, but to fulfill." (Matthew 5:17)

Christianity is superior to Judaism and that is why God has used the Christians to take the Jewish Bible all over the world. Again, He has proved His word that there would be a "times of the Gentiles." Christianity did lose something in forced separation from the Jewish festivals and also on insisting that Jews become completely non-Jewish. In Christ, Jews and non-Jews are equal. In Christ they become the "one new man."

Israel has many enemies just as Bible prophecy stated they would. Their primary enemy seems to be nations that are Islamic. The religion of Islam denies the Bible, the written Word of God, and a billion people are held in the clutches of this oppressive religion. The gospel is reaching lost people in every culture, even in the Islamic world. However, no cultures are as restrictive on religious freedom as Islamic cultures. Leaving Islam is even punishable by death. The word culture has cult in it. Does hatred, violence, oppression of females, radical jihad, and the subjugation or killing of non-Muslims sound reasonable or more like a cult. Islam is a horrendous force against religious freedom. Islam denies the incarnation of God in Yeshua; therefore it is the spirit of Antichrist.

My understanding is that Islam teaches that it was Ishmael (Islam is in Ishmael) and not Isaac that Abraham was going to sacrifice. My question is if this sacrifice was not a type for the sacrifice that God was going to make through His own Son what was the point or purpose? The sacrifice type makes sense through the line of Isaac, but how would it make sense through the line of Ishmael because he was not in the Messianic lineage?

God sacrificed His Son for all people groups and the peoples of all nations. Now, the God of Abraham seems to have everything set in place for a great clash and challenge involving the restored nation of Israel, a West that has been slipping from a Christian world view to relativistic view, and several Muslim nations that have a lot of oil, an important and valuable commodity, combined with followers of Islam that want to defeat Israel and overthrow Christianity. There is a lot of talk of peace, but Yeshua said that there would be war until He returned and destroyed the weapons of war and established His Kingdom. This might be an important time to seek truth, do your own searching and make sure you are on God's side.

A Tribute to the Memory and Mission of

✝ <u>Chris Samuel Nedumkandathil, Evangelist</u> ✝

Chris, a man age twenty-five taught a Vacation Bible School class in Kerala, India the day he died.

This remarkable young man made an impact for Jesus in Kerala, and everywhere he traveled in India and in America. Many people have been inspired to get involved in ministry because of Chris. Tina, his younger sister stated, "All of this is **amazing** to me, and provides a source of joy."

Yes, Tina God definitely is **Amazing**.

I quote from his journal, "If you can preach or teach you are needed. If you can distribute clothes you are needed. If you can give proper medical care you are needed, there are millions in India and around the world in dire need of some spiritual food, the Bread of Life and the Living Water. How long will we ignore them? How long will we continue to worry only about ourselves? Brothers and sisters let us awaken from our stupor and emerge in the world following the footsteps of our Master and walking the paths of our forefathers. The time is now, the opportunities are endless, and the responsibility is ours"

His message and mission needs to continue throughout this nation and other nations around the world. This book was written to increase the Kingdom of God, and this was Chris's mission.

<u>chrissamuelevangelisticministries.org</u>

Order Form

Email orders:	amazingministry@bellsouth.net
Postal orders:	Amazing Ministry
	P. O. Box 3211
	Brentwood, TN 37211

Book Price is discounted from recommended retail.

Amazing Book $15 ☐   CD Lexicon $8   ☐
                        (4 or more $6 each)

Amazing T-shirt $19 ☐   Book & CD $20   ☐

Amazing Annual Membership (newsletter and access to lexicon updates) $12 ☐

Shipping by USPS or UPS ground. Add $4.00 for first product and $2.00 for each additional product up to ten. No additional shipping charge above ten products.

Add 8.75% sales tax for shipments to Tennessee addresses.

Please send more FREE information on:

Speaking ☐   Other books ☐   Interview ☐

Send Gmail submissions to email address. If added to the lexicon you will identified by up to three initials and your state. Example: HDW-VA

Name: _____

Address: _____

City_____State_____Zip_____

Telephone_____Email:_____

CHURCH INFORMATION

Church name

_____

Address	City	State	Zip

www.amazingministries.org

Printed in the United States
202286BV00003B/115-315/P

9 780981 567624